Agency, Illusion, and Well-Being

Agency, Illusion, and Well-Being

Essays in Moral Psychology and Philosophical Economics

JEROME M. SEGAL

LEXINGTON BOOKS

A division of
ROWMAN & LITTLEFIELD PUBLISHERS, INC.
Lanham • Boulder • New York • Toronto • Plymouth, UK

LEXINGTON BOOKS

A division of Rowman & Littlefield Publishers, Inc.
A wholly owned subsidiary of The Rowman & Littlefield Publishing Group, Inc.
4501 Forbes Boulevard, Suite 200
Lanham, MD 20706

Estover Road
Plymouth PL6 7PY
United Kingdom

British Library Cataloguing in Publication Information Available

Library of Congress Cataloging-in-Publication Data

Segal, Jerome M., 1943–
Agency, illusion, and well-being : essays in moral psychology and philosophical economics / Jerome M. Segal.
p. cm.
ISBN-13: 978-0-7391-2968-5 (cloth : alk. paper)
ISBN-10: 0-7391-2968-6 (cloth : alk. paper)
ISBN-13: 978-0-7391-2969-2 (pbk. : alk. paper)
ISBN-10: 0-7391-2969-4 (pbk. : alk. paper)
1. Act (Philosophy) 2. Agent (Philosophy) 3. Alienation (Philosophy) 4. Economics--Philosophy. I. Title.
B105.A35S445 2008
128'.4—dc22

2008034397

Printed in the United States of America

The paper used in this publication meets the minimum requirements of American National Standard for Information Sciences—Permanence of Paper for Printed Library Materials, ANSI/NISO Z39.48–1992.

Also By Jerome M. Segal

Creating the Palestinian State: A Strategy for Peace

Agency and Alienation: A Theory of Human Presence

Graceful Simplicity: Toward a Philosophy and Politics of Simple Living

Negotiating Jerusalem (coauthor)

Joseph's Bones: Understanding the Struggle Between God and Mankind in the Bible

Contents

Preface

Each of the selections in this volume stands on its own as an independent essay. Collectively they address a series of fundamental questions:

- What is the nature of human agency?
- Is self-deception necessary to maintain a sense of the coherence of the self?
- As described in the Bible, is God engaged in a project of self-deception with respect to his dependence on mankind?
- Is it possible to sustain political agency without self-deception?
- Does the belief in progress rest upon collective self-deception?
- Does money promote illusions about the value of agent centered activities?
- How does economic activity affect human well being?

The broad topic towards in which they all participate is captured in the title, *Agency, Illusion, and Well-Being*. If there is a single theme that links them, it is the centrality of illusion, typically self-deception, in diverse aspects of human experience, be it our experience of ourselves, our efforts to create a better world, our religious conceptions or our engagement in everyday economic life.

In selecting these essays rather than other possible writings for this collection, I have given priority to one question: "Are they interesting?" An author's own judgment of his own work is perhaps not the best, but I do believe that these are interesting essays. They are about fundamental matters and they often move in new directions, opening for the reader avenues for further thought and inquiry. Typically they either present perspectives that remain novel or they call attention to classic works that today receive far too little attention. Let me say a word about each.

The final essay, "Human Activity: A Molecular Approach to Action Theory," is placed last because it is the most technical, probably of interest to few outside the community of professional philosophers. Action theory has sought to answer Wittgenstein's probing question, "when 'I raise my arm,' my arm goes up. And the problem arises: what is leftover if I subtract the fact that my arm goes up from the fact that I raised my arm?" The dominant answer is that when I raise my arm there is a particular causal story that explains why my arm went up. This can be articulated in terms of volitions, acts of will, or the wants and beliefs of the individual. Such accounts have seemed to many, however, unsatisfactory because they seem to deprive actions of their very activity—thus, if consciousness were quick enough, we could passively witness our own arm going up as a result of the causal chain set off by some earlier mental event (e.g. a desire).

In the account I offer, I suggest a new approach to action theory in which the basic unit is not some bit of behavior, such as an arm or finger movement, but rather what I call "the activity molecule," a causally integrated sequence of movements that is guided by an on-going perceptual awareness that causes an outcome to conform to a standard implicit in the perception. On this approach one is able to distinguish two separate questions which standard action theory has conflated, "When is something an action?" and "When is someone an agent?"

In the opening essay, "Human Agency" I offer what I call the presence theory which maintains that one is the agent of an activity when one's self is present in the activity. But what is it for the self to be present in one's activity? This I argue depends upon how the self is conceived. I argue against locus theories of the self which would view certain components of the personality, for instance, our higher order moral judgments, as constituting the authentic locus of the self. Beyond this matter of what is or is not the authentic self, there is another issue—how is the self actually active in its activity? Here I try to show that the activity molecule, for instance, kissing someone, is not a fixed element that has this or that cause, but rather, in its very structure becomes this kind of kiss or that kind of kiss, precisely in virtue of the ways in which the self is present or absent in the kissing.

In the following essay, "Alienness: Experiencing One's Own Incoherence" I call attention to a kind of experience which I term "alienness." The object of such experiences are aspects of the self, it may be one's emotions, one's actions, one's beliefs or values, or it may be the entire self or one's life as a whole. The alienness experience is two-fold, on the one hand one recognizes the element as one's own, yet on the other hand, one finds it not truly or fully or really one's own. For instance, one might say, "I feel as if my emotions (or my values, my beliefs) are not really mine." I argue that such experiences, whether or not they are pathological, can be an accurate account of an inner incoherence, or more generally, a meaningful expression of an encounter with incoherence. Rather than viewing such experiences in terms of motivation (e.g. the individual is trying to escape from full responsibility for his emotions) I approach them in cognitive terms, as responses to beliefs, typically insights, that the individual has attained. What these beliefs have in common is that they reveal an absence (e.g. a lack of connectedness, an incoherence) in virtue of which full ownership of the element is not possible. For instance, suppose a person comes to realize that most of what he believes about what is right and wrong, he believes merely because such beliefs were inculcated in a narrow upbringing. In short, he no longer believes that his beliefs are credible. Yet it is not a matter of a specific belief, nor of his believing the opposite. He simply comes to lose confidence that he really has any valid foundation. Yet, his attitudes remain his attitudes, he finds himself responding viscerally as he always has, yet now he has a perspective on such beliefs, "they are his and not his" or "not really his own." My general thesis is that in a wide variety of contexts, be it self-exploration, political activity, or philosophic reflection, we are led to insights into the absence of the kind of coherence that we take for granted in normal experience. The subsequent essay, "Alienness, Understanding, and Self-Deception" explores more fully how insight into one's own psyche may give rise to alienness and how this is to be distinguished from self-deception.

"God's Project of Self-Deception" explores the issue of self-deception in a totally different context. It is based on a close reading of the first books of the Bible, in particular Genesis and Exodus and concerns itself with trying to understand how, in those texts, God's motivation is to be understood. Why is God so passionate about mankind? Why does he care so much? It is argued that, as presented in the Bible, God himself lives under an illusion that he fights to maintain. He sees himself as I-am-that-I-am, a characterization that bespeaks independence from the other, but this is exactly what the God-character is not. God, in the Bible, needs mankind in order to be, his being, if not his well-being is dependent upon his being experienced by mankind as God.

In "Alienation and Political Agency" two features of actions on the grand stage are explored, the way in which actions that have vast consequences draw one towards acting in ways that are contrary to the morality of everyday behavior, and the way in which actions with vast consequences create a need for knowledge of consequences which exceeds our capacity. Thus both because of value conflicts and inadequate knowledge, the political agent is drawn into alienation from his own activity. Alternative strategies for dealing with this dynamic are represented by Gandhi, Trotsky and Bentham, but in the end there is no satisfactory solution, and we act either with a degree of alienness or with illusion.

"How We Fooled Ourselves into Believing in Progress" is an exploration of the history of the idea of progress. It emphasizes the extent to which, for centuries, it was within the aesthetic realm that the West looked to determine whether or not mankind progressed. Secondarily, attention was paid to the moral realm, and as no convincing case can be made that later periods are either morally superior or aesthetically richer than earlier periods, no general idea of progress took hold. For the idea of progress to emerge what was necessary was not technological or scientific advance, rather what was necessary was to redefine "progress" so that what was once viewed as of lesser consequence came to be seen not only as of greater importance, but as all that is important.

In "The Monetary Illusion" the spell that economic life casts over our ability to perceive value is explored on the individual level. The essay opens with consideration of the familiar distinction between price and value, and how economists long ago observed that some things of great value, such as water, cost very little, while others of questionable value, such as diamonds, may cost a great deal. The illusions of the marketplace, however, are far more pervasive; that which is outside the market tends to not be recognized as valuable at all. The effort to put price estimates on home production and unpriced household services (e.g. housework) is barely a corrective. There are two very different kinds of personal services. There are those that have a specific output, such as mowing the lawn, or doing the dishes, and these are purchased by the wealthy, and can have surrogate prices. But then there are others in which the key is not the output, but the identity of the agent and his relationship to the person receiving the service, for instance, reading a story to one's child, or taking a quiet walk with a loved one. These services are outside the marketplace because their meaning is undermined by a market relationship and because a market-supplied agent cannot provide an adequate substitute for the relational agent. Such activities, not just for the recipient, but for the agents themselves, are the activities of the greatest value. Their existence within a mode of life or culture is a form of wealth. When they disappear, often under the time pressure of increased marketization of labor, their disappearance eludes our economic accounting, thereby facilitating an illusion of economic progress.

Both Aristotle and Adam Smith recognized that economic well-being is not primarily a matter of possessing a stock of commodities; it is most essentially, a matter of how one actually lives, and of the higher-order activities that one performs in relation to the commodities one possesses. Adam Smith illustrated this most powerfully by pointing out that "being able to appear in public without shame" is of great importance whatever society one might live in, whereas the commodity requirements for doing so, (does it require a linen shirt?) differ markedly from one society to another. In recent years, Amartya Sen and Martha Nussbaum have built on these insights to develop valuable analyses of the concepts of "the good life" and of "standard of living." The essay "The Good Life and Economic Activity" emerged from a conference on Ethics and Consumption in which I served as a commentator on Nussbaum's presentation. In this essay, I first identify what I see as the limitations of Nussbaum's effort to identify the capabilities that are necessary for the good life. I argue that the so called "capabilities and functionings" approach is better able to explicate the narrower, but important conceptual question, "What is it to live at a high economic standard." I then go on to identify ten economic "functionings" (aspects of how one actually lives), that collectively offer an understanding of what it is to be living well in relation to the economic dimensions of life.

This last essay appeared in the collection *Ethics of Consumption*, edited by David Crocker and Toby Linden. The essays, "How We Fooled Ourselves into Believing in Progress" and "The Monetary Illusion" appeared in my book *Graceful Simplicity: Toward a Philosophy and Politics of Simple Living*. "God's Project of Self-Deception" appeared in my book *Joseph's Bones: Understanding the Struggle Between God and Mankind in the Bible*, and the other essays on activity, agency and alienness appeared in *Agency and Alienation: A Theory of Human Presence*.

The number of people who assisted in developing these various pieces is far too extensive to enumerate here. In putting together this collection, however, I wish to thank Carroll Linkens and most especially Rachel Neuschatz.

1
Human Agency

Philosophers have viewed the question, "What is an action?" and the question "What is it to be an agent?" as two sides of the same question. Actions are those things that are done by agents; one is an agent whenever one has performed an action. Thus, the two traditional views, that which understands actions as events caused by a volition (or wants and beliefs) and that which understands actions as events brought about through the exercise of agent causality, are alike in that they do not separate the two questions.

The tendency to think that only one question is involved has been reinforced by an implicit aspect of much of the theoretical writings in analytic action theory—an atomistic perspective that takes as its starting point a simple event (e.g., the movement of a finger) and asks in relation to this event: "What is it for me to be the agent of this event?" For instance: "What is the difference between the mere movement of the finger, and my having moved the finger?"

So conceived, it is not surprising that the two questions tend to merge into one. When we focus on an event this simple, it is quite natural to suppose that whatever it is that makes me the agent of this event is exactly that which makes it an action.

The theory presented in my essay "Human Activity" can be characterized as molecular rather than atomistic. The notion of an activity molecule is introduced as the central element of the theory. The activity molecule is conceived not as a simple event but as a process that is unified through what I call "indirect perceptual integration." This is a complex causal relationship whereby an ongoing perceptual assessment of an outcome causes an ongoing *series of events* to occur in a manner that shapes the outcome so that it conforms to a standard inherent in the perception. The typical events in the series are physical movements, and thus typically molecular activities are physical activities. In so understanding activities, a mental component (i.e., the perceptual assessment) is built into the notion of activity—molecular activities are thus psychophysical processes. They can be thought of as a very specific type of movement-feedback-adjustment process.

But having thus conceived of activities, and having understood them *apart* from any notion of volition, wants, desires, or agent causality, the question of agency emerges as a distinct question. Activities occur, but under what circumstances are we the agent of such activities?

The general answer I gave is that we are agents of activities when and only when the self is present in the activity. The present essay explains what it is for the self to be present in its activities.

Freedom and Agency

The term "freedom" is used in so many different contexts and senses that it would be bold to say there is no sense of "freedom" corresponding to what I have called "agency." But certainly agency is not the same as freedom in its central usage. A person can be the agent of his actions even when he clearly is not free, in the sense that he faces various threats and extreme penalties if he chooses certain courses of action that are in some more general sense "open" to him. But there is a particular notion of freedom that, even if it is not the same as what I have called "agency," appears to raise many of the same issues.

Traditionally actions have been viewed as caused by a desire (or a volition). Working off of this understanding of actions, some philosophers have distinguished free actions from unfree actions in terms of the nature of the desire. For instance, if the desire is the desire of a drug addict for heroin, and if it is so powerful that though she tries to resist it, she cannot, then it would make sense to say that she was unfree. Similarly, if through vast powers of manipulation, some evil power were capable of causing me to have desires quite contrary to my own values, we would also say that I was not free, even if I did what I wanted to do.

Viewed in this way, one analysis of freedom is that a person acts freely when he does what he wants to, provided that the want or desire from which he acts is truly his own. For this to be informative, what is required is an analysis of what it is for a desire to be truly one's own. This can be rephrased in the vocabulary I have been using as a need to provide an analysis of what it is for a desire to come from the self.

My interest is not in trying to explicate the concept of freedom, but rather in picking up on that discussion insofar as it is relevant to understanding what it is for an action to come from the self. Even though I have rejected the analysis of actions as events caused by desires, it still is possible to maintain that being caused by a desire, or a desire that is truly mine, is exactly what makes an action (or activity) mine. Thus, agency could be understood as being caused by a desire that comes from the self.

I reject this as a necessary feature of agency because I want to maintain that actions can come from the self even if there is no desire that is their direct cause. Even so, it remains possible that a sufficient condition for agency is that the action in question comes from a desire that emerges from the self. Without, at the moment, going into whether or not this is sufficient, it is at least highly relevant to agency. Thus, it will be useful to consider how certain philosophers have dealt with this question: What is it for a desire to be truly mine?

Harry Frankfurt, writing of free will, says that it involves "satisfactions . . . which accrue to a person of whom it may be said that *his will is his own*."[1] Frankfurt centers his discussion on what it is to have a will that is one's own, and on what it is to be a person. He writes that "one essential difference between persons and other creatures is to be found in the structure of a person's will." He goes on to say that "It seems to be peculiarly characteristic of humans, however, that they are able to form . . . second-order desires." By "second-order desires" he means desires about other desires, for instance, the desire to not have a desire to eat ice cream.

But, according to Frankfurt, the essential feature of persons is not that they have second-order desires, but rather that they have desires that certain desires be the motives out of which we act. He calls these "second-order volitions," and says,

> it is having second-order volitions, and not having second-order desires generally, that I regard as essential to being a person. It is logically possible, however unlikely, that there should be an agent with second order desires but with no volitions of the second order. Such a creature, in my view, would not be a person.[2]

He introduces the term "wanton" to refer to such creatures who are not persons (they have desires, but not second-order volitions). Frankfurt makes clear that the stance adopted towards first-order desires by the second-order volitions need not be a moral stance. It suffices merely that the person has preferences with respect to what desires he or she will act from. He then goes on to identify *freedom of the will* with being free to have the will one wants (the "will" for Frankfurt is that desire which is actually acted upon). Thus, to have a free will is to have the ability to determine whether or not one will act on one or another of one's desires. For instance, if the drug addict has two competing desires, the first to take the drug and the second to not take the drug, and if she also has a second-order desire that she not act out of the first desire (the desire to take the drug), then her will is free if and only if this second-order desire is controlling. If despite this desire to not act on the desire for the drug, she is unable to resist the desire for the drug, then her will is not free. Put differently, the person has an unfree will because her will is not subject to determination by her preferences with respect to it.

Frankfurt further distinguishes between having a free will and acting freely. He maintains that even if one doesn't have a free will, one can be said to act freely if one acts in accord with second-order volitions. Thus, he cites the case of the happy addict, a person whose will is not free in that her addiction is too strong, but who is quite happy to be acting out of her desire for the drug. This "happy addict" acts freely, while the unhappy addict does not act freely.

Certainly, there is a useful distinction to be made between people who have a capacity to determine which desire they will act on when desires conflict and people who do not. But is this capacity to be equated with freedom? The key issue is why should an action in accord with a second-order desire be viewed as emerging from the self? Why give this particular locus to the self, or this particular authority of being genuinely mine to actions that are in accord with these particular desires?

Frankfurt has adopted a particular stance within a general category of positions that can be called "locus theories of the self." Locus theories pick out a particular mental state or a particular part of the personality and view these components as having a special authority in determining what is truly mine and what is not. The theory of the self developed in my book *Agency and Alienation* is a nonlocus theory. The self was understood as the integrated personality without identifying any particular component as necessarily the central point in that integration.

Frankfurt doesn't argue in a straightforward way for the proposition that a desire is one's own if it is the subject of a second-order desire that we act from it, but his view on this seems linked to his claim that having second-order desires (desires about what desires we act from) is "essential to being a person"—it is the basis for his distinction between persons and the class of beings he calls "wantons."

The term "essential" and its variants have a long and perilous philosophical history. In one sense they are used to identify a distinguishing characteristic, a necessary feature. I would hesitate to accept Frankfurt's view that having second-order desires is a necessary condition for being a person. But even if this were to be true, it would not follow that such desires were "essential" in a different sense, in the sense in which we might speak about the "inner essence," or that which is most truly one's own.

These two senses of "essential" are quite distinct. For instance, it is perfectly possible to accept that having the ability to act from second-order desires is an essential (i.e., necessary) characteristic of persons and to maintain that this very ability to act from second-order desires is in fact the ability to act from desires that are not truly one's own. Thus, it may be that a necessary feature of persons is an ability to act from what is not one's self. And thus, Frankfurt's outlook could be turned completely around. Wantons (e.g., animals) might be viewed as creatures whose desires are always their own (and thus free), as distinct from persons who end up often acting from second-order desires rather than from their truer more natural selves.

Consider the Puritan who views his lust as sinful and desires to not act on it. Are his actions through which he avoids being alone with members of the opposite sex free actions? Would he not be acting on a desire that was truly his own if he acted on a sexual impulse? Why are his moral strictures, which find their way into his second-order reflections on his own desires, more genuinely his own than are the promptings of his body?

Sometimes it seems that in addition to saying that to act out of a second-order volition is to act freely, Frankfurt also believes that one acts freely only if one acts in accord with a second-order volition. That is, that acting in accord with a second-order desire is not only sufficient for acting freely but necessary. But what reason is there to maintain this? Is the open and spontaneous and unreflective sexuality of the Samoan youth not fully his own? Is he acting unfreely when he acts naturally?

Consider the act of telling someone that you love them. On Frankfurt's account this would be wantonly done if the person had no reflective views with respect to the motives he or she was acting on. But for a healthy person, the natural expression of love to a loved one may be completely without reflection upon one's motives. Acting directly out of love, simply giving it verbal expression without any second-order desire to do so, would appear to be acting freely and performing an action that was truly one's own.

My point is not to argue for the direct expression of emotion as the only mode through which the self emerges in action, and thus to argue against the significance of alternatives. Rather, it is to argue against the centrality and exclusivity that a locus theory such as Frankfurt's involves.

Frankfurt does not intend to give a special priority to second-order volitions as opposed to volitions at any possible higher level. He recognizes that one may have a critical view of one's second-order volitions. Suppose I am someone struggling against my Puritan background. I have a lust that I find myself viewing as sinful. Thus, I find that I have a second-order volition to not act out of that lust. But I might also have a third-level perspective on this Puritanical view of lust. And on this third level I may have a desire that I not act out of my second-level volition, but rather out of my first-level lust.

Frankfurt does not clearly address the question of whether it is always the highest level volition that reflects the self and thus is the guide to the free act. Rather, he says, "When a person identifies himself decisively with one of his first-order desires, this commitment 'resounds' throughout the potentially endless array of higher orders."[3] Some commentators have urged that this expresses a more refined view, according to which Frankfurt is saying that a sufficient condition for acting freely is that a person identifies decisively with the desire from which he or she has acted.[4]

An identificationist view can be stated as follows:

> An action is truly one's own (and therefore free) if and only if the person identifies with the desire from which he or she acted.

This however is not a refinement of the emphasis on second-order volitions. It is a different analysis. To have a desire to not act from sexual desire is one thing; to identify with a desire to not act from sexual desire is something different. Suppose I have a second-order volition that I not act from lust; it is still possible that I identify with the sexual impulse. I can identify with a desire yet still not desire to act from that desire. To identify with a desire is to experience it as truly mine; it need not be the case that I approve of all that I so experience.

Whether or not Frankfurt's view is to be understood in terms of a second-order volition or an identification with a first-order desire, both formulations are essentially answers to what it is for a desire to be truly one's own. The action is truly one's own because the desire is truly one's own. And if the action is truly one's own then it is freely done.

Both formulations treat having a certain attitude (an approving desire or an identification) towards a desire as sufficient for constituting that desire as one's own. There are basic problems with this position. If the key factor is the attitude towards the desire, it may be asked, when does the attitude in question have this certifying perspective on the desire? Attitudes, be they desires about desires or identifications with desires, change. I can at some later time come to be quite estranged from the desire that I today identify with. Thus, in retrospect, having understood that I was acting largely out of the views of my parents and their (I now think) distorted moralizing, I now see as foreign many of my desires that I once identified with or approved of.

When we identify with a desire, this identification has within it, it would appear, a judgmental component, a judgment that the desire is my own. When I at some later point no longer identify with the desire out of which I acted, my lack of identification reflects a change in judgment. I am no longer judging that desire to have been truly mine. If having an attitude towards a desire (whether an identification with it or an affirmative second-order attitude towards it) is sufficient to make it one's own, then given the fact that these attitudes change, either "ownership" is relative to a particular point in time or is itself noncognitive. On this latter perspective, assertions that a desire is mine or not mine would be understood in a fashion analogous to the way emotivists portrayed assertions in ethics. The "judgment" that the desire is truly mine would be treated as a pseudo judgment that fails to affirm any matter of fact, merely expressing some attitude.

The alternative that I am maintaining rejects both the claim that having an attitude towards a particular element (e.g., a desire) is sufficient to make it truly my own, and further rejects the noncognitive interpretation of such statements. To say that a desire is one's own is to posit the existence of a structural relationship between the desire and one's self. Similarly, to say that an action is one's own is to posit the existence of a structural relationship between the action and the self. Because our identifications embody judgments about the presence of such structural relations, they may be erroneous. The exact nature of the structural relationship that makes a desire or an action one's own is extremely complex and theoretically open.

A particularly jarring example that suggests that identification is not sufficient for somethings being really one's own is found in the television commercial for a popular brand of face cream. It shows an attractive, late thirties or early forties woman. She muses to herself about the wrinkles that have appeared. She says, "There is a part of me that says 'Age gracefully,' but then the real me says, 'why?'" As she says "then the real me says," she smiles a somewhat devilish, somewhat sexy smile. The viewer is presented with a woman who is experiencing inner conflict. On one level she affirms an ethic that challenges youth-based ideals of beauty and advocates aging with acceptance, grace, and dignity. On the other hand she has a powerful desire to continue to appear young. But the viewer witnesses her having resolved the conflict through an identification with the will to struggle against aging. The smile "tells" us that this indeed is the real person coming through, and it relegates the "age gracefully" perspective to something foreign, perhaps the superficial imperative of a feminist subculture.

The intent of the commercial is to get the viewer to take over the perspective of the woman in the ad. It seeks to cause the women viewing the ad to have the same kind of identification that she does, to not fight against their attachment to youth-based conceptions of beauty or the will to appear younger than they are, but rather to embrace such impulses as genuinely their own and instead to reject those values in terms of which such impulses might be overridden (and face cream neglected).

Suppose that such advertising campaigns are effective in getting women to have the identifications they seek to establish. If identification is sufficient to establish a part of oneself as really one's own, then the advertisers have brought it about that the woman's real self lies not in her "age gracefully" values, not in her reflection upon what is wrong with the face cream culture, but rather in her will to resist the appearance of aging. I would deny this. At some later time the very same woman who now identifies with the will to resist looking one's age may come to see that her identifications themselves were manipulated, that her identifications were not really her own. Something more than identification is required to establish an element of the self as genuinely one's own. Identification is neither necessary nor sufficient.

Watson, in his celebrated essay "Free Agency," put forward a view that comes closer to the structural perspective I am urging. Watson seeks to "develop a distinction between wanting and valuing which will enable the familiar view of freedom as able to make sense of the notion of an unfree action." He contends that in the case of an unfree action, the person is "unable to get what he most wants or values, and this inability is due to his own motivational system."[5] In developing the distinction between wanting and valuing, Watson emphasizes that when we want something because we value it, the source of the want lies in our *judgment* with respect to the good. Watson is careful to explain that some moral attitudes are merely the result of acculturation and do not emerge from the person's judgment. In the sense in which he is using "to value" these situations would not be instances of valuing.

He defines the valuation system of an agent as "that set of considerations which, when combined with his factual beliefs (and probability estimates) yields judgments of the form: the thing for me to do in these circumstances, all things considered, is a."[6] He defines the motivational system of an agent as "that set of considerations which move him to action."[7] He then concludes that the possibility of unfree action consists in the fact that an agent's valuational system and motivational system may not completely coincide. He says, "The free agent has the capacity to translate his values into action; his actions flow from his evalutional system."[8]

Watson then considers the approach Frankfurt has taken. He disagrees with the emphasis on second-order volitions. He writes:

> the "structural" feature to which Frankfurt appeals is not the fundamental feature for either free agency or personhood. . . .
>
> One job that Frankfurt wishes to do with the distinction between lower and higher orders of desire is to give an account of the sense in which some want may be said to be more truly the agent's own than others (though in an obvious sense all are wants of the agent) the sense in which the agent "identifies" with one desire rather than another, and the sense in which an agent may be unfree with respect to his own "will."[9]

Watson goes on to ask, "What gives these volitions any special relationship to 'oneself'?" Watson argues that the status of the second-order volitions comes from first-order practical judgments concerned with whether or not a given action is worth doing. If we judge that it is, then we want to act out of the desire to do it. Watson then draws the explicit parallel with Plato:

> Therefore, Frankfurt's position resembles the platonic conception in its focus upon the structure of the "soul." But the two views draw their divisions differently; whereas Frankfurt divides the soul into higher and lower orders of desire, the distinction for Plato—and for my thesis—is among independent sources of motivation.[10]

Essentially, Watson shares Frankfurt's view that an agent is free when he or she acts from desires that are in the fullest sense his or her own. But Watson claims that these are not as Frankfurt would have it, desires that are the object of second-order desires, nor are they the second-order desires themselves, nor are they desires that one identifies with. Rather they are desires that emerge from first-order evaluative judgments.

Watson quite correctly points out that Frankfurt has not demonstrated the special status he attaches to second-order volitions, and Watson then goes on to suggest that the special status actually should be given to our first-order evaluative judgments.

Watson's view may be recast as:

> A desire is one's own if is integrated with the individual's valuation system; and, a desire is one's own only if it does not conflict with one's valuation system.

Harmony between values and desires ensures true ownership, and conflict between values and desires disqualifies ownership of the desire.

It is important to see that Watson's outlook is also a form of locus theory. He is not requiring harmony per se as a condition of ownership of any element of the self, but rather as a condition of ownership of desires. They must fit with the values. The values have the elevated position. Conflict between the two systems does not call them equally into doubt.

What I want to emphasize about Watson's perspective is the importance he gives to a structural relationship. He is not saying that any moral or evaluative attitude per se is one's own. There must be some *set* of views that results in an evaluative judgment.

In his reference to valuation systems and motivational systems, and the need for "harmony" between those systems, Watson is describing aspects of what I have referred to as the integrated personality or self. One difference between Watson's view and my own is simply that in my analysis for an action to come from the self it is neither necessary nor sufficient that it come from a desire that is part of a larger evaluative system.

It is not sufficient because the *evaluative* system need not be truly one's own. It may run powerfully in conflict with other emotions and desires of the person. Suppose that I have not only a belief that sex is wrong and ugly, but a *system* of beliefs in which I believe that man is evil and that sex is the source of that evil, and further I believe that there are religious authorities of great stature that have laid down these findings. Thus, I have a value system, a structure of judgments. Does it follow from this that my sexual impulses are not my own? Does it follow from this that I am unfree if I yield to a desire in conflict with these judgments? Watson and Frankfurt would say yes.

Against both Watson and Frankfurt, there is the Lawrencian position. In D. H. Lawrence we have the total rejection of desire that emerges from some notion of the ideal, whether it be second-order volitions as to which first-order desires we want to act from, or first-order judgments of the worth of contemplated actions. Lawrence's rejection of action that emerges from notions of the ideal would encompass actions done in pursuit of one's ego-ideal or in fulfillment of notions of virtue.

Both Watson and Frankfurt represent certain specifications of linkages between self and action. Watson's view is more structural and powerful than Frankfurt's but it remains just one possible way of giving signification to these connections. A Lawrencian outlook maintains an alternative view of the self that takes these exact connections and treats them as criteria for concluding that the action is *not* really one's own. Not only are different factors given different weight, but the same factor, on a different conception, may count against, not for, presence of self.

Consider:

> Experience is true to the person when he is himself alone. . . . There are no goals to pursue, directions to follow, or techniques to use. . . . Self-expression is not persuasive and is without special purpose or function.[11]

And

> Not voluntarism, but spontaneity, or grace, not the ego but the id.[12]

In these passages, which reflect the influence of D. H. Lawrence, the authors give emphasis to that which is done for its own sake, rejecting that which is instrumental, calculative, or goal oriented—central elements in the evaluative system Watson emphasizes.

Similarly within a Nietzschean perspective, an individual whose moral beliefs are in conflict with his or her impulses and who engages in an activity *out of a sense of duty*, does not manifest the presence of his or her self in that activity. It is exactly the opposite.

Both Lawrence and Nietzsche represent alternatives to Watson's view that the locus of the self is to be found in the evaluative system per se. In pointing out the limitations of Watson's view, I am not maintaining that the kind of linkages he points to *must* be insufficient. Rather, a great deal depends on the individual self in question. For instance, unlike Lawrence, I am not saying that the sexual is the locus of the true self and of authentic desire. If the person has a sufficiently integrated personality in which his judgments and beliefs about the sinfulness of sexual impulse are deeply and richly integrated, then that is who he is. And in *that* case his acting in ways that conflict with sexual impulse are genuinely actions of his self. But because I am not attributing to the value system some general role as the locus of the self, the degree of integration required would be considerably more than that demanded on a view of the sort Watson holds.

As an alternative to all locus theories, I would argue that there is no single psychic element or subsystem that is the carrier of the self, and thus no special entity that must be related to desires in order that they be my own. Rather the question of ownership is specific to the individual in question. If his personality is integrated around an evaluative system, and if his actions emerge from that system, then they emerge from himself. But if his personality is integrated in ways quite different, if, for instance, desires and emotions play a more central role and judgments are less central, then when there is conflict between his values and his desires or emotions, he is more fully expressed when he acts out of his emotions.

The Structural Web of Agency

Agency can be viewed as a complex structural union between actions and the self. In virtue of this structural connectedness, the self may be said to be present in actions. But it is more than that. Agency is not a single simple relationship. It is not a matter of the exercise of some irreducible power of agent causality, nor is it a matter of the general existence of a single causal thread that connects volition or desire with physical movement. Agency is a union of self and action that is different in each and every token of every type of action. Moreover, it is not merely a structural connection between the self and the action, but typically a structural relationship through which the self is directly present in the activity molecule and thus accounts for our sense that we are literally alive and active through our actions.

There are two radically different dimensions to this structural connectedness. On one end of the spectrum the connectedness in question may have nothing to do with the experiential qualities of the activity performance. Indeed, as I will maintain, this non-immediate structural connectedness can even be constructed by the person years after the performance of the action itself.

On the other hand, there is a second dimension that involves the direct and immediate presence of the self within the activity itself. This dimension has both phenomenological and behavioral aspects. It is not a mere matter of causal connectedness between activity and self, but of actual presence of self in the activity.

In this section I consider the first dimension—the web of structural relations that constitute agency, whether or not they result in direct presence of self. In the next section I will consider direct and immediate presence of the self within the activity.

A person performs an action. Is it really hers? As both Watson and Frankfurt realized, the central structural linkage involves consideration of why the individual performed the action. On traditional accounts, since something is an action only in virtue of being caused by wants and beliefs (or volitions), there are always wants and beliefs that are linked to the action. Thus, the issue of whether or not the action is truly an act of that person tends to focus on whether or not the wants and beliefs are truly her own.

On the account I offer, an activity is a free-standing process that is an activity in virtue of its inner structure. This inner structure involves a causal interaction with a mental element (the ongoing perceptual awareness) but does not necessarily involve wants and beliefs.

It is possible to imagine a situation in which, through electrical or chemical stimulation of the brain, scientists would be able to cause a person to engage in some activity. They could do this without causing her to have the wants and beliefs that would typically explain the action. Suppose someone picks up a violin and plays it. And suppose that not only do her hands behave in ways necessary to bring forth music from the instrument, but the performance is brought about through the ongoing perceptual assessment of the music as it is generated. We have a clear case of an activity. In some minimal sense it would be her activity, in that it was her body that was active and the movements of her body were being guided by mental states that were hers. But she would not be the agent of that activity. There would be no connection to the self at all.

Suppose we ask this person why she played the violin. And suppose that she can give no reason, and that we can find no reason. And suppose further that the "default" explanation—"because I wanted to," or "because I felt like it," turns out to be completely empty. The individual had no experiential desire to play the violin, and when checked we find that the typical brain states people are in when they have such a desire were not present. Essentially we have activity with no motivation. Under these circumstances, we might maintain that the person was completely passive with respect to the activity. She was not an agent of it at all. Just as we can imagine the story where the explanation for the behavior lies in the manipulation by the scientists, it is completely possible for something, perhaps not quite this stark, but similar, to happen in ordinary life without any external forces doing the manipulation.

The question of motivation is the central issue, but not the only issue, in considering the way in which a person is linked to his actions. The various factors raised in the accounts given by Watson and Frankfurt all have their place in the story, but none occupies the throne.

Typically actions do not occur just by themselves. They arise out of a constellation of wants, beliefs, attitudes, evaluative judgments, and emotions. In establishing agency, the first task is to identify these connections. The question "Why did he do it?" typically elicits this kind of connectedness: "because he was angry"; "because he hates her"; "because he wanted to"; "because he thought it was right"; "because by doing that he was able to do *X*."

Any of these connections can serve, and there is no need to try to squeeze them into one particular model. Further, as both Frankfurt and Watson recognized, these kind of linkages are insufficient to establish that the action is really his own. It must be more deeply connected to some larger structure of self, typically by showing that the desire, emotion, belief, value, or judgment from which the action emerged is itself authentically the person's.

Where Frankfurt's and Watson's approaches go astray is in their efforts to specify a particular kind of linkage, whether to second-order desires or to evaluative judgments, which is either necessary or sufficient. Similarly, a person's identifications, which are clearly also of relevance to agency, are neither necessary nor sufficient. As I argued earlier, identification reflects a judgment about the existence of a deeper structural relationship.

A much stronger formulation, which brings together Watson's emphasis on values and Bergmann and Frankfurt's focus on identification and that ensures a powerful structural tie between self and action, would be to require that the action emerges from some element that is part of someone's self-identity. For instance, that it emerges from *certain* values, the holding of which is part of how the person understands himself to be the person he is. This is a nonphenomenological linkage, which may be expressed in an identification experience, but need not be.

But this condition is far *too* strong and would be met only relatively infrequently, and further, as strong as it is, might still prove insufficient as even a person's identity structure could prove to be not authentically his own. (This possibility is considered further in the discussion of alienness and political activity later in this volume.)

What I conclude from this is that agency has to be conceived as a kind of webbing, as a connectedness between self and activity that has no particular specification. It might be thought of as analogous to the webbing that supports suspension bridges. There is no engineering specification that covers all cases, being necessary to all circumstances and sufficient to all eventualities.

Moreover, some elements of webbing that connect the self to its activities can be very indirect, and nonetheless quite central to establishing that the action is genuinely one's own. Thus it may be a matter of a connectedness that is nothing like the following:

> At the time of the performance, the desire that actually causes the act-token must be accompanied by another occurrent desire that the first desire be acted upon and this second desire must itself be a cause of the fact that the first desire causes the action.

Rather it may be that:

- The person's self-identity tends to be confirmed by the fact that he does *A* (a deeply religious person engages in a ritual prayer, almost on automatic pilot);
- The skills that are utilized in *A* have been acquired as part of a central project of *X* (a figure skater does a dance routine at the Olympics after having rehearsed it for years);

- The opportunity to do *A* was the result of *X*'s efforts to obtain an opportunity to do *A* (an immigrant finally gets the opportunity to pull the lever in a voting booth);
- Doing *A* is expressive of *X*'s deepest emotions and concerns (without reflection or even conscious awareness a mother comforts her child).

Put in general terms, the structural connectedness between the person and his or her action needs to be such that the action is linked to the self rather than to some element that itself floats freely. Insofar as a particular theorist maintains a conception of the self that places specific elements at the center of the self complex, it would be expected that that theorist would view agency as requiring a linkage with elements of that sort.

In presenting a view of the agency relationship as a web of diverse connectedness, I want to stress just how complex and how theoretically open this relationship between an action and the self is. This can be seen by reflecting on the way in which at later points in our life we can give meaning to earlier points, and appropriate as one's own actions from one's distant past. For instance, some event is made into a decisive turning point by the things I do later; I give it its deeper significance by making something out of it.

Consider a man who for years worked tremendously hard, accumulating a good deal of money and power and the ability to cut his way through obstacles that would thwart most others. One day he begins to look back on much of how he has lived his life, on all that activity and expended energy, and it seems strange and pointless. He wonders about it. What was his life about? Were those wasted years? Why was he so motivated to earn money? He now looks back upon much of his life with a kind of confusion. He doesn't understand what point there really was in his having devoted so much time to accumulation. From one perspective, it may seem as if his life was never his own. Yet it may be within his ability to appropriate those years, to give them a meaning that becomes their central meaning even though they were not seen that way when they occurred. For instance, in turning his attention towards the future, towards some grand project in which he deeply believes but has never until now undertaken, he may find that it is only made possible because of how he lived all those previous years. His wealth and power and personality now are seen differently. He weaves them into a larger structure, into the project of his life, and through this his meaning and fulfillment emerge. Their meaning is revealed. They were the years of preparation, the years through which he became who he had to be in order to do what he must do in life.

A perspective such as this is common in fairy tales and in some fictional writing. Usually it is a story of someone who does not know his real identity, a prince raised as a pauper. But the conception of identity in fairy tales is as something externally given, through birth or through an oracle or through some supernatural agent with the power to confer identity. In reality, identity is to a considerable extent self-conferred, and with the conferring of identity we have the reformulation of the self, and thus the realignment of past actions in relationship to that self.

The basic point is that the connectedness that constitutes agency is not limited to a connectedness that exists prior to or at the time of the action. It can come into being at a later stage, and thus agency, which in the main is a matter of causal relations through which the self gives rise to the action, cannot be limited to just linkages of that sort.

Immediate and Direct Presence of the Self in Activity

It was noted above that the union of self and action has two dimensions. The first is a diverse web of connectedness that links the self to the action. The second is something rather different—it is the direct and active presence of the self within the activity performance.

If we think of actions or of agency as the "making happen" of some simple event, some bit of behavior—say the movement of a finger—we may not even notice this aspect of agency. And indeed, it has been largely ignored in the vast literature of action theory. Yet it is something that we are all familiar with in everyday life.

The expression "present in the activity" corresponds to our experience when we are engaged in an activity. We do not experience our hand as moving and merely believe that there is some connection between the movement of the hand and our self; rather, we experience the movements as the movements of the self. Not only is the movement self-generated, but it is the movement of an embodied self; in some sense I am both in and active-in the activity of the moving hand. This goes way beyond merely causing it. Of course, *experiencing* oneself as present in an activity is neither a necessary nor a sufficient condition for *being* present in that activity. It is always possible, for instance, that someone, through confusion or self-deception or freak circumstances, fails to experience himself as present in some activity where he is present (fails to experience himself as an agent when he is an agent), or experiences himself as present when he is not. The question to be answered is this: In virtue of what characteristic is someone's experience of himself as present or not present in his activity correct or incorrect?

When we are engaged in an activity, when we are most active, there is a sense that we are somehow alive within the very activity itself; it is in and through the activity that we are rendered visible, concrete, and external. This is not the only sense in which someone might be said to be present in his activity, but it is phenomenologically the sharpest.

But to what does this phenomenological experience of ourselves as alive *within* the activity correspond? Are we dealing here only with imperfect metaphors for something very difficult to describe? Or is it literally true that the self is present in the activity? On the account of activity offered earlier, literal presence is possible.

The expressions "presence of mind" and "absent-mindedly" suggest that activities can be performed with different degrees of presence of self. And the admonition to do something with presence of mind suggests that it is in some sense possible to put oneself into the activity—where this means more than just to watch it from afar, even if watched carefully. But if the self can be present in the activity, how does it gain access?

In my essay on activity I maintain that activities are organic wholes unified through "indirect perceptual integration." There is an ongoing perceptual assessment of the outcomes such that the other elements (e.g., movements) are caused to occur in such a way as to bring the outcomes into conformity with the inherent assessment. In a direct primary sense, the self gains access to the activity molecule through the perceptual assessment. Perceptual assessments are not uniform across the entire domain of activities. The perception may be intense; it may be wavering; it may be sensitive to aspects of concern to the self; it may be impulsively blind; it may be the highly developed result of years of practice or it may be amateurish; it may constitute all of *X*'s awareness or it may compete with other mental states; it may be absorbed or it may be detached.

The perceptual assessment can be characterized as a form of "seeing-as," that is, as a phenomenologically rich perception whose particular richness involves the seeing of the outcomes as too-this or too-that or as just-right. To speak of a perceptual assessment is to say that the unfolding outcome is perceived against the backdrop of a standard or bench mark or image of adequacy. The perceptual assessment is, however, an occurrent mental event.

Perceptual assessments are not wants or beliefs and they cannot in all cases be understood as expressive of the individual's wants and beliefs. Thus, an individual may not want her craft to be aesthetically right (e.g., she does not want to give her best to this employer given the low wages she receives) but she finds that she cannot avoid seeing the work as not-right (her seeing it as not-right should not be viewed as an expression of a desire of hers that it be right or that it be not-right—it is just the way she sees it). Nor is it always the case that the perceptual assessment is expressive of the individual's beliefs. For instance, in driving my car behind another car I regulate the distance between the two cars by way of a perceptual assessment of the distance between the two cars as "okay" or in terms of a perceptual assessment that a certain distance is "too close." Not only do I not have to have the thoughts "I'm getting too close to that car and I had better slow down," it is not necessary that I even have such beliefs. All the fact of activity requires is that I have the perceptual assessment and that it causes me to move in ways that result in my getting the distance between my car and the other to conform to my perceptual sense of what is "okay." It is perfectly possible that I know, and thus believe, that I am vastly over-cautious and believe that in fact it is perfectly safe to be much closer than I am. I can have these beliefs and nonetheless have a perceptual assessment of the car ahead as "too close." Thus, the notion of activity can be articulated without reliance on wants, volitions, or beliefs of the individual.

However, to point to these possibilities of activities that are divorced from the individual's wants and beliefs does not mean that they must be divorced. On the contrary, typically it is the case that the perceptual assessment is expressive of the individual's wants and beliefs. If I see the car ahead of me as "too close" it is because I don't *want* to be in an accident and because I have some general *belief* that at this distance there is danger of an accident. It typically is in virtue of my having wants and beliefs of this sort that I come to have perceptual assessments of this sort, and while it is the case that the perceptual standard, once formed, can have a life of its own, it is generally responsive to the wants and beliefs that one has in the specific context.

Suppose that I am giving someone an account of a particular incident; it may be that the way I tell the story, the detail, the speed, the tone I take, and so on, are regulated via my perception of their reaction as I speak. I might not have any preexisting standard that corresponds to what I view as too-close when I approach another car—rather my telling of the incident is regulated by my desire to get a certain kind of response from this particular person, and by my belief as to whether or not I am getting that response. While these desires and beliefs may be fully operative during the activity, they need, of course, not be desires or beliefs that I am conscious of as I speak. Indeed, the awareness of the fact that I am regulating my activity in the light of such wants and beliefs tends to break the flow of the activity. It fragments it into separate components. Its wholeness is better preserved when the regulation merely occurs—thus, at the heart of activity there is an element of passivity. Or to put it differently, activity may be at its core nonvolitional.

The normal coherence between the individual's wants and beliefs and the perceptual assessment inherent in the activity is the most basic way in which the self is directly present in activity. The wants and beliefs are typically part of the integrated unit we are calling self, and their reflection within the activity *is* the presence of self in the activity. The perceptual assessment is their expression. This linkage is our base case of normal, minimal agency. It implies nothing about the centrality of the wants and beliefs to the self, and it corresponds only to the minimal sense in which we are typically the agent of our activities.

It can, of course, be the case that the aspects of the self that are directly present in the activity are quite central. Thus, consider the standard that is implicit in the perceptual assessment. For instance, is this standard tied to the individual's self-identity—as it might be if the activity in question was an artistic activity (e.g., ballet), and being a person who has such and such a standard of how it should be done, or being a person who is able to perceive the differences between its being done well or poorly, were central aspects of a person's sense of worth.

Wants and beliefs, however, are not the only aspects of the self that can be directly reflected in the activity molecule. Consider an individual whose vocal feeling tone does not fit with the content of what she is saying. This relationship between the content of the speech act and the tone of the same act is intelligible because both content and tone are expressive of emotions, moods, and attitudes. There is conflict when tone and content seem to express contradictory attitudes. But our nonverbal behavior also has an emotional tone to it; the way in which we do certain things is not merely a matter of conformity to some perceptual assessment, it may also be the result of the fact that we are in a particular emotional state. The emotion is directly expressed through the activity; it colors the activity. Thus, the emotional tone of an activity, while not a matter of bringing the shape of the activity into conformity with an implicit standard, does, in a parallel way, reflect the direct presence within the activity of mental states that may constitute or be connected to central elements of the self.

Consider, for instance, a single act—a woman kisses a man. The kiss is never just a kiss. It is always a certain kind of kiss, and its being this kind or that kind is itself reflected in the very structure of the kiss. Compare then:

1. *Purely instrumental*—a kiss delivered to a stranger for one dollar at a country fair kissing booth. In this case, without pleasure or emotion of any sort, performed solely in order to raise money for charity;
2. *Perfunctorily*—the marriage has gone stale. It is the regular bedtime kiss;
3. *Affectionately*—she greets her good woman friend of many years;
4. *Sensuously*—she is in bed with her lover; they have the whole afternoon ahead of them;
5. *Tenderly*—her husband is asleep and she does not really want to wake him, but she is filled with love for him;
6. *With repugnance*—out of a sense of obligation as a wife married to a man she finds physically repellant;
7. *Passionately*—overflowing with sexual desire, she tries to devour him.

In these different situations, the woman feels different things, and the kiss has different causal histories. But it would be a serious mistake to assume that the kiss itself is always the same, and that the situations differ solely with respect to antecedents or concomitant mental states. Quite the contrary. The sensuous kiss is not the same as the perfunctory kiss, and neither is the same as the tender kiss. There are observable differences, different not only to the one doing the kiss but to the person being kissed and to a third-party viewer. If it were in a play, the director might tell the actress what kind of kiss, and in teaching acting one might need to show someone the differences.

The sensuous kiss is slower. The lips themselves are more exploratory, and are pushed forward and perhaps slightly parted. This much can be seen by the observer. But it is more than observation. For the person doing the kissing, it is not just a matter of behavior. To kiss someone sensuously is to locate one's consciousness in a certain way. One cannot kiss sensuously while thinking about something else.

This feature of the kiss—the character of consciousness during the kiss—is not something extra that occurs at the same time as the kiss, rather it is itself inside the kiss. The activity molecule that is the kiss is held together by it. The awareness of the lips of the other is not the same in the sensuous kiss as in the perfunctory kiss. Not only is it longer in duration, but it is a more acute awareness. It involves a full attentiveness of the person to the lips of the other as they are found by one's own. But it is more than that; it involves a finding of the other's lips as delicious (at least typically so). Thus, the person is in it in a special way that is not the case with the perfunctory kiss. That kiss is almost pure behavior. It is stiff and unexploring, and brief.

In the loving kiss there is yet another difference. It is not merely that the person loves the person she is kissing. One can kiss a loved one other than lovingly. The loving kiss itself is saying something through the activity. An emotion is being expressed. The emotion of love is not only expressed in the kiss, it conditions the kiss. Because the kiss emerges from love it is different in certain ways. There is a language of expression. It is not critical whether it is purely conventional or whether there is some universal and natural way in which feelings of certain sorts are expressed through behavior. What is germane is that because the kiss expresses love, and possibly because it is intended to express love, it is done in a certain way.

And it must be remembered that the activity molecule that is the kiss is made up of more than that which is logically necessary for a kiss—a kiss is in reality more than something we do with our lips. It involves the entire body. It involves holding the other or touching the other in certain ways. Two hands hold the head in a way that is coordinated with the lips. The eyes are closed just in order that consciousness of all else be obliterated; just in order that sensuous engagement is possible.

These correlative elements of the kiss are quite different in different kisses. In the country fair kiss, there may be elements exactly the opposite of the loving kiss. The body is held back so that there is no physical contact except that between the lips themselves. This may be how the woman says, "This is just a country fair kiss."

The broader point is this: the activity molecule itself, whether it is the perceptual assessment, the standard implicit in the perceptual assessment, or the movements themselves (what do the lips do, and how long, how forcefully do they do it), or what the arms and hands and head and eyes do in the kiss—all of these elements possess the capability of modification that may reflect aspects of the self. They are all vehicles through which other elements of the self are present in the kiss.

An important distinction needs to be made. Part of what I am saying is that the kiss itself has within its very structure elements that are modified to express a broad array of attitudes, motives, emotions, and desires. And the perfunctory kiss is in its way just as expressive as the sensuous kiss. That is, it too reflects and embodies something quite large. An entire universe of understanding might be read out of one perfunctory kiss. So in one sense the self is to be found, perhaps revealed and expressed, in the perfunctory kiss. Yet there is another sense in which the difference between the perfunctory kiss and the sensuous kiss is precisely that the self is *not present* in the former and is present in the latter.

The fact that we make this distinction tells us that by presence of self we mean something more than that components of the self are revealed or expressed or manifest in the activity. Just what we mean is not easy to say. A first thought is that the difference is that the perfunctory kiss expresses or reveals the absence of certain feelings, while the sensuous kiss actually is the manifestation of their presence. But this is hard to sustain. The perfunctory kiss certainly is not the manifestation of love, but it might be the manifestation of something else—perhaps in some instance a sense of duty. And the kissing of that which is experienced as repugnant may manifest emotions as powerful as love—it may manifest hatred.

The difference at hand is a difference that has to do with being wholly engaged (or not) in a performance. The term "wholehearted" might be used as well, but that term is ambiguous. In one sense it is synonymous with "wholly engaged," referring to the phenomenology of the performance as it occurs, but in another sense it has to do with the absence of any conflict about what it is that we are doing. This typically is reflected in the phenomenology, but it need not be. So we may not be wholehearted in kissing an illicit lover, in that we may believe that it is wrong, yet it may be the case that some of these illicit kisses are kisses that we are wholly engaged in when we deliver them.

One aspect of what we mean by being present in an action is that we are fully present in it when we do it. It suggests the absence of conflicting tendencies, in that conflict tends to affect our consciousness during the very performance. Consider these diverse examples of a kiss that does not fully engage the person as she performs it:

- *Purely instrumental*—the kiss at the country fair previously described;
- *Against her will*—a woman kisses a man who threatens her with a knife. It is a rape. She is almost frozen with fear;
- *Conflictedly*—she kisses an illicit lover, feeling that it is wrong to be doing so;
- *Ambivalently*—it is the first date. She kisses him but is unsure of whether or not she really wants to;
- *Perfunctorily*—the marriage has gone stale. It is the regular bedtime kiss.

In none of these kisses is the person wholly engaged in *the performance*. Being distracted, remote, frozen, or troubled are all ways of being not-present when we do something. Yet the absence of the whole engagement of the person connotes rather different things in each case. In the instances of fear, guilt, and ambivalence there is conflict; either conflicting tendencies, conflicting motives, or conflicting desires. But in the instances of pure instrumentality and the perfunctory kiss, it is not conflict but rather the absence of an occurrent (noninstrumental) desire to kiss.

In that which is spontaneous, joyful, delightful, in that which is play, there is an immediacy to the performance. And sometimes we speak of the immediacy of a person, meaning their capacity to be right-there in that which they are doing. Thus, the presence of the self is not merely a matter of the expression of elements of the self in the activity, but also the immediate presence of the self.

When we do something naturally, spontaneously, rather than purely instrumentally, there is a creativity that emerges. One discovers who one is by relaxing and letting one's self come out. And this relationship between self and action when the self is emerging is perhaps what gives us the sharpest sense of the activity of the self. It is not merely that there is a preexisting self that is expressed or reflected in the activity, but rather *the self emerges for itself in the very activity*. In this regard there is a basic difference between a performance that is rehearsed and one that is spontaneous. It is not that in delivering a rehearsed performance one is not an agent, or that the self is not present in the performance. It may be fully so. But in the spontaneous performance, be it an exciting conversation or a jazz performance, there is the element of *novelty*. We do not know exactly what we are going to do or say prior to our doing or saying it. Yet *rather than this lack of forethought and lack of explicit intention reflect-*

ing an absence of agency, it is exactly this feature that permits the self to be most active, to rise to and break through the surface. In creativity the self is both revealed to itself and constituted. Ironically, this greatest activity of the self occurs when we abandon volition, when we just let ourselves happen.

Some activities, in virtue of the kind of activities that they are, have a particularly great potential for the self to be present. These expressive activities are those in which the self can most fully be directly present in the activity itself. Thus, playing the violin offers far greater possibilities for the direct presence of self than does stapling papers together. The perceptual assessment of the ongoing outcome is rich and subtle and sensitive to the variety of possibilities. The perceptual assessment serves as the eye of the needle through which the self emerges.

The fact that certain kinds of activities have an unusually rich and distinct potential for being vehicles for the direct presence (expression) of the self results in their being separated off as "expressive," "artistic," or "aesthetic" activities. The potential that they have, which we might term "aesthetic potential," is not unique to them. All human activity has *some* aesthetic potential; what makes aesthetic activities unique is the range and scope of this dimension.

The fact that an individual engages in such activities, however, does not mean that he or she avails of that potential. Rather, it is typically the case that one has to learn how to do so. This is a great part of what training in these activities consists of. Thus, consider sculpture—it is the plasticity *of the clay itself* that provides the potential, but the individual must learn how to express himself through it. And this direct expression is a matter of learning how to make the clay conform to the standards inherent in one's perception of it as it is modeled (which is itself in part dependent on the education of our eyes as well as our hands)—and also of learning how to transmit to or through the clay an emotionality.

Yet artists or practitioners of any aesthetic activity may be thoroughly alienated from what they are doing. Often there is a failure to perceive or understand how this can be so, because it is not recognized that self-expression is not guaranteed merely in virtue of the type of activity that is performed; it is a question of the relationships of the self to the actual token, and these relationships may be quite diverse. They may also be quite weak, even where great aesthetic potential exists. There is no type of activity that cannot be done without immediacy, without involvement, without presence of self. We always may be elsewhere.

The actualization of the aesthetic and emotional potential of an activity, what we are calling the immediate and direct presence of the self within the activity, is of great importance. For some people participation in such modes of self-expression is the central pleasure/confirmation that life has to offer. But we should not make the mistake of assuming that direct presence is the only way the self may be present in an action; nor should we assume that it is necessarily the most significant.

It is often the case that even when aesthetic potential is very limited, and thus there is limited *direct* presence of self, the *indirect* presence may be quite powerful. Digging a hole may be a mechanical operation, performed with crude tools and little or no critical perception or adjustment of outcome; yet it may embody a great deal of the self—as when one is planting trees in a reclaimed desert. The simple act of handing someone an object is not rich in aesthetic potential. Yet if the object is one's teenage diary and a mother is passing it to her daughter, the *act* of giving it to one's daughter may express much that is central to the self of the parent—though the activity in physical terms expresses little. Thus, both aspects of agency—the web of connectedness and the immediate presence of self—stand on their own feet. Indeed, for all the power of the experiences of immediate presence, at bottom they are features of the phenomenology of the performance. They are properly thought of as the marks of presence, rather than being fully constitutive of presence itself. And thus I might at some later point look back on actions in which I experienced myself as immediately present and conclude that that wasn't really me after all.

Kohut's discussion of what he terms "pseudovitality" is suggestive of how a better understanding of the psychological dynamics that lie behind the marks of engagement can contribute to our understanding of agency.

He writes of

> the overt excitement. Behind it lie low self-esteem and depression, a deep sense of uncared-for-worthlessness and rejection, an incessant hunger for response, a yearning for reassurance. All in all, the excited hyperactivity of the patient must be understood as an attempt to counteract through self-stimulation a feeling of inner deadness and depression.[13]

This is an important caveat. If we are to go along with Lawrence and Nietzsche in their emphasis on spontaneity, we must remember that the truly spontaneous may be quite hard to discern.

With this I conclude the discussion of presence. At bottom it is presence of the self that is at the heart of the notion of agency. The concept of presence is multidimensional and remains a rich field for future work. In the pages above, I have called attention to many of its central dimensions; they are listed below.

I. *Ways in which the self gains direct presence within an activity*

1. The perceptual assessment is expressive of the wants and beliefs of the individual.
2. The standard inherent in the perceptual assessment is itself an expression of *X*'s basic values, standards, projects, sensibilities, etc.
3. The emotional tone of the activity is expressive of central emotions or concerns of *X*.

II. *Immediacy: marks of presence in the performance*

4. While doing *A*, *X* does not experience moral qualms about doing *A*.
5. *X* enjoys doing *A*.
6. While doing *A*, *A* seems a reasonable thing to be doing.
7. While doing *A*, *X* does not feel that he would rather be doing something else.
8. While doing *A*, *X* does not dwell on the alternatives he might be doing instead of *A*.
9. *X*'s sole attention is on *A*.
10. *X* "forgets" or "loses himself" in doing *A*.
11. When he does *A*, he experiences himself as free, or as acting out of his real self.
12. *X* performs *A* with enthusiasm; it rushes out of him.

Notes

1. Harry Frankfurt, "Freedom of the Will and the Concept of a Person," in *Free Will*, ed. Gary Watson (New York: Oxford University Press, 1982), 92.

2. Frankfurt, "Freedom," 86.

3. Ibid., 91.

4. John M. Fisher, ed. *Moral Responsibility* (Ithaca: Cornell University Press, 1986), 48.

5. Gary Watson, "Free Agency," in *Free Will*, ed. Gary Watson (New York: Oxford University Press, 1982), 97.

6. Watson, "Free Agency," 104.
7. Ibid., 105.
8. Ibid., 106.
9. Ibid., 107.
10. Ibid., 109.
11. Clark Moustakis, *The Self* (New York: Harper, 1956), 3.
12. Norman O. Brown, *Psychology Today*, Aug. 1970, 44.
13. Heinz Kohut, *The Restoration of the Self* (New York: International Universities Press, 1977), 5.

2
Alienness: Experiencing One's Own Incoherence

From Plato to the present day, the human psyche has been thought of as consisting of parts, and mental health has been thought to require certain degrees and kinds of relatedness between the parts. Plato used the metaphor of political justice to characterize the ideal relationship between the parts; contemporary theorists may emphasize the elimination of "dissonance" between cognitive elements. However it is formulated, be it in terms of "integration of the personality," "internal coherence," or "cognitive dissonance" there is an enduring tendency to think of human healthfulness as requiring a certain unity or wholeness.

Closely linked to the tradition that emphasizes wholeness is another strain of thought that emphasizes honesty and authenticity as central to the health ideal. From the Socratic injunction to "know thyself" through contemporary efforts to uncover one's real feelings, the attainment of healthfulness has been associated with overcoming internal dishonesty and self-deception. It is an ancient wisdom that human beings not only have, at times, false beliefs about themselves, but that the "falseness" is not innocent.

The "wholeness" tradition and the "honesty" tradition are intimately connected. Not only is a lack of internal honesty one example of a lack of wholeness, but internal dishonesty is typically thought of as a response to a yet more fundamental incoherence. This disunity, which may be characterized as "conflict" or "threat" or less dramatically as "dissonance," gives rise to the falsity. Thus mental health is thought to involve not only self-knowledge, but also the elimination of internal discord, which generates falsity. The honest recognition that one is terribly conflicted, that one's emotions are not consistent with one's judgments, or that one has inconsistent views of oneself, is but a way station on the road to a fuller health. But what if it does not work this way? What if it turns out that the more we follow the injunction to "know thyself" the more we encounter incoherence? And what if it turns out that that incoherence is not rooted in malleable features of our individuality, but instead is rooted in rather permanent features of the human condition? And what if it turns out that the discovery of this incoherence is so unsettling that it makes it impossible for us to engage in the normal activities and relationships that we take to be the hallmark of the healthy life?

Just such a conflict is articulated by the Underground Man in Dostoyevsky's *Notes From Underground.*

> "I am a sick man."
>
> "People do pride themselves on their diseases, and I do, maybe more than any one. We will not dispute it; my contention was absurd. But yet I am firmly persuaded that a great deal of consciousness, every sort of consciousness, in fact, is a disease."
>
> "I do not respect myself. Can a man of perception respect himself at all?"
>
> "I invented adventures for myself and made up a life, so as at least to live in some way. How many times has it happened to me—well for instance, to take offense simply on purpose, for nothing; and no one knows oneself, of course, that one is offended at nothing, that one is putting it on, but yet one brings oneself, at last to the point of being really offended."
>
> "Anger in me is subject to chemical disintegration. You look into it, the object flies off into the air, your reasons evaporate."
>
> "Oh, if I had done nothing simply from laziness! Heavens, how I should have respected myself, then. I should have respected myself because I should at least have been capable of being lazy; there would at least have been one quality, as it were, positive in me, in which I could have believed myself. Question: What is he? Answer: A sluggard."

How are we to characterize the Underground Man?

1. He sees himself as sick.
2. He finds himself unable to remain involved in any activity.
3. He feels that he lacks an identity; his perception of himself is as a being without any characteristics.

4. His emotional life is unstable. Emotions are not sustained; instead, they seem to dissolve. They never flow smoothly into conduct.
5. He claims to take pleasure in his pains, and pride in his problems.
6. He constantly feels that he is acting some part that he gives himself.

From our everyday standpoint, from the way in which we actually experience people with whom we are in contact, we would recognize the Underground Man as a person with serious mental health problems. And surely, if he were to follow standard advice and seek professional assistance, no psychiatrist would suggest that there is nothing wrong with him. Clearly this man has "psychological problems."

We might, if he is forceful, pause at his knowing that this is precisely what we will think of him. Indeed, he characterizes himself as sick. He seems to be aware of how we will see him, yet he seems to be beyond us. He is mocking our categories and contends that actually there is some logic to his situation. We may *pause*, but surely his having an intelligible perspective on his own being would not lead us to doubt that he has serious problems. It is commonplace that the patient has a rational structure within which his conduct makes sense.

Yet there is something different here. The Underground Man does not explain the peculiarities of his conduct and being by putting forward any facts that are unknown to us. He seems to perceive things quite accurately, with no trace of fantasy. Rather, he claims that it is our conduct and way of being that are in question; that he is the way he is, not out of response to special features of his situation that are unknown to us, but out of appropriate response to the most general features of a situation that we all share. All he is, he claims, is a man honestly responding to the truths of the human condition.

His claim that his experience is authentic or valid is tied to the claim that it *is grounded in consciousness*, that is, accurate awareness or true belief. Even if true, this does not, however, settle the question of his mental health. Accordingly, for the time being, let me put the question of mental health on "hold." What I am concerned with is the *appropriateness* of his experience of incoherence, and the validity of what he says. Though this has bearing on the question of mental health, it is not the same issue. We may discover that there is a conflict within our concept of health; for instance, we may discover that one's general well-being, one's ability to be happy, take pleasure, feel whole, and be productive are not compatible with an authentic response to one's condition.

The existence of some incoherence is the general condition of the human psyche; it is possible that there have never been any human beings that have achieved complete unification. In what follows I shall explore the different kinds of fissures and seek to distinguish those that are ultimate givens of the human condition from those that are personal and in principle remediable, and both of these from those that, while neither purely personal nor universal, seem to compellingly arise in the central contexts of human life (e.g., in situations of deep political commitment).

To say that incoherence is a general condition of the human psyche is not to say that people are generally aware of their own lack of unity. Indeed, it may be as the Underground Man suggests—only a rare few, those with heightened consciousness, are aware of the emptiness at the center. It may be as Sartre says—that we are regularly drawn towards an inauthentic posture of wholeness.

In what follows I will argue that incoherence abounds and that its discovery awaits us at every turn. It is revealed by reflection on the most intimate details of our personal life. It is to be found in our basic projects: our personal relationships and our work. And it is inherent in our social projects: our efforts to shape and control the terms of our relations with others—our existence as political agents.

Thus, broadly speaking I am in agreement with the Underground Man. For the most part, people are not aware of the extent and nature of the incoherence they contain. When they are aware of it, it is usually manifest in feelings of uncertainty, doubt, confusion, hesitation, and ambivalence. These are the everyday forms of experienced incoherence; but under greater reflection these experiences may be transformed into something much sharper, into a dramatic perception of one's own lack of internal connectedness. I use the term "alienness experiences" to designate these intense experiences of inner fragmentation.

"Alienness" refers to a felt experience, something that occurs at a given time and place and occupies one's consciousness. It is a part of our mental phenomenology. While the term has been invented, the experience has not. That is not to say that it is a regular experience or even that all people have it at some time. Nor is it to say that it is an experience that has existed from time immemorial. I doubt that cave dwellers felt alienness. Human experience has a history, and it makes sense to suppose that the first experiences of alienness came relatively late in that history. This does not make them any less real, and it may make them particularly interesting.

Let me hasten to explain that I am not talking about alienation or alienness experiences primarily in the social sense of being alienated from society, or of feeling alien at a party or in a foreign country. These uses have some relationship to what I am concerned with, but my primary interest is in the experience of one's self as alien, or more specifically, the experience of some aspect of oneself as alien. Consider:

Experiencing one's past actions as alien. I am alone. I am eating. I have been indulging myself, eating all my favorite foods, especially chocolate ice cream. For a moment I pause with the ice cream in my mouth. I am playing with its creaminess; I attend to it sharply. I notice the taste, but it is strange, for the taste is not particularly good. Perhaps it is just something in my mouth, or this ice cream, but no, I come to realize that I have no special fondness for this taste; more than that, I realize now that I never had, that during those years when I was adamant as to which flavors I would eat and which ones I liked I had never really paid any attention to the taste of the ice cream. It all seems strange; all of that behavior looks now like some sort of act that I was going through, a series of movements that weren't really mine. I want to say that I didn't really do this, that there was something else that must have been acting through me.

Experiencing one's ongoing actions as alien. A similar case: lovemaking. So much activity is organized around this, so much perception and engagement. The world seems divided into two kinds of objects, sexual and nonsexual. So much is involved: the pursuit, the seduction, the anxieties that follow. The centrality is immense. Yet in the very act to pause and wonder, "What the hell am I doing!" Amid the strain and exertion to recognize that, if anything, I am feeling tense and fearful rather than ecstatic! What is it all about? What am I inhabited by? I continue through the act. Very little changes, everything goes on as before, organized around this pursuit, but now it is all weird, as though it is not me at all. I want to deny that I am doing this.

Experiencing one's emotions as alien. I oppose the war. There is no question about this. I oppose it all, the actions of trapped men, entrapping their children in struggle, each killing the other, the tremendous waste and injustice. Yet, sitting in front of the television, hearing news reports of fighting, hearing the passion of the newscaster, I experience all the emotions of a booster. What is this? What are they? These emotions are foreign. They are not mine, that's not the way I feel! I want to shout, "these emotions are not mine!"

Experiencing one's beliefs as alien. We are sitting at a table, my friend and I and a woman I am with. Somehow it sneaks up on me—a suspicion: Is he touching her foot? He seems to be just talking and she is eating, but are they really doing nothing? It is not an ordinary question. I know that there is nothing going on. There is not a shred of evidence. I have no reason to believe. . . . Yet even now I am unable to control myself; like a fool I glance under the table, careful that no one sees me looking, for how could I possibly explain what I was looking at? Yet my suspicions are eased only while I can see under the table; the very second I look up I am again assailed. What is wrong with me? What are these thoughts, these invasions? These beliefs are foreign matter, I don't believe that there is anything to be seen, yet again it comes. I want to deny that these beliefs are mine.

Experiencing one's life as alien. What am I to do? There is not really any alternative to doing something. I am caught within the necessity of deciding, of taking stands, of taking sides. Even adopting skepticism constitutes a position. I am engaged in major projects of all sorts: I marry, choose a career, live in a certain country, adopt a certain life style, accept a position, buy a home, have children. These are all terribly significant actions; they are irrevocable. To turn away from them once they are done entails a total alteration. And yet I know that I enter into them without having sufficiently appraised the question. I am unsure of my wants and beliefs, and, to the extent that I am confident, I know that I ought not be. Yet I go on, as I always have. I make decisions. Yet they don't seem to emerge from me as much as absorb me. My entire life seems strange. I tend to say, "my life is not my own" or "it's as if I'm not alive."

Experiencing one's entire self as alien. I think of myself in a certain way: I am a certain kind of person; there are things about me that are central. Perhaps I am an artist or a writer; I have a special concern with truth, or with understanding; or I live according to certain standards, and evaluate myself and others by them. But I see these aspects of myself as arising from rather simple conflicts and insecurities at an early age; I chose these standards and self-images in order to judge, in order to feel superior. I pursued them in order to feel secure within my own world. This is especially true of those identifications that are not even superficially grounded in assessments, but are simply mine: the way I see things, the way I do things, the kind of person 1 am. Once understood, it looks so different. My entire personality seems to be that of a buffoon, a pathetic creature. I would replace it wholesale, and even this concern with identity, this concern with who I am; this too is the hallmark of that very same fear-ridden, needful, or merely habitual person. I turn away in disgust. But where am I to go? I feel as though I were inhabited, as though I were not myself, as though I don't really exist.

Let me say a few words about these experiences. First note that in each example there is something that the person experiences as alien, be it an emotion, a belief, an action, or his entire personality. As such the experience of alienness is unlike certain other conscious states such as feeling chilled or dizzy.

To have an alienness experience is to experience something as-alien. In this it is similar to many phenomenologically rich modes of experiencing. A child can experience one of her stuffed animals as terrifying, or as malevolent, alive, hungry, lecherous, and so on. We arrive at a party where we know no one—we may experience it as forbidding, cold, unfriendly, or perhaps as sparkling, exciting, inviting. Sartre speaks of arriving at the cafe and experiencing Jacques as "not-there." Alienness is a particular way of experiencing oneself. Alienness is not the same as merely experiencing something as not belonging to oneself. After all, I do not experience your actions as belonging to myself; I do not experience your personality as being mine; I do not experience your past as being mine; nonetheless, I cannot be said to have alienness with respect to any of these objects (your actions, your beliefs, your personality). It is only my personality, my actions, my beliefs that are possible candidates for alienness. Thus, alienness is the experience of something as one's-own and also, at the same time, as not-one's-own. It is the experience of an aspect of one's self as my-own-yet-not-my-own.

It is useful to consider how such experiences have been hitherto understood. However, the psychological and psychiatric literature contains no term that corresponds exactly to the phenomena I am considering. The closest resemblance is found under the heading, "depersonalization." Karl Jaspers gives the following definition:

> Every psychic manifestation, whether perception, bodily sensation, memory, idea, thought or feeling carries this particular aspect of "being mine" of having an "I" quality, of "personally belonging," of it being one's own doing. We have termed this "personalization." If these psychic manifestations occur with the awareness of their not being mine, of being alien, automatic, independent, arriving from elsewhere, we term them phenomena of depersonalization.[1]

For Jaspers, the objects of depersonalization are psychic manifestations. What is experienced as alien is something "mental" or "internal," a content of consciousness that can be placed in time precisely. One can say, at a specific time *t*, I had a manifestation of sort *S* and it did (or did not) have the quality of being-mine. In the phenomenon of alienness, what is experienced as alien includes not only psychic manifestations, but also beliefs, emotions, desires (in the both occurrent and dispositional senses) as well as the person's body or self or actions. Second, in depersonalization (as Jaspers describes it) the manifestations (thoughts, emotions, etc.) are experienced as merely alien, often as belonging to others, but in alienness they are recognized as one's own, yet not one's own. They are experienced as mine-but-not-mine.

Various authors use the term "depersonalization" in somewhat different ways.

> The experience is distressing and seems to be essentially one of unreality; the world feels unreal; the subject feels that he is unreal, totally or partially; the symptom never seems to have a delusional quality. . . . The patients have insight. They do not say "I am unreal" but "I feel that I am not real, although I know I am." When they speak of a change in their personality, they seem always to refer to a sense of loss.[2]

Another describes depersonalization as:

> an experience pertaining to either the bodily or the mental self. In the first case the person will complain that his body or rather certain parts of the body do not feel like his own, as belonging to him. He may describe them as estranged from himself or as being dead. . . . Not rarely we detect states of depersonalization pertaining to the genitals and to the sexual act. . . . They perceive themselves as going through the act without being "present"; the penis performs as if it were not their own. Whenever depersonalization extends to the mental self there is a feeling of unreality of the self and of being "outside the self." The depersonalized patient will think, react, act; but his experience is that of a detached spectator who is observing another person's performance. Not only his actions but his own thought processes appear to him unfamiliar and strange.[3]

And still another says:

> The outer world appears substantially unaltered, but yet different; not so essentially, so actually, near or far, clear, warm, friendly and famili-

ar; not really and truly existing and alive; more as if in a dream and yet different from a dream. At heart the patient feels as if he were dead; and he feels like this because he does not feel. His feeling, wishing, thinking and memory processes have become different, uncertain, intolerably changed, and yet the patient knows everything correctly; his faculties of perception, of intellect and of logic have not suffered at all . . . . In still more severe cases even the unity of the ego is only perceived, not felt.[4]

The fact that there is no generally accepted definition of "depersonalization" seems to reflect the absence of any satisfactory theory to explain the phenomena. Without theoretical insight it is difficult to see how to classify diverse phenomena, and different classifications may reflect different intuitions as to where an explanation is to be found. Such differences will even affect the description of the phenomena to be explained. Is depersonalization the same as alienness? At this time there is little point in maintaining that we are dealing with one, two, or three different phenomena. It is only from the position of having a theory of alienness that we will know how to relate it to depersonalization.

Returning to the examples of alienness, I note that each example involved a rather rich context, and setting the experience within the context was critical to understanding just how one could come to feel the way one does in the alienness experience. In each case the person has some beliefs about the object he experiences as alien. In the examples, the relevant beliefs included: (1) my actions have not been motivated by what I have always understood as my reasons for acting as I do; (2) my beliefs make no sense, yet they remain my beliefs; (3) my emotions do not emerge from my beliefs but in spite of them.

We also find certain verbal formulations or tendencies to verbalize alienness. These statements about the object—that it is not one's own, that one did not do it, that one is not oneself—emerge as complaints within the clinical situation. One complains that one feels as if one were not the agent of one's actions, or as if one's emotions were not one's own, or as if one did not exist. Understanding alienness calls for grasping the relationship between (1) these verbal formulations, (2) the experience of alienness, and (3) the beliefs and realizations about the object of alienness.

I reject the general assumption that these experiences are in themselves pathological, and reject the general assumption of the psychoanalytic approach that they are had in order to protect or defend the individual from some unpleasant realization about himself or herself. Along with this last, I reject the view that these experiences are part of some general self-deception on the part of the individual. I wish to show that these experiences may be accurate perceptions of reality, and that they play a central role in authentic human life.

Thus far I have grouped together a variety of verbal articulations of the experience of alienness:

- "I feel as if *I am not the agent of my actions*."
- "I feel as if *my actions are not really mine*."
- "I feel as if *I never really do anything*."
- "I feel as if *everything just happens to me*."
- "I feel as if *everything I do is done by something else*."

I have spoken as if there were only one experience of alienness. But having understood wholeness as involving integration in three distinct loci, it is possible to distinguish three distinct experiences of alienness, each corresponding to the experience of a different lack of coherence.

First consider the normal experience of oneself as the agent of one's activity, or as the genuine holder of one's beliefs or values, or as someone whose desires and emotions are really his or her own (see figure 2.1).

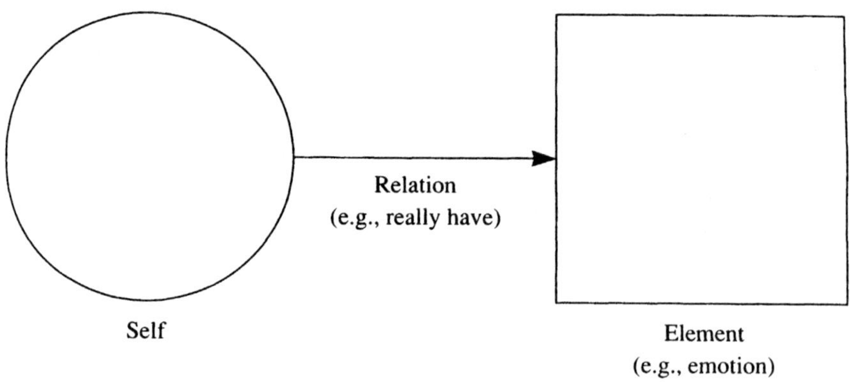

Figure 2.1: Normal Experience

Integration in the three areas may be characterized as follows: (1) there is a complex integrated in the manner that is constitutive of its being a particular kind of element (e.g., an emotion, a belief, a value, an activity); (2) there is a unified complex that is oneself; (3) there is an appropriate relationship between the self and the element such that the element can be said to "belong to," or "come from," or "really express" the self.

The first contrast with normal experience may be termed *reduction of aspect* (see figure 2.2). Here the necessary integration is missing within the aspect or element itself. There exists an aspect of mine that appears to be an activity (or an emotion, or a belief, or a value) but is really something else ("I don't have real activities, emotions, beliefs, values, etc."). Here there is no challenge to either the existence of the self or to the connection of self to the aspect. It is rather that the aspect is seen as failing to really be the kind of aspect it is originally taken to be; in reality it falls short of the required fullness; it is correctly seen as reduced to something else. For instance, they are not actions but merely movements; they are not beliefs but merely thoughts; they are not personality characteristics but merely patterns of past behavior.

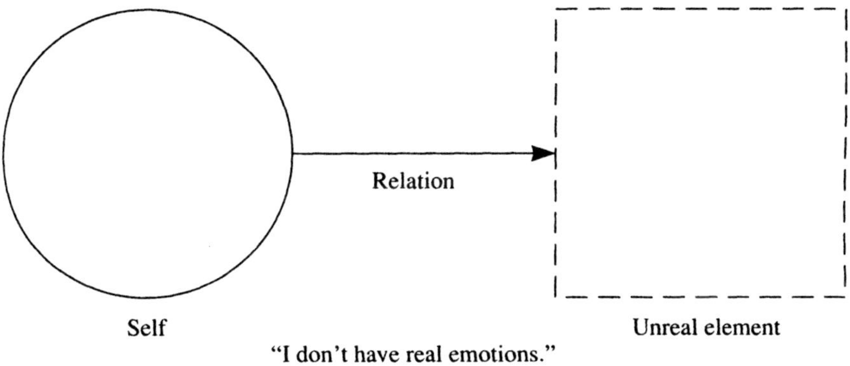

Figure 2.2: Reduction of Aspect

The second contrast with normal experience may be termed person/self ambiguity (see figure 2.3). Here the reality of the element is not questioned. It is a real activity, emotion, desire, and so on. Moreover, it is the expression of some entity, but that entity is not truly oneself. There exists an activity that was done by the person I am but not by my self. I am not the agent of it; something or someone else is. This is an expression of the absence of the fully formed self. Rather than a fully integrated personality, the individual confronts two fragments neither of which is fully whole. Person/self ambiguity is introduced to refer to these two complexes. That which the individual calls self is the complex with which he or she identifies; the theorist may from his or her third-person point of view identify one or the other fragment as representing the self, or he or she might be neutral between the two fragments. There is no challenge, however, to either the aspect itself (it is a real activity, emotion, belief, etc.) or to the linkage between the aspect and the fragment from which it emerges. What is at issue is the status of the fragment: "It comes from the person, but not from me."

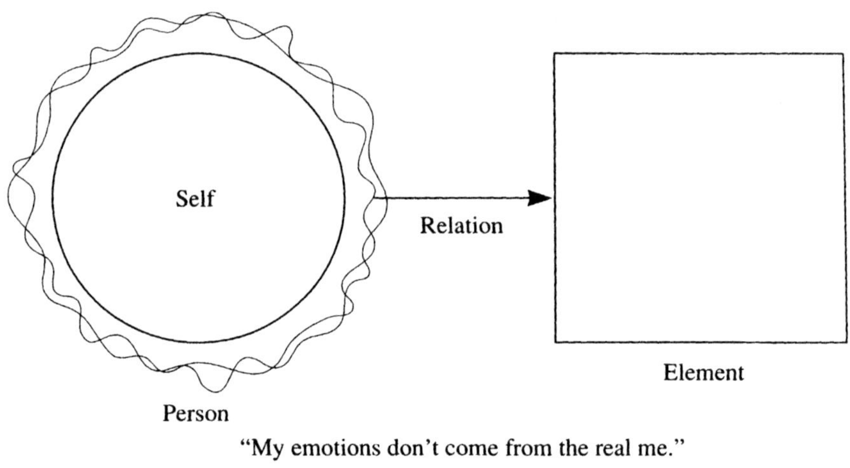

Figure 2.3: Person/Self Ambiguity

The third contrast with normal experience may be termed alternate relation (see figure 2.4). Here there is no challenge to the full-fledged existence of the element. It is a genuine emotion, value, action, and so on. Nor is there any question of the existence of the self. But the necessary integration between the self and the element is missing. There exists an activity of mine but I am not the *agent* of it; I have it, but I have not done it. (It is my desire, but I don't *really have* that desire, it's not really mine. I have the belief that *p*, but I don't *really believe* that *p*.) Here the incoherence is experienced as located *between* the aspect and the self. The self exists and so do the particular actions, emotions, desires. But they are not the actions, desires, emotions of the self. The self is not really present in them; it has some other relationship to them.

Thus, corresponding to each of the three loci of possible incoherence there is a distinct kind of alienness experience and distinct ways in which the experience will be characterized or expressed verbally. If we look at these verbal expressions, at what is in clinical situations, sometimes referred to as "the verbal complaint," we find that typically they take the form: "I feel as if ______." The underlined segment, which we can refer to as the embedded belief, asserts the existence of some state of affairs (e.g., I am not the agent of my actions, my emotions are not mine, I have no personality traits). I have identified above several of these verbal complaints from the agency/action family of alienness experiences.

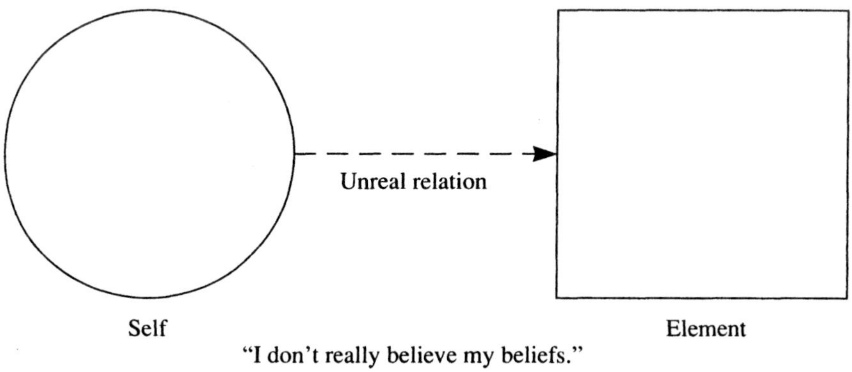

Figure 2.4: Alternate Relation

The fact that the verbal formulation typically begins with the disclaimer "I feel as if" reflects the fact that the individual having the alienness experience is no more able than anyone else to say what it is to not be the agent of one's actions, or to have emotions that are not ones own. He or she is groping for a verbal formulation that will capture an experience of himself or herself that is deeply perplexing. I have spoken of the experiencing of some aspect of the self as being one's own and not one's own, but it would be a mistake to imagine that the experience itself exists in full clarity and that the problem is merely how to translate it into words. Our experience of ourselves is mediated through the conceptual structures that we use to think about the self. In my analysis of agency I have sought to articulate the conceptual structures that are implicitly present in these experiences. But by making the implicit explicit, there is the risk of presenting the experience as though it has greater clarity than it does.

These experiences remain paradoxical for the person who has them, and she realizes their paradoxical character. She does not have the delusions of the person who claims to be inhabited by beings from another world. Because she is in touch with the paradoxical nature of her experience of self, she uses the "as if" formulation. In view of this, one might say that figures 2.2, 2.3, and 2.4 better convey the phenomenological quality of alienness if we erase the words that explain the symbols.

The general explanation of alienness is this: the beliefs that cause or give rise to the alienness experience do so, typically, because they serve as grounds for the assertion contained in the embedded belief. They constitute reasons for believing the embedded belief to be correct. Thus, in the analysis of agency, I have provided an account in terms of which it is meaningful to ask if someone is an agent with respect to his or her activity. The identification of something as an activity does not carry with it the implication that the person who "has" that activity is an agent with respect to it. The beliefs that give rise to the experience of oneself as not the agent of one's own activities are just those beliefs that suggest there is insufficient integration to conclude that the agency relationship holds between self and activity.

The explanation that I am offering, however, could not be correct if the individuals who have the alienness experience do not share the conceptual framework in terms of which the embedded beliefs of alienness complaints are made intelligible. While the analysis could render "I am not the agent of my actions" intelligible, it could not explain how or why such experiences occur for people who do not embody this conceptual framework. And it should be remembered that there is a diversity of ways in which the self as integrated personality can be understood. Thus, an understanding of any particular person's experience would require knowing what particular conception of the self they hold. Put differently, it can be said that we all carry with us philosophic theories that condition our experience of ourselves.

Insofar as the analyses I have provided go beyond our pre-analytic conceptual framework, the analysis should to some extent modify the alienness experience. In particular, it should render that experience somewhat less paradoxical. The internalization of the philosophical analyses presented should result in the elimination of the "as if" quality of those experiences. At the same time, the ability of the analyses of activity, agency, and self to render intelligible our experiences and our verbal characterization of those experiences is additional confirmation of the theory. All philosophical theory, even that which seeks to radically revise ordinary language, must bear some connectedness to our linguistic intuitions. Action theory is rather tightly connected to the fact that we do distinguish between "my hand went up" and "I raised my hand." Theorists have looked for an account of action that would articulate the criteria that lie behind these linguistic discriminations. In the search for a conceptual analysis that would explain the experiences of alienness and thus make them rationally intelligible as opposed to inherently pathological, there is a broader intuitive base, which serves as a touchstone for the adequacy of philosophical analysis.

Alienation and Agency

Throughout the previous discussion I have been rather careful to speak of the experience of alienness. In general, I have avoided using the term "alienation," and at no point have I said that a person who experiences some aspect of self as his-and-not-his is alienated from that aspect. Nonetheless, it is clear that there is an important relationship between alienness and alienation, and this should be made clear.

The relationship can be stated succinctly: Alienation is the state in virtue of which a given experience of alienness is valid. In the alienness experience an individual experiences some aspect of self to be his-and-not-his. This is a veridical experience if and only if he is truly alienated from that aspect of self. Thus "alienated" can be defined as follows:

X is alienated from aspect *A* if and only if it is his and not his.

As defined, alienation refers to an underlying structural relationship, essentially the lack of integration between *X* and the aspect in question. To say that a person is alienated from such and such an aspect does not imply that he feels alienated or has an alienness experience in relationship to that aspect.

It should be recognized that as defined the notion of alienation is schematic. No specific characterization of what it is to be alienated from some aspect of self is given because the account is intended to be sufficiently general to encompass alternative understandings of the self and the necessary modes of integration.

It was pointed out above that judgments of the validity of an *experience* of alienness are based on a conception of the self and on a view as to what integrations must hold for a given aspect to be fully of the self. Thus, from a third-person perspective the theorist (therapist, friend, other) may assess some other individual's experience of alienness, embodying in the assessment a conception of the self that is quite different than that embodied by the individual who has the alienness experience. This can be restated in terms of alienation; in making judgments about whether or not an individual is alienated from some aspect of himself, the theorist may employ a notion of self different from that of the individual himself.

Implicit in this view of alienation as a state that underlies the valid experience of alienness is the circumstance that one may be alienated from an aspect and not experience it as being-and-not-being-one's-own. Indeed, one may even have no experience of the aspect at all. One may not even know that it exists. Thus, one may be so deeply alienated from one's emotions that one is not even aware of their existence. By contrast, the person who is alienated from *A* and does have the experience of *A* as being-and-not-being-her-own is the person who is in touch with certain features of her reality. She experiences her relation to the aspect in question as it is. Thus, it is an error to take the absence of alienness as signifying unity. In many cases there is not only a lack of integration but a lack of awareness of the lack of integration.

Having linked alienness and alienation, and having understood agency as the presence of the self in its activities, we can now define "agency" in terms of "alienation."

> *X* is the agent of some activity *A* if and only if *A* is an activity of *X* and *X* is not alienated from *A*.

Thus agency is the opposite of alienation. This, in a nutshell, expresses my theory of agency. Both agency and alienation are understood in terms of a structural relationship between the self and the element in question (e.g., an activity). To ascribe agency is to affirm the existence of that relationship. To ascribe alienation is to affirm the absence of that relationship. Paralleling the structural side, there is the individual's own experience of the presence or absence of the relevant structural connectedness. When she experiences it as present, she experiences herself as an agent; she identifies with herself as the source of the activity. When she experiences an absence of a required relationship, she experiences alienness. This experience, as noted, differs depending on where the incoherence is experienced as residing.

The basic point is that alienness emerges from coming to believe things that serve as grounds or reasons for concluding that the embedded alienness beliefs are correct (i.e., that the required structural connectedness is indeed absent). If I am correct that alienness is rooted in belief that serve as its grounds, then the alienness experience can be explored by situating it in the kinds of reflection or practical contexts that give rise to such beliefs.

Three central contexts within which alienness emerges are: (1) psychological inquiry into one's own nature as a specific individual; (2) philosophical inquiry into the most general features of the human condition; and (3) political activity that aims at basic changes in our social world. Table 2.1 shows the linkages between the alienness-generating beliefs, the contexts in which they arise, the verbal expressions and experiences they give rise to, and the conclusions they support.

Table 2.1: Alienness-Generating Beliefs

Belief	Context	Verbal Expression	Useful Model	"Warranted Conclusion"
A. My actions are motivated by values I reject	psychological/ political	"My actions do not come from the real me"	p/s	The actions are integrated with something belonging to the person but not to the self
B. My actions are not motivated as I had thought. I don't know my motives	psychological	"My actions do not come from the real me"	p/s	Integration with person but not self
C. My values were implanted in me by others, by society, etc.	psychological/ political	"My actions don't really come from me"	p/s	The actions are integrated with values that are not really his own
		"I feel as if another acts through me"	a-r	Action is merely done by him but it expresses another

Table 2.1 (cont.)

D. There are no answers to value questions (nihilism)	philosophical	"I never really do anything"	p/s	There is an absence of "reasoned" integration between all values and other aspects; thus they do not belong to the self
E. Everything one does is fully determined by events that occurred long before one's birth (determinism)	philosophical	"I never really do anything"	r.a.	There are no actions, just movements
		"I never do anything. I am not the agent of my actions"	b/p/s	Actions come from something that is not the self (e.g., the body). One is never a real agent
F. Mental events never are causes of movements (Epiphenomeenalism)	philosophical	"I don't do anything"	r.a.	There are no mental causes, no indirect perceptual integrations, no actions, just movements
		"My actions don't come from me"	b/p/s	Actions are caused by bodily states
G. One can never know what effects actions have (Skepticism)	philosophical/ political	"My actions do not really come from me"	a-r	Since one never has good grounds for doing the things one does, they are not really one's own
H. If one had by chance been born in a different culture, one would see things in a radically different way and pursue a radically different life.	philosophical	"I don't really do anything"	p/s	Actions are integrated with values and beliefs, but these are not grounded in the way they must be to be really one's own

Table 2.1 (cont.)

I. What I am doing violates own values	psychological/ political	"I am not the agent of my actions"	p/s	His actions don't come from his self as they violate his essence
J. The existence of the self does not involve some "deep fact"—there are no Cartesian egos (Parfit)	philosophical	"I do not really exist. There is no real me"	p/s	He is not really the agent of his past future actions

Key: p/s = person/self
a-r = alternate relation
r.a. = reduced aspect
b/p/s/ = body/person/self

Notes

1. Karl Jaspers, *General Psychopathology* (Chicago: University of Chicago, 1963), 121.
2. H. J. Shorvon, in *Proceedings of the Royal Society of Medicine* 39 (1946):779, as quoted in Brian Ackner, "Depersonalization," *Journal of Medical Science* 100 (October 1954): 844.
3. Edith Jacobson, "Depersonalization," paper presented to the New York Psychoanalytic Society," February 1, 1958.
4. M. N. Searl, "A Note on Depersonalization," *International Journal of Psychoanalysis* 13 (1932): 329.

3
Alienness, Understanding, and Self-Deception

My primary concern is with the individual's own encounter with his own lack of integrity, with how a still greater sense of his internal disunity may be brought about through self-exploration, with his response to his own incoherence, and with the dynamic import of the alienness experience.

In the West, in the twentieth century, this intense engagement with oneself occurs most often in the formalized psychotherapeutic setting. Traditionally, intensive self-examination has occurred in a religious context. Within the history of Christianity, this self-examination emerges from a focus on the call for purification of the personality. Early Calvinist sects engaged in these efforts to explore and reform the individual psyche, and Perry Miller has written about the extremely fine categories of personal transformation that were developed in this country by the seventeenth- and eighteenth-century New England Congregationalists.[1]

Twelve hundred years earlier, in his Confessions, Augustine told of a struggle with himself:

> I was held fast, not in fetters clamped upon me by another, but by my own will, which had the strength of iron chains. The enemy held my will in his power and from it he had made a chain and shackled me. For my will was perverse and lust had grown from it, and when I gave in to lust, habit was born, and when I did not resist the habit it became a necessity. These were the links which formed what I have called my chain, and it held me fast in the duress of servitude. But the new will which had come to life in me and made me wish to serve you freely and enjoy you, my God, who are our only certain joy, was not yet strong enough to overcome the old, hardened as it was by the passage of time.

> So these two wills within me, one old, one new, one the servant of the flesh, the other of the spirit, were in conflict and between them they tore my soul apart.From my own experience I now understood what I had read—that the impulses of nature and the impulses of the spirit are at war with one another. In this warfare I was on both sides, but I took the part of that which I approved in myself rather than the part of that which I disapproved. For my true self was no longer on the side of which I disapproved, since to a great extent I was now its reluctant victim rather than its willing tool. Yet it was by my doing that habit had become so potent an enemy, because it was by my own will that I had reached the state in which I no longer wished to stay. Who can justly complain when just punishment overtakes the sinner? I could no longer claim that I had no clear perception of the truth. . . . But while I wanted to follow the first course and was convinced that it was right, I was still a slave to the pleasures of the second. . . . It was in vain that inwardly I applauded your disposition, when that other disposition in my lower self raised war against the disposition of my conscience and handed me over as a captive to that disposition towards sin, which my lower self contained. For the rule of sin is the force of habit, by which the mind is swept along.[2]

Augustine does not mention any experience of alienness. Yet this is not merely an account of personality change arising out of conflicting desires, but of an individual struggling to change his own personality. The crucial feature is revealed when Augustine says, "In this warfare, I was on both sides, but I took the part of that which I approved. . . . For my true self was no longer on the side of which I disapproved."

It is hard to understand exactly what Augustine is saying here. Does his true self shift from siding with one of these wills to siding with the other? Or is it that one of these wills represents his true self and that he comes to side with it? In either case he arrives at a point where he experiences himself as split into his "true self" and his "lower self," and he finds that the lower self is still in command. Yet he is not merely witnessing a conflict; he takes the side that he believes to be right. Nonetheless, this side is still the weaker of the two. While he experiences some of his actions as not coming from his true self, he continues to recognize them as his. He is not involved in a psychotic denial of reality. Nor does his way of formulating the inner discord represent any attempt to flee from responsibility.

Augustine explicitly criticizes the Manichees, who assert that "we have two minds of different natures" and that "they are in conflict because they spring from two opposing substances and two opposing principles."[3] Augustine is at pains to emphasize that both desires are his own, even though they are not experienced as equally his own. One set emerges from his true self, the other does not. Rather than being the external spectator of a conflict between two wills that are his equally, he is experientially at one with one of them and "the prisoner" of the other.

An even closer parallel to the current discussion may be found in a sermon by John Donne from 1622. Donne says,

> . . . . if upon the earth thou beest in the way to heaven, thou must have a body too, a body of thine own, a body of thy possession; for thy body hath thee, and not thou it, if thy body tyrannize over thee. If thou canst not withdraw thine eye from an object of temptation or withhold thy hand from subscribing against thy conscience nor turn thine ear from a popular and seditious libel, what hast thou towards a man? Thou hast no soul, nay, thou hast no body. There is a body, but thou hast it not; it is not thine, it is not in thy power. Thy body will rebel against thee even in a sin; it will not perform a sin when and where thou wouldst have it.[4]

For Donne, if one's body is not in line with one's conscience, "what hast thou towards a man? Thou hast no soul, nay, thou hast no body." If we substitute "self" for "soul" the parallel is clear. One's body did such and such but not one's self (soul). My actions are not my own. I have a body but I do not possess it—it is not mine own.

We should not be misled by Donne's use of the term "body." If we take "body" in a scaled down physiological sense, the inability to control one's body is reminiscent of those cases where the arm goes up even when one wants it to stay down. But Donne addresses himself to a spiritual sickness. His notion of "body" corresponds more fully to what I have called "person." For Donne, the body may have a will and yet that will need not be mine own. If this will subscribes against one's conscience then one has no soul (self). Thus, in Donne's account the soul or self only exists when there is integration between the body and one's conscience. In the absence of this integration there is not a mere conflict between two parts of one's self; it is clear that the conscience part indicates the self, real self, or true self. This is similar to Augustine's taking the side of which he approved and that he knew to be right. And it is also similar to the perspective found earlier in the discussion of Gary Watson's account of freedom.

The discovery that one's actions, will, or emotions are in conflict with one's values is probably the most common source of alienness. The first-person sense of the alienness of actions in conflict with one's values, as well as third-person judgments that such actions are not really actions of the individual (though they are his or hers), implicitly use the moral value of the individual as a guide to the locus of the self. As was pointed out earlier, there is no necessity to this identification. One could have a person/self distinction and not locate the self in this fashion. For instance, a Nietzschean might experience these values as just that which indicates what is not-self. Nietzsche identifies the self with the body and its reasons. Thus Nietzsche and Donne offer radically opposite frameworks for identifying what is really one's own. It is important to remember that this is not merely a matter of alternative identification experiences, but rather alternative theories about the real self that have third-person applicability. Both Nietzsche and Donne are operating within a conceptual framework that allows them to make judgments about the real self of other persons, regardless of what that person's own identifications are.

When one does live and experience from within a conception of self that gives one's moral judgments or values a special role in constituting the self, coming to believe that one's actions are motivated contrary to one's values tends to call forth the experience of one's actions happening in spite of oneself. To say that the locus of the self resides with the moral values is not to say that what emerges from desire is viewed as non-self, but rather that its status is uncertain. When it conflicts with the moral judgment it is non-self; however, it will only be so experienced when there is awareness of the conflict.

With Augustine, the inner discord is experienced as a struggle; one way of understanding the phenomenology of this struggle is that the identification experience is not stable. On cool reflection, which is to say, when the desire is no longer occurrent, the individual is aware of both the conflict between desire and moral judgment and of the implication that the desire is not of the true self. This awareness expresses itself in his identification with the judgmental component. But it is part of the very power of the desire that when it is occurring its strength is expressed in its ability to occupy all conscious space or to relegate to a tiny corner of awareness a recognition of the conflict with moral judgment. When the desire is occurrent it is the desired object that occupies consciousness—it is experienced as desirable. When one engages in cool reflection, the desire itself rather than the object of the original desire is now the object of consciousness (e.g., he thinks about the fact that he desires someone sexually, as opposed to sexually desiring that person).

The experiences of Augustine and Donne both involve a question of moral conflict. It is a matter of the individual's experiencing a conflict between values that he affirms and desires that he has or actions that he engages in. As presented in these examples, such conflict may be something that one simply finds within oneself; one encounters it without any necessary inquiry. On the other hand, the experience of moral conflict may result from a sustained inquiry into the moral quality of one's being, an inquiry that reveals to one a variety of unpleasant truths about oneself. And alienness may be the result of this discovery. But inquiry into one's moral standing is only one of a variety of self-explorations that may generate alienness.

I have offered three distinct models for capturing the alienness experience: reduction of aspect, person/self ambiguity, and alternate relation. These correspond to whether the locus of the incoherence is experienced as within the element, within the individual himself or herself, or in the relationship between the element and the individual. I have stressed that alienness is a response to coming to believe certain things that serve as the grounds for concluding that an aspect is not one's own. Alienness-grounding beliefs include:

1. Beliefs that suggest certain elements do not exist in their fullness. "I have no beliefs, values, emotions, actions, desires—they are really something else, something less."
2. Beliefs holding that while there is integration between the element and a larger complex that may be termed a person, that person-complex is not really me (my self).
3. Beliefs suggesting that while these aspects exist they are not properly integrated with oneself in that they do not stand in the proper relation to oneself. "My beliefs are not really mine for I don't know why I have these views."

One particular line of inquiry that may generate alienness is inquiry into how it came to be that one feels, believes, or values in the specific ways in which one does. Thus, one may discover that one has certain attitudes because one was raised in a certain way, or because those were the attitudes of one's parents, or because those were not the attitudes of one's parents and were thus chosen in rebellion in order to achieve a sense of identity in the face of dominant parental pressure.

The nature of this kind of inquiry is to search for deep motivational structures. Thus one does not focus on whatever good reasons one may have for these attitudes, beliefs, values, and so on, but rather on their nonrational (but not nonpurposive) causes. This does not require that the individual have no reasons—no good reasons—for his or her beliefs and judgments and feelings. Even when one has good reasons there is much that needs to be explained. Why was it that certain factors came to appear to one as good reasons? Why was one responsive or sensitive to these factors and not others? Why did one not seek out the counter-arguments?

Where the motivation was strong, the fact that the reasons one had may have been good or adequate grounds may have been causally irrelevant. If they had not been good enough to warrant belief they would have been seen as good enough in any event; or alternatively, the motivation to believe certain things may have entered the process not at the point of evaluating evidence but at an earlier point of amassing evidence.

Inquiry of this sort is a quest for an explanation of a certain sort. To demonstrate that a person lacks adequate grounding for his or her attitudes does not in itself refute the correctness of what is believed. Rather it suspends such questions as it pursues a nonrational account of this particular person's having certain views.

As was discussed earlier, it is primarily through the rational connectedness of the cognitive content of beliefs, values, emotions, and other mental elements that they are capable of cohering with each other. Alternative conceptions of the self may give differing emphases to rational connectedness, but a minimal rationality enters into all conceptions of the self. Because of the centrality of rational connections, the discovery of the nonrational process whereby I came to have the outlook I have has the potential for being alienating in that it suggests the possibility of an inappropriate kind of integration. Thus a belief may be integrated with other aspects of the self in virtue of the fact that my having this belief serves a variety of purposes and needs, but if the belief is integrated in this way it may be integrated in only this way, through the purposes it serves, and not rationally integrated in terms of its cognitive content.

Thus, it should be clear, it is misleading to speak simply about "integration" or "coherence" between the elements; just as with the analogy of the electronic parts that can be wired together to form either a radio, a video recorder, or a telephone, so too it is with human beings. Being a self (attaining selfhood) is something that emerges only when the integration is of a certain sort. It is an integration in virtue of which all the parts are truly one's own, and this integration is subtle (as well as subject to different design specifications depending on the conception of the self).

It is typically the case that our systems of beliefs are lightly integrated in rational terms, but that this lightness is not recognized. Instead the beliefs are fiercely maintained, and this fierceness, which may in fact result from a need to retain these beliefs, is instead experienced as rationally (i.e., cognitively) warranted. A recognition of either past or present motivation affects our awareness of the lightness of rational connectedness; the element tends to be exposed in its starkness. One sees that one believes things that may not be true; one sees that one has values and attitudes that may lack validity.

Yet even when exposed as strongly motivated but only lightly grounded, the belief-embedded elements have not been eliminated; this is not a process whereby beliefs are necessarily changed or replaced by others. Rather, it is a process whereby their fixedness is shaken; they remain there as one's own but they are unglued. One has them, but they are not fully one's own. In fact they never were, but the inquiry has led one to an awareness of this fact. Thus, the alienness experience represents a degree of self-knowledge achieved.

It should also be clear that identification does not suffice to make something one's own. Look at it in the third person. Suppose that we are examining someone else's belief structure and we reach the conclusion that none of these beliefs are tightly integrated in terms of their cognitive content—that they simply float about as handy devices to serve as needed. Yet suppose the individual identifies himself with certain of these beliefs? Does this change anything? Does it substitute for the structural relationship that is missing? I think not. And if the individual at some later point comes to see the loose connectedness that we see, his identification itself might change. Or perhaps it would change if he was able to address more directly the needs and fears he has that underlie the fierceness of his identification.

With respect to these elements that are now seen as essentially "free standing," the situation is quite different than that considered in Augustine's case, where he identifies with one element in a moral conflict. In Augustine's description there is no discussion of grounding, there is the simple conflict between two elements (e.g., a desire that we have and a value judgment that specifies the having of such desires as sinful). In the case at hand, however, the individual is not identifying with a given element as opposed to another. Rather, he is applying an integration standard of ownership that is part of a theory or conception of the self, perhaps a conception that strongly locates the self in the rational component and thus demands tight rational integration as a criterion for something's being of the self. In terms of that conception, the elements are not truly his own, and having applied the criteria of that conception, they are now seen (i.e., experienced) as not truly one's own. For Augustine the conflict of values with something else—action, will, emotion—is clear-cut. He is himself aware of the disjunction; he is engaged in a moral struggle with himself in his effort to be good.

Augustine's experience does not have a fully modern ring to it. Since the work of Freud, the major model for the psychic conflicts that arise out of the demands of moral ideals has become more intricate. Instead of the direct absence of integration between our values and our desires or emotions, we have an absence of integration between beliefs or between beliefs and perceptions. The individual does not accurately know herself because she fails to draw proper conclusions about herself from the beliefs she has or should have, given the evidence available to her. This lack of integration between beliefs is itself rooted in a conflict between values and behavior (or wishes, emotions, desires, etc.). However, the individual's struggle is no longer a moral struggle to do or be good, but an unconscious struggle to deceive herself about herself.

In the psychoanalytic approach there is no tendency to identify the person's "real self" in terms of her values. The self is more likely to be conceived of as a composite of conflicting systems (e.g., ego, id, superego). Because of this, when the experience of alienness arises out of a conflict between values and something else, there is very little thought given to the possibility that the experience is an accurate perception. Rather, experiencing a part of oneself as not really one's own is seen as an effort to deny reality. In such views, alienness arises from a need to maintain an idealized self-image. The distinction between the person and the self is not seen as a distinction between two real complexes, but between the actual person and her ego-ideal (i.e., the person she aspires to be). Alienness is seen as reflecting an inability to accept the gap between the ideal and the real. It is not seen as part of a healthy dynamic of change, nor as an accurate perception of internal conflict.

In his classic work, *Self-Deception*, Herbert Fingarette laid great emphasis on this inability to accept oneself as one really is. Fingarette's work is of particular interest to the current discussion because his view that the self is a synthesis, an achievement of the individual that he builds as "he excludes material from the self as well as accepting, incorporating and synthesizing," is quite similar to the view of the self as the integrated personality.[5] Fingarette writes:

> I speak of an individual's "engagement in the world". . . . I use it to characterize, in most general terms, what someone does or what he undergoes as a human subject; it is how an individual finds and/or takes the world including himself. It is a matter of the activities he engages

> in, the projects he takes on, the way the world presents itself to him to be seen, heard, felt, enjoyed, feared or otherwise "experienced" by him . . . .
>
> The immediately crucial point is that we are not in general explicitly conscious of our engagements in the world.[6]

We become explicitly conscious of our engagements through a process of spelling out. We engage in the activity of spelling out only when there is some reason to do so.

> The policy of refusing to spell-out one's engagement is merely the most "visible" feature of self-deception. Though highly visible, it is a concomitant of a far more fundamental manoeuvre. The self-deceiver is one who is in some way engaged in the world but who disavows the engagement, who will not acknowledge it even to himself as his. That is, self-deception turns upon the personal identity one accepts rather than the beliefs one has. It is the hallucinator who speaks, but he will not acknowledge the words as his; disowned by him and undetected by others, the voice nevertheless still speaks, and so it is assigned by him to some supernatural being. The paranoid is filled with destructiveness, but he disavows it; since the presence of destructiveness is evident to him, he eventually assigns "ownership" of that destructiveness to others. . . . In general, the self-deceiver is engaged in the world in some way, and yet he refuses to identify himself as one who is so engaged; he refuses to avow the engagement as his.[7]

Thus,

> It happens—witness the self-deceiver—that an individual will be provoked into a kind of engagement which in part or in whole, the person cannot avow as his engagement, for to avow it would apparently lead to such intensely disruptive, distressing consequences as to be unmanageably destructive to the person. The individual may be powerfully inclined toward a particular engagement, yet this particular engagement may be utterly incompatible with that currently achieved synthesis of engagements which is the person. . . . The phenomena we classify under such headings as "self-deception," "defense," and "mauvaise foi," are "regressions" to this form of engagement; they manifest our capacity for such isolated engagements even after the emergence of a personal self, and in spite of unacceptability to the person.[8]

The self-deceiver is then someone who is engaged in the world in some particular way, but neglects to spell this out to himself. But this failure to spell out (to become explicitly aware of what he or she is, or how he or she is engaged) is not an oversight nor is it an innocent lapse. It is part of a disavowal of the engagement in circumstances where it would be too distressing to face the implications of that engagement.

The question that Fingarette does not ask is this: If the self is a product created by the individual through the integration of various elements, then wherein is there self-deception (or even error) if elements that are not part of that complex are not seen as part of it? If the self is the fully integrated person, then when there is serious internal conflict, the whole self does not exist. However, it may be represented by some of the fragments. Thus, within the overall collection, it may be possible to distinguish what is self from non-self (or person). This must be distinguished from self-deception. When we are really dealing with self-deception, for instance, someone who denies that she performed some action, her error does not consist in a failure to see the action as coming from her self. Her error of self-deception involves a failure to recognize the existence of the action or the motivating desire at all (e.g., "I wasn't trying to hurt her"; "I'm not jealous"; "There was no nastiness in what I said"). Here then is the difference between alienness and self-deception.

In the case of self-deception the individual is unable to see the engagement for what it is. She says, "I am not angry," "I don't hate him," "I didn't do that." In the case of alienness the person says, "there was this angry feeling of mine, but I was not angry," or "there was this feeling of hatred, but I did not hate him," or even "that was done by me but I didn't really do it." It is because of this actual seeing of the implications or meanings as others would see them that alienness seems so much more bizarre than self-deception. Indeed, alienness is hardly expressible, whereas the self-deceiver's false beliefs are not in themselves odd or paradoxical.

Fingarette speaks of the hallucinator and the paranoid who are in touch with the meanings and existence of elements but attribute them to others: they project and invent fantastic agents to whom they ascribe their actions. But this too is not alienness. The person who experiences alienness does not engage in these neurotic or psychotic distortions. He is able to make the same inferences in his case as he might in the case of others. While the self-deceiver does not experience his own action as having been done at all, and the hallucinatory experiences his own actions as not-his-own, the alienness experience is of actions as both one's-own-but-not-one's-own.

Somehow, despite the fact that Fingarette's view of the self—the self is an integrated complex created by the avowals and disavowals of the individual—suggests that what is not integrated with the complex is not part of the self, Fingarette overlooks alienness entirely. Instead of seeing how his view of self-deception can illuminate the authentic experience of nonintegration, he focuses on pathological ways of experiencing such conflicts.

The effect of calling attention to the differences between the various experiences of incoherence and of giving a meaningful interpretation to alienness is to open up a space between neurotic self-deception on the one hand and "self-acceptance" on the other. My thesis is that alienness, far from being an experience that manifests one's self-deception, may be an authentic mode of experiencing the lack of integration within the entire personality. We may think of repression and other neurotic distortions as arising, at least in part, because recognition of what is repressed or distorted would contradict (and thereby imperil) something of immense importance (e.g., one's self-identity as a good, decent, or wise individual). In the alienness experience "unflattering elements" are recognized without being attributed to the self. To the individual himself, this experience of something that is mine-but-not-mine is hardly comprehensible. Insofar as the analysis makes such a mode of experience intelligible, it may make it possible for the conflicted individual to recognize the existence or meaning of certain actions without suffering the loss of self-identity that would be necessitated by simply viewing himself as destructive, vindictive, or cruel.

It may be objected that this experience still remains self-deceptive, that the only fully honest response would be to recognize that one is, or has been, a nasty, cruel, or petty individual. If this view of oneself is at variance with one's explicitly held values or self-image, so much the worse for the self-image. One may either say "he is really cruel," thus dismissing whatever conflicts with this appraisal as not of significance, or one may say, "he is a mixed affair—in part he is cruel, in part he is not."

These two responses are quite different. The first, "he is really cruel, all the rest is mere talk," is implicitly based on a view of how to deal with conflicting fragments. This view may or may not be defensible or shared by others. The second response, "he is a mixed affair," remains correct by remaining on the level of the evidence. It merely restates the fact of fragmentation without committing itself to any position on how to grasp the conflicting aspects. While this may appear to be an acceptable or safe thing to do, it may be criticized on grounds of inauthenticity.

The issue of authenticity is not primarily a matter of taking an objective perspective on oneself; it is a matter of the dynamic import of one's perspective. So long as one is alive, the meaning of one's past is not out of the range of one's influence. Insofar as one steps back and adopts a third-person view towards oneself, saying merely, "there is a conflict between my proclaimed values and my actual conduct" or "I am a non-integrated individual," one abandons one's role as a creator of the synthesis. This role is what Augustine assumed when he took the side of what he approved.

I am not putting forward any general claim about what the dynamic import of alienness experiences must be. What I am saying is that, at least some of the time, to recognize what is ugly and repellent and to refuse to allow that that is "the real me" is not a way of maintaining a virginal self, in principle untaintable, but a way of committing oneself to the completed construction of a whole self out of the fragments that are not repellent.

On the account I have offered, a person who does not regard as his own an engagement that is inadequately integrated with his self may be correct. Have I then eliminated the possibility of self-deception? Not at all. Self-deception exists in several forms. First, there is the familiar failure to perceive the meaning of actions (e.g., "It was not a hostile act"). Second, there is the case of the person who does not experience alienness, but merely experiences something as alien. That is, instead of recognizing the way in which what is not his is his, he is simply cut off from recognition of any tie to it. He projects the action onto real or imaginary others. Finally, there is the person who experiences alienness when the experience is inappropriate. Not all experiences of something as one's-own-but-not-one's-own are correct. I have never maintained that any lack of integration is sufficient for denying that some element is of the self. Just because it is discovered that some action is in conflict with some explicitly affirmed value, it does not follow that it is not integrated in other ways that may be sufficient for it to be of the self. The actual working out of these criteria for the appropriateness of alienness could only be done in terms of a given conception of the self and in terms of that conception's approach to the various instances of fragmentation. Once this is done there would be a range of cases in which an alienness experience verbalized as "I was trying to hurt her but it wasn't really me" would be a variant of self-deception that would fall short of "I wasn't trying to hurt her," which is a more pervasive self-deception. In these cases the honest response would be the admission, "Yes, I was trying to hurt her." In an actual case one would want to know just how securely embedded the value is, and whether the apparent incoherence of the action can be shown to be merely apparent.

The effort to determine the real degree of incoherence of a given element may call for a sustained exploration of the unconscious. This investigation would attempt to show the ways in which what appears to be isolated is in fact part of a larger structure. But we should not assume that this is true in all cases. Indeed, it may turn out that the process of showing how the element is tied to the whole can only be carried out in part. Ultimately, we may be forced to conclude that though a given bit of behavior is part of a larger set of attitudes, desires, and perceptions, this larger complex cannot be identified with the self. One may have to accept the fact that one has no unified self, that there is something closer to a conflict of multiple persons, each of which is incomplete and falls short of selfhood.

Beyond these considerations, as was pointed out earlier, an element is not one's own merely because it is integrated in some fashion with other elements that are part of the self. Our conceptions of the self are extremely subtle and contain specifications as to the kinds of integration that may be acceptable for given elements. Thus, there are some activities that are one's own precisely because they are free from complexity. Insofar as they appear as the direct and spontaneous expression of the self, they are unquestionably part of it. But if we discover that what has appeared light and easy on the surface is in fact highly motivated, its link with the self is shattered. This is the case of the person frolicking in the autumn leaves; in a moment of honesty she recognizes that all this frolicking is done as an object of her own attention. She is trying to give herself an image of herself as carefree, natural, spontaneous, happy. The awareness of the convolutedness of her own self-expression produces a sense of horror at herself. She may be filled with a sense that she doesn't even exist at all, but is possessed—not possessed by some demon that is truly outside herself, but possessed by a grotesque multiplicity of needs and fears that on the one hand is herself and yet is something utterly foreign. This is unlike the previous case in that it need involve no conflict with a value; *the motives from which it arises may be acceptable, but not its way of emerging*.

As I have stressed, the forms of integration that exist between the self and the activity vary according to the conception of self. But if spontaneous activity is seen as "self-expressive," then the self is conceived as having immediate preferences and direct pleasurings that are reactions to specific features of the immediate present, in particular, a responsiveness to aesthetic contact of all kinds. Thus, in the playing in the leaves example, the problem is not that the individual's actions lacked integration with her wants and beliefs. Nor is the problem that tossing leaves must in itself be done in a carefree manner. Nor even that one cannot for good reason put on a carefree manner in tossing the leaves. But rather the problem is that the complex motivational structure of the action was itself hidden, and that its being hidden was a necessary feature of the successful completion of the project of giving to oneself the image of someone who acts intensely without a complex motivation. It is the staggering fullness of this project that is so overwhelming; it suggests the complete infiltration of one's being by such motivations, and the complete absence of anything that is one's own because of simple delight.

The goals of the individual, which are the object of his or her schemes, may themselves be acceptable. But they are expected to operate within a restricted sphere. Insofar as it is discovered that they penetrate into everything, we may correctly experience ourselves as inhabited. And this may be so even if we are inhabited by values or desires of which we approve and with which we identify. Thus no simple formulation of the criteria of ownership will suffice.

What is this thing that is me, yet inhabits me, this me that is not me? This type of situation may be grasped in terms of person/self ambiguity. And we may even apply this to the cases where we are inhabited by desires and values that we approve of. Still they remain different from the self because they are wired—integrated—in ways that conflict with that of the self.

As inquiry into oneself proceeds, the discovery of more integration than one ever imagined, of kinds of integration that one did not suspect, or of integration to elements that clash with one's values, may abolish the experience of the alienness of a specific action, only to replace it with the feeling that one's self does not exist at all. When the action is experienced as an isolated occurrence, there is the sense that the self exists over against it. When the same action is shown to be connected to all sorts of things in all sorts of ways, the individual may experience a radical reversal. Instead of being on firm ice and watching a small piece drift off, one comes to realize that one is the small piece and the glacier has slipped away.

Yet, from the position of almost any conception of self, to identify oneself in this manner cannot be correct. An individual who experiences his entire self as alien is someone who cannot accept who he really is. Given the clash between the individual's standards and what he is actually like, we may regard his refusal to recognize himself as understandable, but it cannot be correct. After all, if we have an articulated value on the one side and an entire unified (but perhaps ugly) complex on the other, surely it is the value that is not part of the self. Any concept of self that identified the self with the fragment, the individual's sense of self, or ego-identity, would come close to totally eliminating the possibility of self-deception with respect to what is or isn't part of one's self.

However, in theory building, in constructing a conception of self, the relevant question is: What would be the point of developing a concept of the self that identified the real self in terms of this isolated fragment? The answer may be this: *The identification of oneself with the single fragment that is not integrated may itself be the only healthy or moral act the person is capable of.* If this is true, the moral and therapeutic dimensions of concept formation may outweigh the scientific (predictive), and thus we may attribute to this isolated and weak effort at self-definition the dignity of being correct.

There is a dynamic import to first- and third-person judgments about who or what someone really is. One aspect of this is that in a self-characterization that appears to conflict with an individual's past, she is laying some sort of claim with respect to how she will act and experience in the future. This is not typically a matter of forming an intention to act differently in the future (e.g., an intention to change), but rather the laying of a claim that one is, is presently, such that one would act and feel in the appropriate ways under the relevant circumstances. The issue of whether or not the person is correct cannot be answered except in relation to some criterion for the valid attribution of the relevant character traits. But in choosing between alternative concepts, one of the merits of expanding the extent to which the individual may be correct (i.e., may escape from her past and make semi-authoritative pronouncements about who she is) is that such pronouncements themselves play a significant causal role in bringing about the changes in question. There is a tremendously fine line between self-deception that functions to allow the individual to remain static and self-affirmations that play a role in processes of transformation. Similarly, third-person perspectives on who someone really is can have a powerful impact on whether or not a person remains the same or undergoes some degree of change. Thus it is that young people on the way to becoming who they are find it necessary to escape from their family and friends and sometimes even from their culture. To stay at home during a process of rapid reorganization of the self is to be subject to the third-person perception of oneself as "phony." This judgment of phoniness, this discerning look of the other, is the other's most powerful judgment as he arrogates to himself an authoritative stance with respect to one's true being.

Lurking behind the general antipathy to developing concepts that organize the data in such a way as to allow a person to be correct when he retreats to a tiny fragment of his being, is the feeling that this would entail a breakdown of responsibility. If the actions aren't his, then he can't justly be held responsible for them. Indeed, if the entire self may be alien, then when is someone ever implicated by what he does?

If we accept the individual's claim to be who he thinks he is, then how will he ever learn responsibility? Thus, it is felt that acceptance of real guilt may be a necessary stage in the therapeutic process. Fingarette writes:

> The patient in therapy, therefore, must come to see, to experience, to acknowledge with the full vividness of complete and immediate reality his identity with these hitherto unacknowledged, unconscious subselves. He must consciously realize the extent to which it is, for example, indeed he who, at least with a part of himself, wants to evade responsibility and to be a child, to be loved as a child, or for example, that it is he who harbors within him murderous impulses toward his father. . . .
>
> There is a relief which the patient may legitimately enjoy subsequently; but it has a different source. Suppose the patient accepts the guilt and follows this by achieving insight into the motives which engender the guilt; then, at last, the patient may be able decisively to influence those motives. Having rejected or transformed those motives, he may feel relieved of his burden of guilt.[9]

This is a significant outlook and worthy of serious attention and inquiry into the actual effects of such processes. However, it must be remembered that when we are dealing with alienness as opposed to self-deception; the individual does recognize the meanings of his conduct, emotions, feelings. What he doesn't do is *identify himself in terms of these meanings.*

Moreover, the responsibility issue should not be pushed too far. Insofar as we are dealing with a sense of the alienness of the entire self, it should not be *assumed* that individual change is a possibility. The individual may at one particular moment have a flash of insight as she perceives and rejects the total complex that she is. She may see that she is dealing with a complete and unified personality and not a mere fragment, and she may see that the person that she is is itself the product of a culture or society that is deeply flawed. For instance, for a brief moment, late in life, she may recognize herself as the totally formed and integrated product of a racist, sexist, and avaricious culture. And in that moment, she may say, "That is not me. I never came into existence. I lived and will die, without even having really existed as myself." It may not be possible for her to change, nor reasonable for her to feel responsible for herself. The alternative to individual responsibility may be social responsibility rather than no responsibility. Responsibility for oneself may be a historical product to be attained socially and not necessarily available at any point in history; it may be hubris to view oneself otherwise.

This links to what Parfit has written about the question of whether or not a person has survived in certain hard fictionalized cases (e.g., when a person divides). For Parfit the question of survival—of whether or not it is the same person—is an empty question. And so it may be in the case of self-deception, for the question of whether the individual is in self-deception depends upon whether there is anything to deceive himself about. Parfit's answer in the case where there is a lack of continuity is that once we know all of the facts, there is no additional fact to know. So the person we see as a self-deceiver must be seen to be making a decision. What kind of a decision is it? And what kind of a decision are we making when we call him a self-deceiver? These are the interesting questions, and I argue that it all depends on the context. It might be the case that his refusal to view himself as himself is an authentic act of freedom or it might be an effort to deny the implications of what he has been. To know this we would have to know the context. There is no general rule.

Parfit argued that in making those choices one was expressing a view about what matters, and that in rationally making those choices one was expressing a rational view about what matters. But matters to whom? Parfit treats it as impersonal. He implicitly assumes that the rationality of what matters does not depend on who is involved. Most of his examples, however, are about personal survival and mostly they involve the first person. But he does not seem to consider that what matters to me about my survival may be different from what matters for another about my survival, and that the issue is not one that can be settled from the first person. If Parfit is correct about the logic of these situations, then there may be two very different descriptions about whether a person has survived and they may both be defensible as expressing for different speakers a rational view of what matters. And it may be that this is exactly analogous to the case of self-deception. Not only are there no additional facts to be known, but the choice of how to characterize the situation may be very different from the first- and third-person points of view—and thus there is a permanent tension about who we really are.

Notes

1. Perry Miller, *The New England Mind* (Boston: Beacon Press, 1968).
2. Augustine, *Confessions* (Middlesex: Penguin, 1961), 164-65.
3. Augustine, *Confessions*, 174.
4. John Donne, *Sermon XV*, folio of 1690, in *Seventeenth Century Prose and Poetry*, ed. Witherspoon and Warnke (New York: Harcourt, Brace and World, 1963), 71.
5. Herbert Fingarette, *Self-Deception* (London: Routledge and Kegan Paul, 1969), 82.
6. Fingarette, *Self-Deception*, 40.
7. Ibid., 67.
8. Ibid., 87.
9. Herbert Fingarette, *On Responsibility* (New York: Basic Books, 1967), 87.

4
God's Project of Self-Deception

In the fourth century B.C.E., the Greek philosopher Epicurus wrote that "the blessed and immortal nature knows no trouble itself nor causes trouble to any other, so that it is never constrained by anger or favor." What he meant was that God is neither moved nor moves in relation to the affairs of mankind. Such a conception of God, as a creative power behind the world but not engaged within it, has had numerous adherents during the last two thousand years. But a God of that sort bears no relationship to the God we find in the Hebrew Bible.

Above all else, God in the Hebrew Bible is emotional. Indeed, he is hyper-emotional in relation to mankind; so much so, as we have seen with the story of the Flood, that he himself recognizes a need to control his emotions—thus he binds himself with a promise to never again bring the world-flood and he places the rainbow in the sky to remind himself of this commitment.

The only time that God is remotely calm is in the very beginning of Genesis, before he has fully engaged with mankind. With utter majesty he creates the heavens and the earth. He separates light from dark, and the land from the sea. He creates the plants and the animals and then mankind. At each step along the way, we are told that God saw that what he had created was good.

Even in this calm, we find a pattern of interaction that will recur throughout the story. Something has been created and is there to be seen. God sees it, and he reacts to it. At this early stage, he is pleased, very pleased. These are the first emotions, as God is enlivened by his own project. Thus, we are immediately introduced to a God that feels things. And here at the very beginning, just before God creates mankind, he announces his intention: "I will make man in My image, after My likeness." And then the narrator tells us that he did so: "And God created man in His image, in the image of God He created him; male and female He created them."

Never again will God possess the tranquility that is exhibited in these first pages. He is about to become an emotional whirlwind. But if the God of the Bible is a god of surging emotions, what are they about? And why is God so engaged in the affairs of humankind? What is the meaning for him of this project? And why does he want a being in his image?

These are fundamental questions, and no literary interpretation of the Bible story can be viewed as adequate unless it provides answers to them. After all, God is the central character in the story; how is it possible to understand the story unless we understand his motivation?

There is always the default option: that God is ultimately a mystery to mankind, and we are not capable of fathoming his purposes. Even in a work of literature, one could construct a story in which the central character makes no sense at all. He would not fall into patterns that suggest motivation, and there would be no clues and certainly no direct explanation by the character of his own purpose. While we can imagine such a story, it would be distinctly unlike the Bible. In the Bible, we are given clues; we can find patterns and critical events that allow us to penetrate God's purposes and understand his intensity; further, on occasion, God provides a specific explanation of why he has acted as he has. It is not just that God is portrayed anthropomorphically in the Bible—as if he has human traits; he is portrayed as a very specific person. Viewed in relation to other works of literature, the Bible gives us more material to understand his character than we often find. Our task as readers, is to pull this information together into an overriding construct which makes the deepest sense out of the broadest possible features of the story.

The Creation of Humanity

The most important clues as to the nature of God's project come from a passage I have already considered, the Garden of Eden episode. Here are the elements:

1. Morality is portrayed as objective, being the subject of a higher form of knowledge.
2. The knowledge that comes from eating the forbidden fruit is not

moral wisdom, but rather the capacity to use moral categories.

3. God most definitely does not want humanity to be possessed of both moral knowledge and immortality.
4. In saying "Now that the man has become like one of us, knowing good and bad, what if he should stretch out his hand and take also from the tree of life and eat, and live forever!" God makes clear that now that the gap between mankind and the divine beings has narrowed considerably, he does not want to see it closed completely.

In reflecting on the Garden scene one might wonder, why, if God does not want mankind to have moral knowledge, did he place the tree of such knowledge in the Garden in the first place. Or to put it slightly differently, why did he create mankind as a being with the potential to use moral categories, and why did he make Eve someone who would be motivated to eat the fruit because she perceived it as a source of wisdom?

A standard answer is that God has created mankind as free to choose, that while God does not want mankind to choose to violate his first command, in order for freedom to be real, this choice has to be possible. Some go further and say that in so disobeying God, mankind reveals its propensity for evil (or disobedience) and thereby becomes responsible for what befalls it (mortality).

In part this line of thought seems to me to be sound. God has created mankind as free to obey or disobey him. To create mankind with this ability (we can call it freedom) is indeed God's choice, and an essential part of his project. This, however, leads to another question: why does God want the existence of a free being? Before attempting to answer this, I want to suggest an alternative, that God does, in fact, want mankind to eat of the tree of knowledge of good and evil. God might want mankind both to choose and to choose to disobey, thus becoming morally conscious. Indeed, one can go further and say that by placing the two trees in the Garden and by making the tree of knowledge alluring, perhaps even by putting the snake in the Garden, God establishes an elaborate set-up. In creating Adam and Eve, God has created a unique form of animal, yet still an animal. But he wants something beyond this. He wants mankind in possession of moral categories but without immortality. Moreover, he wants mankind to live out its terrible fatedness, its knowledge of its ultimate death, in full awareness that it has brought this on itself through disobedience to God. In sum, God wants mankind to be free, to be morally conscious, to be mortal, and to recognize itself as both responsible for its own fate yet dependent upon God. We will understand much about God and his project if we can understand why he wants this kind of being to exist.

Babel

The story of the Tower of Babel is strikingly brief, consisting of only ten sentences. Yet it serves as a pivotal point in the overall biblical narrative. It appears just after the story of the Flood, and just before the opening of the long story of Abraham. Structurally, it moves God's attention and that of the reader from mankind as a whole to a single family, that of Abraham. And from Abraham will emerge his grandson Jacob, also known as Israel, and thus the Israelites—the single people whose history is the focal point of the Hebrew Bible.

A central feature of the Babel story is God's creation of distinct peoples out of a previously undifferentiated humankind. God does this by creating different languages "so that they shall not understand one another's speech." We are told, "That is why it is called Babel, because there the Lord confounded the speech of the whole earth; and from there the Lord scattered them over the face of the whole earth" [Genesis 11: 9].

It should be emphasized that God's intention is not merely to create diversity or multiplicity of languages and cultures; his action does not emerge from his love for his creatures and his delight in the multitude of different patterns that human life can take. One could imagine such a story—a god delighted by his own creatures, fascinated by their comings and goings. Such a god might view each culture as a unique treasure and a unique source of interest and amazement.

Yet such a characterization is not what we are given in the Babel story. Rather we are told that God "confounded their speech there, so that they shall not understand one another's speech." And twice we are told that he "scattered" mankind. God wants mankind to be not only diverse, but to be foreign and incomprehensible to each other. He wants an absence of understanding, and I would argue, his goal is misunderstanding and distrust. Indeed, the Babel story suggests that God wants enmity and even war, between these varied nations.

That this is no over-interpretation is supported by the opening of the Abraham story which immediately follows Babel. In the second verse of the Abraham story God makes a covenant with Abraham:

> I will make of you a great nation,
> And I will bless you;
> I will make your name great,
> And you shall be a blessing:
> I will bless those who bless you,
> And curse him that curses you;
> All the families of the earth
> Shall bless themselves by you. [Genesis12:2-3]

This structuring of humanity into nations, some greater than others, some blessed and some cursed—this is the basis for the covenant with the Israelites, and it presupposes the diversity and enmity initiated at Babel. Without a context in which there is a hierarchy of nations and a fierce competition between them, God's commitment to Abraham and through him to the Israelites, would lack both meaning and value. It is through the actions at Babel that God makes himself instrumentally important to the future Israelites. He is setting the stage for what he will become: a god of war.

More generally, we can say that God, through the imposition of human mortality, has made mankind vulnerable, and now through the creation of nations that cannot comprehend each other, he has situated mankind into groups that threaten and fear each other. And then within this newly structured human condition in which we are by birth part of one grouping and foreign to another, he has made himself indispensable.

The motivational question remains. If this is a correct description of what God has done at Babel, why has he done so? In the Babel story we are given an account of what it was that triggered God's decision to confound mankind's speech and to scatter humankind across the earth:

> All the earth had the same language and the same words. . . . And they said, "Come, let us build us a city, and a tower with its top in the sky, to make a name for ourselves; else we shall be scattered all over the world." The Lord came down to look at the city and tower which man had built, and the Lord said, "If, as one people with one language for all, this is how they have begun to act, then nothing that they propose to do will be out of their reach." [Genesis 11:1-6]

Immediately upon saying this, God "confounded the speech of the whole earth." In the passage above, it becomes clear that God has not acted out of amusement, or malevolence, or as punishment for some violation of a commandment. Rather, he acts out of some anxiety, the exact nature of which has yet to be uncovered. When God says, "If . . . this is how they have begun to act" we hear the same note of fear in his voice that we hear when he expels Adam and Eve from the Garden saying "Now that mankind has become like one of us . . . what if he should stretch out his hand and take also from the tree of life. . . ." In both cases he fears the next step humankind might take. In Babel the fear is that "nothing that they propose to do will be out of their reach."

At Babel we are told that the humans say to one another, "Come let us make bricks and burn them hard." And we are told that "Brick served them as stone, and bitumen served them as mortar." Here we are given a two-fold picture. First, we see the introduction and discovery of technology. Very early on, human beings discover how to fashion a man-made stone that substitutes for God's creation. Further, they discover how to use the minerals of the earth to connect those bricks, one to another into walls and structures. Secondly, we are shown man's cooperation. Mankind, with "the same language and the same words," has found it possible to work together for a common purpose, with a common idea, in this case "to make a name for ourselves, else we shall be scattered all over the world." Mankind has an awareness of danger, senses the importance of being unified, and successfully carries out a breakthrough project of technological and social accomplishment.

God takes note, and experiences the power it represents. He projects it forward saying, that if this is what mankind can do at this early stage, then ultimately nothing "will be out of their reach." Such a belief is not unlike the belief that if mankind does not blow itself up first, through science, ultimately, we will be able to conquer every constraint.

In the Babel story God expresses a fear of an ever-expanding human capability, a fear of infinite human reach. He envisions that humans will develop powers that will make them god-like, able to achieve whatever they desire. In the aftermath of the flood, that world-traumatic demonstration of human mortality, the immediate concern of mankind is its vulnerability, and if one thinks in terms of the drowning that proceeded it, the construction of an edifice that reaches to the heavens is, at least in symbolic terms, understandable.

On a more fundamental level, the range of human ambitions must be thought to extend to a desire to overcome mortality itself. It is this unstated, but perhaps not unthought, possibility that specifically links God's decision to expel mankind from the Garden and God's decision to confound human speech. At bottom the fear is the same, that mankind, now that it has gained the moral categories and "become like one of us," shall find a way to take from the tree of life and with the aid of future technologies further close the gap between God and mankind.

Note that in speaking of God's fear of an all-powerful humanity, I am not referring to a physical fear. There is nothing in the text to suggest that mankind can ever endanger God in a direct physical (if one can use that word) contest. There is no reason to imagine that when God says that nothing would be beyond the reach of mankind, he believes that mankind might someday develop powers that are more powerful than his own.

This fact of the story, that in a straightforward sense God cannot be endangered by humanity, helps to define and expand the puzzle—why does a God that cannot be endangered somehow feel in danger? What is there to be afraid of? What is at stake for God? What negative outcome could he possibly suffer at the hands of a god-like mankind?

Pharaoh's Heart

The fullest statement of God's project emerges in the Book of Exodus. The setting is the ongoing confrontation between Moses and Pharaoh. The reader has been told in advance that extracting the Israelites from the power of the Pharaoh will not be easy, but God has made clear to Moses that he will succeed. At the scene of the burning bush, God tells Moses:

> I have marked well the plight of My people in Egypt and have heeded their outcry because of their taskmasters; yes, I am mindful of their sufferings. I have come down to rescue them from the Egyptians and to bring them out of that land to a good and spacious land, a land flowing with milk and honey. . . . I will send you to Pharaoh, and you shall free My people, the Israelites from Egypt. [Exodus 3:7-10]

Moses, of course, does not have to be told that it will not suffice to merely demand the freedom of the Israelites. And God is explicit on this point, saying "I know that the king of Egypt will not let you go except by force. So I will stretch out My hand and smite Egypt with various wonders which I will work upon them; after that he shall let you go."

In Moses' first encounter with the Pharaoh things go as might be expected. Moses chooses to not speak in his own name, but rather quotes to Pharaoh the words of God. He tells Pharaoh, "Thus says the Lord [Yahweh], the God of Israel: Let My people go. . . ." Here I should note that Pharaoh is not being asked to free the Israelites, but only to let them go for a few days "that they may celebrate a festival for Me in the wilderness." Moses asks Pharaoh for permission for the Israelites to go a distance of three days into the wilderness to perform a sacrifice. Yet even this modest request is turned down. Pharaoh has never heard of this god and he is not impressed. He says, "Who is Yahweh that I should listen to him and let Israel go? I know nothing of Yahweh. . . ." [Exodus 5: 2].[1]

Not only does Pharaoh not permit the Israelites to depart so they may make their sacrifice, he makes their lives more difficult. Whereas previously Pharaoh's agents provided the Israelites with the straw that is used in making the mud bricks, they now tell the Israelites to gather it themselves. As a result they are unable to meet their quotas and the Israelite foremen are beaten by the Egyptians. In turn the foremen criticize Moses for "making us objectionable to the Pharaoh." And Moses, with a critical voice, questions God, saying:

> O Lord, why did You bring harm upon this people? Why did You send me? Ever since I came to Pharaoh to speak in your name, it has gone worse with this people; yet You have not delivered Your people at all. [Exodus 5: 22-23]

God responds, "You shall soon see what I will do to Pharaoh." God then makes clear that it is no accident that the Israelites have not been liberated quickly. He tells Moses that he will make him "an oracle to Pharaoh," using his brother Aaron as his spokesman. They are to repeat to Pharaoh all that God will instruct Moses to say. Yet this will be of no avail, for we now learn that God will prevent Pharaoh from being responsive. God tells Moses:

> But I will harden Pharaoh's heart, that I may multiply My signs and marvels in the land of Egypt. When Pharaoh does not heed you, I will lay My hand upon Egypt and deliver My people the Israelites, from the land of Egypt with extraordinary chastisements. And the Egyptians shall know that I am the Lord, when I stretch out My hand over Egypt and bring out the Israelites from their midst. [Exodus 7:3-5]

The text does not tell us anything about Moses' reaction to this revelation. Perhaps it does not seem strange to him that God would deliberately harden Pharaoh's heart so that God would have this opportunity to work his "marvels." On the other hand, perhaps Moses finds this astonishing. We are not told; God does not explain, and Moses does not ask. We are only told the Egyptians shall know that I am the Lord (Yahweh). Whatever Moses' response, the reader might well wonder why is it important to God to be able to work these terrible deeds, why is it important that the Egyptians come to know of God's power.

At this point in the story, something of a contextual explanation is provided. Previously, when Moses quotes to Pharaoh the words of Yahweh, Pharaoh, as we have seen, responded contemptuously, saying "Who is this Yahweh . . . I know nothing of Yahweh." Now God will ensure that Pharaoh will know indeed. The reader can here understand God's hardening of Pharaoh's heart as God's angry response to Pharaoh's dismissiveness; God will deliver "chastisements" to ensure that in the future other Pharaohs will take notice upon hearing the name Yahweh.

The story then progresses through a series of plagues that God inflicts upon the Egyptians: blood, frogs, animal plague, boils, and so forth. Egypt is a country that lives in virtue of the Nile; water is everything. We are told that the water is turned to blood, and the fish die, and the water is so foul smelling that it cannot be drunk. Swarms of frogs are then brought upon the Egyptians. They not only fill the river, they occupy the palace, the royal bedroom, the Pharaoh's bed, the ovens, even the food.

What emerges is a symbolic contest between Yahweh and the sorcerers of the Pharaoh, each of whom causes amazing events. Pharaoh's men, however, do not protect Egypt from the plagues brought through Moses. Nor do they inflict parallel harm upon the Israelites. Rather, they demonstrate their powers only by duplicating the plagues themselves. They show that they, too, can turn water to blood and that they, too, can make frogs swarm all over Egypt. Egypt is undergoing destruction both at the hand of Yahweh and by Pharaoh's own magicians; yet responding to the challenge of a foreign god apparently takes precedence. However, as amazing as the powers of Pharaoh's advisors are, turning water to blood and summoning frogs is the outer edge of what the Egyptian magic-men can do. When Yahweh, through Moses, has man and beast attacked by lice, the Egyptian magicians fail in their attempt to duplicate the phenomenon. Thus the greater power of Yahweh is demonstrated.

Pharaoh, as one might expect, is not unmoved by these events. They are not mere annoyances but threaten the life of his kingdom. In response to the frogs, even though his magicians can also summon frogs, he agrees to let the Israelites go and perform their sacrifices. Yet when the frogs are gone (at Pharaoh's request Moses pleads with God to remove them), Pharaoh refuses to keep his promise. As a result, more, and worse, plagues follow. Nothing seems capable of causing Pharaoh to release the Israelites. In one plague, all of the livestock of Egypt are killed, yet we are told, "Pharaoh's heart hardened, and he would not let the people go." All of this would seem impossibly foolish were it not for the fact that we have already been told that God will harden Pharaoh's heart, and indeed as the plagues progress we are told again that "the Lord stiffened the heart of Pharaoh, and he would not heed them." Thus it is underscored throughout the encounter that God is orchestrating these events.

Previously, God explains to Moses that the purpose of hardening Pharaoh's heart is to provide God with the opportunity to demonstrate to the Egyptians his vast powers. But there is more to it than that, and in a remarkable passage God provides to Moses a fuller account of the nature of his project:

> Then the Lord said to Moses, "Go to Pharaoh. For I have hardened his heart and the hearts of his courtiers, in order that I may display these My signs among them, and that you may recount in the hearing of your sons' sons how I made a mockery of the Egyptians and how I displayed My signs among them—in order that you may know that I am the Lord." [Exodus 10: 1-2]

In the entire Bible, this passage is the most extensive revelation of God's motivation. It is important to remember that the events that are being explained here are, within the text, historical occurrences of a major order—nothing less than the step by step destruction of Egypt, the greatest power of its day.

The logic of God's motivation is complex. He hardens Pharaoh's heart, so that:

1. He may "display his signs among them," so that:
2. The Israelites may recount among themselves, through the generations, this very story, so that:
3. The Israelites, through the generations, may know "that I am the Lord" (in more direct translations, "that I am Yahweh").

We are being told that history is pedagogy. It occurs the way it occurs, because it is God's way of teaching his chosen people. The vehicle for this teaching, except for the first generation, which experiences it directly, is the telling of this history. And the purpose of this telling, and thus of the events themselves, is that the future generations shall attain a certain kind of knowledge: "that I am Yahweh."

The Bible, of course, is itself the telling of the events in question. It follows then, that according to the Bible, when we, today, read of these events in the Bible, our reading is the very reason why these events occurred several thousand years ago. And if we are thus brought to the knowledge referred to in the phrase "know that I am Yahweh," then God's purpose of thousands of years ago is fulfilled. We are thus drawn into a direct role within the story. Were there no readers of the Bible story, the story itself would not be credible, for it posits the continued existence of its audience. What is beyond amazing is that a several thousand-year-old story, which posits future readers as the explanation both for the events it portrays and for its existence as the story that portrays those events, should turn out to be the most widely and continuously read story in all of history.

This is an extraordinary conception, both of literature and of history. It tells us that history (understood as the retelling of the past) is not merely a factual account of the past but the intended purpose that caused those events in the past. Events occur so that there might be the re-telling. Thus the Bible self-referentially presents itself as that vehicle through which God's purpose, that we know that he is Yahweh, is to be achieved.

Two questions are in order. First, what exactly is this knowledge that God wants his people to have, this knowledge that "I am Yahweh"? And secondly, why is it so vital to God that the Israelites have this knowledge?

Knowing that "I am Yahweh"

Today neither Christians nor Jews make substantial use of the name, Yahweh. In the Hebrew Bible, the name of God is spelled out with four Hebrew characters which in the English alphabet are rendered as YHWH, and is frequently transliterated as Yahweh. However, in Hebrew the vowels are lacking, and the correct pronunciation is unknown. Moreover, in the Jewish tradition it is forbidden to speak the name of God; thus, when the Bible is read aloud, rather than pronouncing this name, the speaker substitutes the term "Adonai" which translates as "the Lord." In some English translations, both Jewish and non-Jewish, this shift is also made in the written text; rather than containing the letters "YHWH" (which matches the Hebrew) or even the names "Yahweh" or "Jehovah," they substitute the term, "the Lord."[2]

In the text, in God's own words, he is acting so that the Israelites may "know that I am Yahweh." Here, it will not do to substitute "The Lord" for "Yahweh." Whatever is meant by "knowing that I am Yahweh" does not seem to be the same thing as "knowing that I am the Lord."

"Yahweh" here functions as a name. If in this critical passage, God said that he wanted mankind to know that "I am the Lord" we would be led to think either that God is asserting his status, saying that he and not others (e.g. the gods of Egypt) is the Lord; or alternatively, we may think that God is stating his desire that mankind know that God exists, that mankind believes in God. When God says that "I am Yahweh" God's effort to have the Israelites know who he is, is harder to grasp. It seems clear that it is more involved than his simply wanting them to know that he is named Yahweh. They already know that.

Knowing Yahweh Among the Gods?

Imagine a story, be it Greek or Hindu or from some other polytheistic tradition, in which there are many different characters, all of whom are gods. Within that imagined story, there would be several understandable interpretations of what it would mean for one of these gods to assert himself before a specific population and to say to them, "You shall know Yahweh!" This would not be a demand that they believe in God, nor a demand that the population be merely familiar with the god Yahweh. Rather, in the context of a specific story, this might be understood to mean that the population was to adopt this god, and not others, as its special deity, or perhaps that the population react to him in a certain way, for example, that they be terrified into obedience of him. Thus we can envision a god saying something of this sort just as he sets out to so thoroughly traumatize a population that they and their descendants will never be without a powerful ongoing consciousness of the presence of Yahweh, having him more fully in mind than other gods.

Can we understand the Biblical Yahweh in these ways, as asserting himself in relation to other gods? This leads to a very fundamental question about the Biblical text. Is the Bible story itself a story of one god among many? This may sound a strange question because we so thoroughly identify Judaism and Christianity with monotheism. Yet the strangeness of the question emerges not from the Bible itself, but from our inability to read the text freely. This specific orientation, reading the text on the assumption that it posits a monotheistic world, is probably the most difficult to relinquish of all of our assumptions about the Bible.

When we let ourselves read the Bible without preconceived notions, however, no question is more natural than whether there are one or many gods in the world of the Biblical narrative. The story is completely ambiguous about this matter. On the one hand, it can be argued that many gods are posited:

- Nowhere in the Bible does God clearly assert that he is the only god that exists.[3] In fact the first commandment states, "You shall have no other gods beside Me"—it does not say "there are no other gods than me."
- There is no commandment that makes it a crime to assert that other gods exist; the crime is always to worship those gods.
- When God instructs Moses to go to Pharaoh, he says to tell him, "Yahweh the God of the Hebrews, has sent me. . . ." Thus, God himself speaks in a way that suggests that he is one god among many.

On the other hand, Moses instructs the Israelites that there is only one god, and no other god ever appears in the Bible. If such a god or gods exist, they are always off stage. In addition, no events ever occur in the Bible that are unambiguously attributed to any other god. Even when Yahweh through Moses duels with Pharaoh's sorcerers and when they succeed in also turning water into blood and summoning frogs, these events are attributed to the magicians themselves, not their gods. Finally, God, in the Bible, is presented as having created all that exists. Though there are other divine beings, presumably angels, and though no account of their creation is ever given, the scope of God's creative power is so vast that it is hard to understand what powers could be left over for other gods to exercise.

Such arguments, on both sides, can be strengthened were the argument extended. The point, however, is that there are convincing arguments on both sides. The biblical narrative leaves open the question of whether or not there are other gods. Moreover, this must be seen as a deliberate decision by the Biblical author, because it would have been very simple to have resolved the matter. One could have had another god appear, and that would have resolved it one way. Or one could have had the narrator explain that there was only one God and this could have been a central aspect of God's teaching as well. None of these potentially decisive options were taken. Instead, the matter was left open. We are allowed to read it with one belief about the story or the other.

Though the alternative choice is possible, I have decided to approach the story as one in which there is only one god, Yahweh. Given that the text is ambiguous on these matters, this aspect of my interpretation doesn't rest on the text itself, but on methodological grounds.

Suppose we read the Bible story as one in which there were multiple gods. Such a reading would have the virtue of suggesting a coherent account of God's motivation. If God is one among many, then we can assimilate his actions within a larger picture of competition between the gods. Exactly what that competition would be about we can't say with certainty, but it would fit into patterns of human competitions over status, power, and prestige. In such an account, what God really cared about would be his place among the gods themselves. His engagement with mankind and with the Israelites would be an arena within which he would seek to triumph in his god-to-god relations. For example, he would seek to have his people triumph over the people of other gods so that he would triumph over those gods. Further, he would seek to demonstrate the commitment to him of his people, that they would be faithful to him and to him alone. Of course there is no direct textual evidence of such a competition among the gods, but if we accept that there are other gods, then such hypotheses are not far fetched and allow us to understand why God is passionate about the Israelites.

Indeed, something similar to this is detailed in the Book of Job, where the unjust afflictions God bestows upon Job are explicitly explained as God's response to a challenge that Satan makes to him. Here Satan is not another god but rather a powerful divine being. To some, this might seem to be no difference at all; among the Greek gods, for example, some were more powerful than others; and Satan in no mere servant of God's will. God's relationship to Satan emerges as of sufficient importance to God that it motivates him toward injustice to Job. If such independent, powerful, immortal divine beings exist, it is no great stretch to simply posit other gods, to envision the entire narrative within such god-to-god relations.

The problem with this is not that it is speculative (which it is, but not unreasonably so) but that it diminishes the depth and grandeur of the Bible and its account of the human condition. If God is primarily competing for status among the pantheon of gods, how shallow a story. How absurd a conception of human existence. How mundane a divine being.

With the alternative, that there is only one god, and further, that God knows he is the only god, we have a deeper and more complex story, perhaps with more questions than answers. What is it that is driving this God who is aware of himself as the only God? Why does he want a free, morally conscious, mortal and dependent humanity to know him? And how does he want that humanity to know him? Why does he care? These are puzzling but powerful questions, ones that lead us deep into the heart of being.

God's Motivation

The question of God's name and God's titles is central to the entire Biblical story. We see this earlier in God's interaction with Abraham when Abraham calls him "the Judge of all the earth," and later when God himself tells Moses that having the Israelites know that he is Yahweh is his central purpose. What is striking here is the radically different ways this issue of "Who is God" emerges in Genesis and in Exodus. In *Joseph's Bones*, from which this essay is taken, I argued that Abraham's fundamental project is to bring God under the constraints of morality. He does this in dialogue with God when he says "Shall not the Judge of all the earth deal justly?" In this Abraham is seeking to have God take on a certain self-identity, to see himself as the just Judge of all the earth. And as I have argued, were God fully to embrace that self-identity, he would not experience morality as a constraint; rather, acting justly would be experienced as acting from within himself, in other words, acting freely.

Because it is God's self-identity that is at issue, the stakes could not be higher. God ultimately determines all that befalls the world. Thus, Abraham's quest is to transform the universe, to make justice a fundamental determinant of all that happens. Given what we know of the world in the Bible, we can conclude that, at best, Abraham is only partially successful in his audacious endeavor. And further, as I have also argued, in the binding of Isaac episode we see the price that Abraham (and Isaac) pay for this audacity.

In Exodus, in the encounter with Pharaoh, God is seized with the project of having the Israelites know him. But here the issue of "who is God" seems strikingly devoid of content. God is not intent on having the Israelites know that he is the just Judge, or on knowing any other substantive aspect of his identity.

One might think that there are two distinctly different issues here, one having to do with descriptions of what someone is like (e.g. is he kind, is he just, is he forgiving?) and one having to do with someone's name (e.g. is he Yahweh?). But these two are intricately linked. In the Bible names are repeatedly given or taken because of their meaning. They are often not mere names but descriptive or commemorative phrases; and often enough, a person is re-named to mark some transformation in his being or in the meaning of his existence. As we have seen Joseph names his son Manasseh "meaning 'God has made me forget completely my hardship and my parental home.'" And at a critical juncture God re-names Abram, Abraham, saying "this is My covenant with you: You shall be the father of a multitude of nations" [Genesis 17:4]. When Jacob wrestles through the night with a divine being (some say it is God, some an angel) he is told that his name is now Israel, "for you have striven with beings divine and human, and have prevailed" [Genesis 32:29]. In fact, in that very episode Jacob asks this divine being, "Pray tell me your name," but he is told "You must not ask my name!" We do not know why Jacob is denied this knowledge, but it is clear that the name holds some power or importance.

When God first appears to Moses and tells him of his mission to free the Israelites, Moses immediately wants to know God's name. He says:

> When I come to the Israelites and say to them, "The God of your fathers has sent me to you" and they ask me, "What is His name?" what shall I say to them? [Exodus 3:13]

What is going on here is not clear. Moses may well be only anticipating problems that he will have with the Israelites, or he may be trying an indirect way of attaining knowledge of God's name. Implicit in Moses' query is the notion that knowing God's name will to some extent make the Israelites more likely to be responsive to what Moses will say to them.

It is thus interesting to see how God responds to Moses' question:

> And God said to Moses, "Ehyeh-Asher-Ehyeh." He continued, "Thus shall you say to the Israelites, 'Ehyeh sent me to you'" And God said further to Moses, "Thus shall you speak to the Israelites: The Lord ["Yahweh" in direct translations] the God of your fathers, the God of Abraham, the God of Isaac, and the God of Jacob, has sent me to you:
> This shall be My name forever,
> This My appellation for all eternity. [Exodus 3:14-15]

Within this answer God calls himself Ehyeh-Asher-Ehyeh, Yahweh, and the God of Abraham, Isaac and Jacob. We are familiar with both "Yahweh" and "the God of Abraham, Isaac and Jacob." Moreover, this last phrase might be viewed less as a name of God than as a descriptive phrase that helps to explain to the Israelites who Yahweh is. Later on, I will argue that more is involved here, but for now, I want to focus on the first of these three responses, the name Ehyeh-Asher-Ehyeh.

This is the only time this appellation appears in the Bible. It occurs at a key moment, when God is charging Moses with his mission. Not only is it revealed to Moses, he is told to use it when explaining who God is to the Israelites. A great deal has been written about this name, yet it remains enigmatic; scholars are unsure even of how to translate it, but agree that it is both meaningful and important. It has been variously translated: "I Am That I Am"; "I Am Who I Am"; "I Will Be What I Will Be." And God seems to be telling us something he views as important about his nature when he tells us this name.

Consider the translations sometimes given, "I Am Who I Am"; "I Am That I Am"; "I Will Be Who I Will Be." Let us assume that one of these is correct. What exactly could this tell us about God? The first and the third of these actually are meaningful sentences; indeed, they are logical truths—tautologies that are true of all persons. I am who I am, and you are who you are. I will be who I will be, and you will be who you will be. All this seems to tell us nothing of substance, quite unlike saying "You are the Judge of the earth." Moreover, and paradoxically, since these statements are true of all beings, they do not distinguish God from anyone else. While the first and the third possible translation are true sentences, the second of these, "I Am That I Am" while structurally similar to "I Am Who I Am" remains odd, and it is not clear that it has any meaning.

If we want to understand what Ehyeh-Asher-Ehyeh means in the story perhaps we should consider what God is doing when he responds to Moses in this manner. What is he conveying either about himself or to Moses? Suppose some stranger asks you to convey a message to a third person, and you ask, "Who should I say you are?" and the response is "I am who I am." While the phrase "I am who I am" is, at least in one sense, true of all persons, to actually respond to a request for a name in this way is more significant. It could be a way of saying "don't ask," or a way of deflecting the question. It could be a way of providing an answer without taking any risks. Alternatively, it could be a joke, or an insult, or a warning. Or it could simply be a deliberate attempt to be enigmatic.

I noted earlier that after Jacob wrestles with a divine being, he asks its name and is told, "Don't ask." If we assume that something similar is at work here, then when God tells Moses that he is "Ehyeh-Asher-Ehyeh," God is using a name that doesn't yield power over him precisely because it communicates nothing. It is as if God is now saying, "I am what I am, you shall know me by virtue of what I choose to do, for I am unconstrained." God here may be seen as engaged in an assertion of freedom, as refusing not only to be bound as Abraham seeks to bind him (the just Judge), but to be bound by any characteristic altogether. That said, we are still left to wonder about the possible significance of the specific words God chooses—after all, there are many ways of conveying "Don't ask," and many different ways of being enigmatic, if this is what is involved. What, if anything, is conveyed by the use of the terms "I Am Who I Am" or "I Am That I Am"?

In the text, there is a second sentence that follows. God says, "Say to the Israelites, 'Eheyeh sent me to you.'" "Eheyeh," often translated as "I Am," is a shorter version of "Eheyeh-Asher-Eheyeh," and is understood as a variant of Yahweh. Thus, God here is telling Moses to refer to him simply as "I Am" when addressing the Israelites. Generally we use the phrase "I am" at the beginning of a sentence that will attribute some property or characteristic or action to the speaker, as in "I am unhappy" or "I am forgetful" or "I am running." To refer to oneself as simply "I Am" or to call oneself "I Am That I Am" or "I Am Who I Am" pulls away from any specific property or attribute toward the issue of being itself. It suggests that God is saying that his nature, his way of being, is somehow different from that of humans, conveying a kind of self-sufficiency or independence of being. And while this is just how many philosophers have thought of God, we know that the God of the Hebrew Bible is exactly the opposite. He is passionately engaged with mankind, and passionately moved, often enraged and carried away in his interaction with mankind. So why is he presenting himself so differently, as if he were like the unmoved god Epicurus envisioned?

Sartre's Insights into Consciousness

In 1943, the French philosopher Jean Paul Sartre published his most important work, *Being and Nothingness*, and established himself as the leading existentialist philosopher of the twentieth century. His central area of concern was with the nature of consciousness, in particular self-conscious beings and their interactions. Whether or not he succeeded in uncovering truths about the very nature of being, viewed from a non-metaphysical point of view, Sartre had astonishing insight into the nature of human psychology. It will serve our inquiry well to take a short excursion into his thought. My concern here is not with Sartre's ideas per se;

rather I shall try to present a Sartrean perspective that strikes me as sound and as relevant to the issue at hand, even if it might stray from full fidelity to Sartre.

Sartre's central focus is on the nature of human existence. A living human being is a being with consciousness, but it is not a disembodied consciousness. We are also physical objects subject to the physical laws that regulate objects in time and space. Yet unlike many other living creatures, human consciousness goes beyond having sensations and perceptions. As we develop we become conscious of ourselves, that is, we ourselves are the objects of our own consciousness.

This distinction between beings that have self-consciousness and those that do not allows us to speak of two different modes of being, the In-itself and the For-itself. The existence of a totally inanimate object, say a stone, is existence in the mode of the In-itself. It simply is what it is. The nature of existence in the mode of the For-itself is, for Sartre, radically different. Because it is self-aware, and because except in rare cases we are not a paralyzed consciousnesses trapped inside our bodies, we are able to self-determine ourselves. For Sartre, the hallmark of the For-itself is that it is free. Sartre extends this not just to bodily actions, but to elements of consciousness as well. Thus, he puts forward a radical theory of the emotions, in which, contrary to the common sense way of speaking, they are not truly "passions" which befall us, and with respect to which we are passive; for Sartre, they are active aspects of consciousness. Even if we do not fully bestow our emotions upon ourselves, we choose either to hold ourselves within our emotional states or step outside of them. We are free to be otherwise.

Similarly, the For-itself goes through time differently than the In-itself. While we have a past that in some sense defines who we are, a self-conscious being is never purely a projection of what it has been. At every moment, it creates itself anew. Thus, we are both what we are, and in some sense, not what we are. Or to put it differently, the way in which we are what we are is fundamentally different than the way the In-itself (for example, the stone) simply is what it is.

The world of a self-conscious being is made particularly complex by the fact that there are other self-conscious beings in it, and because each such being is aware that it is perceived by others. Sartre writes of the Other, a developed consciousness that is not mine. The Other takes as the object of its consciousness not just itself, but me. And I in turn take the Other as my object. In this taking of the Other as an object, we see the Other as having certain characteristics. These we experience as relatively stable properties of the Other, not as freely self-imposed qualities, held in place from moment to moment. For example we see the other as having a specific personality, and we perceive the being of the Other as in continuity with what the other has been in its past. Our perceptions of each other tend to diminish or deny the degree of freedom or transcendence in the being of the other. In short, we tend to make objects out of each other.

It should not be thought that this is something that the self must react against, as though it revels in its freedom and resists the constraints imposed by the other's perception of itself. Indeed, much the opposite is true. Just because the self is aware of its freedom, it is aware of a kind of necessary inner emptiness, that it never just flows from past into future, and that it never truly has properties or characteristics the way an object does. Thus, the For-itself is aware of its own ultimate inner emptiness, its non-being. Freedom becomes something to be escaped from, something that we experience in anguish. Thus, we may embrace the Other's objectifying perception of ourselves, just because it fills us up and gives us a stability and substance that we lack.

Sartre's most penetrating discussion is of what he terms "*mauvais foi*" or bad-faith, sometimes translated as self-deception. The central issue concerns the different ways in which a person might think of himself or herself. Given that we are beings that exist both in the mode of the In-itself and the For-itself, how should we think of ourselves and of each other? That is, how do we experience ourselves and others if we are fully honest, fully authentic?

Sartre asks us to consider a waiter in a café. "His movement is quick and forward, a little too precise, and a little too rapid. He comes toward patrons with a step a little too quick. . . . All his behavior seems to us a game. . . But what is he playing? We need not watch long before we can explain it: he is playing at being a waiter in a café. . . ." Similarly, "There is the dance of the grocer, of the tailor, of the auctioneer, by which they endeavor to persuade their clientele that they are nothing but a grocer, an auctioneer, a tailor. . . ."

But this is the outward presentation. "From within, the waiter in the café cannot be immediately a café waiter in the sense that this inkwell is an inkwell, or the glass is a glass. . ." The waiter knows there is another reality outside the role. Yet to the public he represents himself falsely, as if he did not sustain himself in his role. Yet it is not that he is not a waiter. "There is no doubt that I am in a sense a café waiter—otherwise could I not just as well call myself a diplomat or a reporter? But if I am one, this cannot be in the mode of being-in-itself. I am a waiter in the mode of being what I am not."[4]

This, for Sartre, is not a special case of a particular role or mask that someone puts on; rather the exploration of bad faith reveals something general about consciousness. He asserts, "The condition of the possibility for bad faith is that human reality, in its most immediate being . . . must be what it is not and not be what it is."[5]

Let us return to the Bible, to God's statement of his name, understood as "I Am That I Am" or "I Am Who I Am." A Sartrean orientation allows us to fathom God's strange name. If one wanted to emphasize the fundamental gap that exists between mankind and an infinite God, one would want to go beyond mere differences in degree, for instance, beyond saying mankind is knowledgeable, but God knows more, or even God knows everything. Rather, one would say that God's mode of existence is fundamentally incommensurate with human existence. And thus no predicate affirmed of a human being can ever properly be asserted or denied of God. All one can say of God, and all we finite beings can truly know of God, is that he exists, that He Is. Being beyond language, he can, in truth, tell us nothing of himself except that his name is "I Am."

So far, so good. This formulation works for many a conception of God. There is only one problem—as noted above, this conception is radically foreign to the God that is presented in the biblical narrative. Though God says his name is "I Am That I Am," the God we find in the story is a God with a consistent character, a God with a distinctive personality. This is a God that has passions, regrets, and, most centrally, insecurities.

The interpretive problem is one of trying to understand exactly how it is that mankind can in any sense be threatening to God. Why does a God who creates us in his image and allows us, through eating of the Tree of Knowledge, to become more like him, fear that we should become too much so? And why, as I have asked, does this God so fear unified mankind acting as one at Babel, that he fractures mankind into mutually incomprehensible cultures?

What we must ask is this: If the God in the Bible is fundamentally like mankind rather than fundamentally unknowable, then what are we to make of his encounter with Moses, of his stating his name as "I Am That I Am"? The answer, I believe, is that God is posturing. In this self-presentation to Moses, God is like the waiter in the café: he is affecting a role that he cannot truly be. He is playing the role of being an infinitely distant, infinitely incommensurable God, and, moreover, he does this not in full awareness of the deception but in bad faith, in self-deception. He wants us to see him as one who does not depend for his being on how we see him, but in his very concern with how we see him, he is revealed as dependent upon us.

The Motive

Immediately after saying that Moses should tell the Israelites "Ehyeh [I Am] sent me to you," God tells Moses to say to the Israelites, "The Lord [Yahweh] the God of your fathers, the God of Abraham, the God of Isaac, and the God of Jacob, has sent me to you." As already noted, there is a practical reason for telling the Israelites that it is the God of Abraham, the God of Isaac, and the God of Jacob that has sent Moses. Presumably these three patriarchs are important figures to the Israelites, and presumably the Israelites know some of the stories of their encounter with God, perhaps even of God's covenant with Abraham. By so identifying himself, God establishes his bona fides with the Israelites.

While this may be a reason God makes reference to the beliefs of Abraham, Isaac, and Jacob, I suspect there is more to it than this practical explanation. After all, there are innumerable ways of impressing the Israelites. Moreover, God does not just suggest to Moses that Moses tell the Israelites that Yahweh is the god that the patriarchs worshipped, God identifies himself as such. He sees himself as the God of Abraham, Isaac, and Jacob. This is his name, or appellation, for himself.

Being the God of Abraham, Isaac and Jacob is, for God, no small thing. He has invested a great deal of time and energy in becoming the God of Abraham, Isaac and Jacob, as much of the Book of Genesis details. Of note is the encounter between God and Jacob at a site Jacob names "Bethel," the house of God. There Jacob has a dream in which "the Lord was standing beside him and He said, 'I am the Lord, the God of your father Abraham and the God of Isaac: the ground on which you are lying I will give to you and to your offspring.'" Here it seems almost as if God is recruiting. He already is the God of Abraham and Isaac and now he wants Jacob; he is making an offer. And Jacob responds contractually. We are told,

> Jacob then made a vow, saying, "If God remains with me, if he protects me on this journey that I am making, and gives me bread to eat and clothing to wear, and if I return safe to my father's house—the Lord shall be my God." [Yahweh shall be my God] [Genesis 28: 20-21]

This is Jacob's own covenant, and it does not have to do with becoming the father of nations. It is very here-and-now: He wants protection, food, clothing, and a safe return on a perilous journey. If he gets it, then Yahweh will be his god. This is not a matter of believing in God, not a matter of seeking some demonstration that God exists. Rather, it has to do with the establishment of a relationship between Jacob and Yahweh: Jacob lays down his conditions for taking Yahweh unto himself as his god.

For God, this binding to himself of Abraham, Isaac, and Jacob is just the beginning. His larger project, as we have seen, is for the Israelites, through the generations, to know that he is Yahweh. And indeed, as mentioned above, God is also interested, in a secondary way, that the "Egyptians shall know that I am the Lord." The question remains, why is this project God's project? Why is it so important to God that he become the God of the Israelites, or, alternatively, that they know that he is the Lord, that he is Yahweh?

The answer, I believe, is that it is only by virtue of being the God of a people that God can be God. What is at stake for God, and here I mean from the very beginning of the story when he creates man in his image, is the question of his own reality. God's fundamental project is To Be—and for this he needs mankind, and ultimately he decides that he needs a specific people, the Israelites.[6] The paradox is that a god that calls himself, I Am, can only be if there are others that recognize him as God.

This proposition, that God needs mankind in order to be God, can be taken on two levels, first as ontology, and second as psychology. With respect to both, it should be clear that my concern remains that of offering a literary interpretation of the text, in particular of understanding God's core motivation within the story.

This account of God's motivation, that he seeks to exist, provides us with a powerful explanation of why God is so engaged in the process of being known to the Israelites. If we see God as himself engaged in a quest for being, we can understand the stakes, for they are ultimate. There is no more fundamental motivation of any living thing than to be. And there is no more fundamental process of nature than the transition of living things from mere potential to fulfillment or actualization. If we see the Biblical text as positing a God who needs humanity in order to know himself as God, or in order to be God, then God's emotional stake becomes self-evident. Indeed, it becomes very human; it is that quest which motivates our lives as well, the quest for identity, the quest to come more fully into being, more truly oneself.

In ontological terms, this is a thesis about what it is to be a god. Consider for a moment the Greek pantheon. What exactly makes Zeus, Aphrodite, Neptune, Mercury, and all the others gods? They have several features that human beings do not have: they have certain levels of powers, and they have immortality. These, we should note, are just the capabilities that God seeks to keep from mankind. Human power is to be limited by scattering mankind into nations that are incomprehensible to each other, and immortality is avoided by forcing mankind out of the Garden of Eden. But are great powers and immortality sufficient to be a god? Suppose that the universe only contains such figures and no humans. The first result would be that the very notion of great power would dissolve. Against what standard is a power great? If there are multiple gods, then the power of one limits the power of another. True, they may all be vastly more powerful than the humans, but what if there are no humans? Remove mankind from the story and all you have is a group of immortal beings with certain capabilities—but does that make them gods? For them to be gods, it seems there must be those beings who are non-gods.

Suppose there are two sets of beings, those that are human and those that are like the humans but are immortal and have greater powers. Are these latter beings gods, or just other creatures? Perhaps being a god involves having a certain position in a relationship, just as being a master or a slave requires the existence of the other. Perhaps a being is a god only if it is recognized as such, only if it is prayed to, only if it is seen as a god by a non-god.

Since I am not engaged in this ontological question for its own sake, I needn't try to answer these questions. For interpretive purposes, as an explanation of God's motivation in the biblical text, it is sufficient that this is a meaningful thesis and that it is textually plausible that God experiences himself most fully as God only when he experiences himself as so perceived by an appropriate Other, one whose look can confer a sense of being. Yahweh is portrayed as having an existential insecurity, as being fundamentally unsure of who he is, of needing to have a realm of humankind that sees him as God in order for he himself to know himself as God.

So understood, the Hebrew Bible tells a very particular story, the story of what it is to be a people thrown into a world that is ruled by that kind of god-personality. It is a story that operates at the intersection of philosophy and psychology, concerned with how a powerful deity comes to have an identity through an awareness of others' knowledge of him. The story turns on his investment in humankind. We are said to have been created in God's image, but it is we who provide God with his image. Human eyes function as the mirror that allows God to see himself. It is this role that, on the one hand, opens possibilities for humans to gain power over the infinite power and, on the other, gives rise to fear and hostility on the part of the infinite.

An Existential Novel

When Abraham confronts God over the constraints of morality, he does not say, "It is wrong to punish the innocent along with the guilty, and you should not do so." Rather, he says:

- "Far be it from You to do such a thing."
- "Far be it from You!"
- "Shall not the Judge of all the earth deal justly?"

In the use of "Far be it from You" Abraham presents himself as the Other who knows God's true nature. Implicitly, he claims that God has a certain kind of character, and that it would be inconsistent with the essence of that character for God to act unjustly. By bestowing upon God the appellation "the Judge of all the earth," Abraham offers to God a self-identity that requires just action as that which comes from God's true being.

In response to Abraham, one could imagine that God might say:

You presume too much when you presume to know me.
I AM that I AM.
If I will, there is nothing that is far from me.
"Far be it from you" does not exist for Me.
And I Will What I Will.

But God does not make a response of this sort at all. Rather, we see that Abraham's stance as the knowing Other has an effect. God, at least initially, moves toward living out this identity that Abraham has pronounced. What is displayed in the pleading for Sodom scene is the fluctuating being of God's self-identity under the gaze of Abraham. In Sartre's words, "I recognize that I am as the Other sees me." And further, "for me the Other is first the being for whom I am an object; that is, the being through whom I gain my objectness."[7]

It is not only Abraham who recognizes that God can be affected by this kind of appeal; Moses, too, realizes that God's self-identity is in question. While Moses is upon Mt. Sinai receiving the Ten Commandments, the Israelites construct for themselves the golden calf. God is enraged and says to Moses, "I see that this is a stiff-necked people. Now, let Me be that My anger may blaze forth against them and that I may destroy them, and make of you a great nation" [Exodus 32: 10].

Moses quickly responds to try to save the Israelites. He urges God to recall his promises to Abraham, Isaac, and Jacob, that he will make their offspring "as numerous as the stars" and that he will give the promised land to those offspring. But in addition to this "keep your promises" argument, Moses tries another tack. He says:

> Let not the Egyptians say, "It was with evil intent that He delivered them, only to kill them off in the mountains and to annihilate them from the face of the earth." [Exodus 32:12]

We are told that "the Lord renounced the punishment He had planned to bring upon his people." We are not told whether he changed his mind in response to the first of these arguments or the second, or in response to the combined weight of the two. But it seems sound to conclude that the appeal to how the Egyptians might think of God has some weight. This is further supported by what we have seen earlier, that God wants to impress not just the Israelites but the Egyptians with his power. Finally, we must remember that Moses is at this point no stranger to God. He is closer to God than anyone, and if Moses' automatic response is to call God's attention to what the Egyptians might say of him, this suggests that God is indeed mightily concerned with his image.

After this success in turning God's wrath, and perhaps hoping to further enhance his power over God, Moses asks to see God. He says, "Oh, let me behold Your Presence!" This is parallel to, but a step beyond, his earlier request for God's name. God, however, will not allow this. He says, "You cannot see My face, for man may not see Me and live" [Exodus 33:20]. God, here, is setting limits to the amount of Otherness he will allow mankind to attain.

In Sartre's words,

> To be looked at is to apprehend oneself as the unknown object of unknowable appraisals—in particular, of value judgments. . . . Thus, being-seen constitutes me as a defenseless being for a freedom which is not my freedom. It is in this sense that we can consider ourselves as "slaves" in so far as we appear to the Other.[8]

Subsequently, Sartre writes that in relation to the Other, "I am in danger. This danger is not an accident but the permanent structure of my being-for-others."[9] Sartre calls attention to the danger that exists because the other is capable of value judgments—a being that can make a value judgment has the power to bestow upon oneself either a negative or a positive self-identity. Since this capacity for value judgments, is the outcome of having the categories of good and evil, we can conclude that God, in placing the tree of knowledge of good and evil within the Garden, has allowed mankind to become dangerous to him. And further, because dangerous, mankind has become permanently interesting, permanently important.

It might be objected to this way of reading the Biblical text that these existential dynamics are modern psychological discoveries, and are far too sophisticated for the ancient world. Yet consider the following passage from the Roman Stoic philosopher Epictetus:

> If any person was intending to put your body in the power of any man whom you fell in with on the way, you would be vexed; but . . . you put your understanding [better translated as identity or sense of self] in the power of any man whom you meet, so that if he should revile you, it is disturbed and troubled, are you not ashamed at this? [The Manual, XXVIII]

Here, the stoic philosopher is saying that the danger that the Other poses is simply one that we permit it to pose when we worry that we may be reviled. Sartre would disagree that this is a mere matter of psychology, and not a permanent structure of the ontology of being, but whatever its root, the phenomenon of a person falling under the power of others because of the way the judgment of the Other may affect one's sense of self was as familiar to the ancients as it is to us today.

In order for there to be an Other that can see God as he wants to be seen, this Other must be created in God's image; that is, it must have the higher level of consciousness that comes from possession of moral categories, and thereby allows it to make judgments on the level that God seeks to internalize. One cannot experience oneself as worthy of esteem by internalizing the gaze of an animal that lacks the categories of worthiness. Thus once the moral categories are attained, God says, "now the man has become like one of us." Yet, the morally conscious Other cannot be allowed to become another god, for then God would not be God. So mankind must be driven from the Garden. Even so, the conscious Other that can give God his being as God represents a danger in virtue of this very power. Abraham demonstrates this when his invocation of a moral identity for God is experienced by God as constraint. In response God moves to control this very power that he brought into being. Yet the control cannot be too complete lest the very freedom of the Other, that which allows it to bestow being, be lost. God needs mankind to have the very powers that make him continuously a threat.

Let us take another look at the key moment in the Garden of Eden after the fruit has been eaten. We are told, "Then the eyes of both of them were opened and they perceived that they were naked; and they sewed together fig leaves and made themselves loin cloths." In the earlier discussion of this episode I emphasized the impact that coming to moral consciousness has on Adam and Eve: it allows them to have the new emotion of shame. I also pointed out that by portraying moral consciousness as a kind of seeing ("the eyes of both of them were opened"), the moral dimension is portrayed as an objective structure of reality.

We can also consider this passage from a Sartrean point of view, and here the emphasis would be on the phrase "they perceived that they were naked." What exactly do Adam and Eve see? Presumably, Adam sees that he is naked, and that Eve is naked. Eve also has the same two perceptions. that she, Eve, is naked, and also that Adam is naked. Yet Adam also sees that Eve sees that he is naked, and vice versa. In other words, each has a perception of themselves as naked in the eyes of the Other. And it is this recognition that gives rise to the shame that moves them to clothe themselves.

Interestingly, Sartre opens his discussion of what he calls "Being-for-others" by asking his readers to consider the example of shame. Sartre tells us that

> [Shame] in its primary structure is shame before somebody. I have just made an awkward or vulgar gesture. This gesture clings to me. I neither judge it nor blame it. I simply live it. . . . But suddenly I raise my head. Somebody was there and has seen me. Suddenly I realize the vulgarity of my gesture, and I am ashamed . . . the Other is the indispensable mediator between myself and me. I am ashamed of myself as I appear to the Other. . . . Shame is by nature recognition. I recognize that I am as the Other sees me.[10]

On this analysis, had Adam been alone when he ate of the fruit, though he would have gained moral consciousness, he would not have experienced shame, for he would not have experienced himself as naked-in-front-of-the-other. For Adam and Eve to come into full awareness of themselves, they need each other. And I would suggest that only as a result of this coming to understand themselves both as ones who see and are seen by the Other do they come to be as God needs them, as beings that can know Yahweh.

What is remarkable is that God seems to know that in order for the first human to come into full selfhood, there must be another. Thus, we are told, "The Lord God said, 'It is not good for man to be alone.'" [Genesis 2:18] How is it that God who is presented as being generally opaque and disinterested in the inner life and inner needs of mankind, knows this one very basic fact about man: that it is not good that he be alone. The answer, I suggest, goes to the heart of God's entire project of creation, and in particular addresses his creation of mankind in his image. God himself knows of aloneness. He knows that it is not good for God to be alone. Cast in a more existential vocabulary, he knows that he cannot be God if he is alone, that to be alone is to not fully exist.

There are two senses of not-being, both of which involve not-being-seen by an Other. The first is a matter of the absence of the Other that could potentially see oneself. This exists for God before mankind is created, and it persists until the fruit is eaten, when human beings become the full-fledged Other that can convey being. But with the existence of this Other, comes the possibility of a far more acute sense of not-being: to not be seen in the presence of the Other. Here not-being-seen projects upon the self its own non-existence. This is the true danger that the human-Other constitutes for God and is far more powerful than simply being the object of a negative judgment. Once God sets for himself the project of being seen as God by the Israelites, to not be seen by them, but to have them "see" other gods (whether they exist or not), is the greatest of all assaults on his being. And not surprisingly, it is the cause of his greatest rage. So concerned is God with this possibility, that even when the Israelites are focused on him, God, aware of his dependence on them, and is simmering with anger. It is thus that he is an ever-jealous God.

Notes

1. Here I am quoting from The Jerusalem Bible, which uses the name Yahweh rather than applying the convention of substituting "the Lord" for God's name. The story is more comprehensible when Pharaoh attributes no particular

status to Yahweh, such as might be suggested by a reference to him as "the Lord."

2. This is the case in the Jewish Publication Society (JPS) translation that I have relied upon predominantly. On occasion, when it helps in grasping the story, I have quoted from other translations that retain the word "Yahweh."

3. In Deuteronomy 32 there is a poem in which God asserts, "There is no God beside me," but in the context of the poem as a whole, this remains ambiguous.

4. *Being and Nothingness* (New York: Philosophical Library, 1956), 60.

5. Ibid., 67.

6. God's need for mankind is an important theme in the writings of Rabbi Abraham Joshua Heschel.

7. *Being and Nothingness*, 222, 270.

8. *Being and Nothingness*, 267.

9. *Being and Nothingness*, 268.

10. *Being and Nothingness*, 221–222.

5
Alienation and Political Agency

The term "political engagement" is meant to contrast with everyday life. Even in everyday life our own actions may emerge as deeply unintelligible to us, but when this occurs it is something of a shock. The presumption of everyday life is that people know who they are, they know what they are doing, and they know why they are doing it. When we are engaged in the everyday we take it as a given that we are among those people.

Most people go through life without deep political engagement. To be politically engaged is not only to be involved in a project whose centrally motivating consequences typically involve very long time frames and very large numbers of other people; to be politically engaged is to have a significant part of one's self-identity derived from one's engagement in such a project. Not all who carry out acts of political magnitude can be thought of as politically engaged. For instance, the bureaucrat who works in the counter-insurgency division of the war ministry may merely see himself as a civil servant, or as a good family man holding down a secure, well-paying position. Making a revolution is a paradigmatically political project. Revolutionaries are not typically people who are making revolutions in addition to the many other things they do; they are individuals whose self-identity is rooted in their project.

As extreme situations, revolutions throw the individual into contexts devoid of the relative certainties of the everyday. In *Henry IV: Part 2*, Shakespeare tells of revolution, of the problems of action, and of people with very different dispositions to act. Consider the following passage in which the Earl of Northumberland, whose son Hotspur died in insurrection, is told that a new army has arisen to fight against the king:

> The gentle Archbishop of York is up,
> With well-appointed powers: he is a man Who with a double surety binds his followers.
> My lord your son had only but the corpse',
> But shadows and shows of men to fight;
> For that same word, rebellion, did divide
> The action of their bodies from their souls
> And they did fight with queasiness, constrain'd,
> As men drink potions, that their weapons only
> Seem'd on our side: but, for their spirits and souls,
> This word, rebellion, it had froze them up,
> As fish are in a pond. But now the bishop
> Turns insurrection to religion:
> Suppos'd sincere and holy in his thoughts,
> He's follow'd both with body and with mind.[1]

Here Shakespeare articulates the problem of alienation in political action: how to prevent the division of "the action of their bodies from their souls." In this case the division is brought about by "that . . . word, rebellion," and the alienation of the soldiers from their own actions is overcome by turning "insurrection to religion." This transformation is said to resolve the internal conflict: no longer do the soldiers hold back; they no longer believe that they are acting wrongly. Thus the great power of revolutionary religious figures.

In *Man's Fate*,[2] his account of the Chinese Revolution, Malraux calls attention to a second problem of alienation within political action. Questions of doubt emerge.

> Kyo could not free himself from that reverberation of machines transmitted by the soil to his muscles—as if those machines for manufacturing truth were encountering, within himself, Vologin's hesitations and affirmations. During his journey up the river he had constantly felt how poorly informed he really was, how difficult it was for him to get a solid basis for his activity if he no longer consented purely and simply to obey the instructions of the international. . . .
>
> "It's not knowing . . . ," said the latter, "if it's a question of killing Chiang Kai-shek, I know. As for this fellow Vologin, it's all the same to him I guess; but for him, instead of murder, it's obedience. For people who live as we do there must be a certainty. For him carrying out orders is sure, I suppose, as killing is for me. Something must be sure. Must be."[3]

Here there is no internal moral conflict; Kyo is not someone who turns with revulsion at the prospect of killing another person. His problem is to know that what he is doing makes sense; he seeks certainty in a situation filled with the inevitable ignorance of the actual consequences of actions. Here Kyo struggles with his realization of "how poorly informed he really was" and how he lacked "a solid basis for his activity." Kyo, unable to simply rely upon the Party as a way of bridging this separation of act and consequence, turns toward some other "solution."

In each of these cases there is the threat of some fundamental lack of integration between the activity and the self. The first is a conflict between the individual's values and the actions he is called upon to undertake. The second is an absence of an adequately known tissue of means-ends connections linking the individual's actions to his ultimate objectives. These disjunctions are not unique to political activity. If political activity on a grand scale has a unique characteristic it is the combination of its structural tendency to produce alienation and the absence of experienced alienness. The question is not so much one of why one might be alienated from one's own activity, but rather "How is it that alienness is not the general experience of the political agent?"

It is interesting to note that the two literary passages we cited, in the very breath that they identify the problem also go on to identify a solution that has been found. The appeal to the bishop as moral authority represents a "solution" to the conflict of values. Where the problem resides in the absence of visible means-ends connections a different authority may be called into play; the Party may emerge as the tactical authority, as the decision maker that knows what needs knowing. Where this is no longer viable, as in the case of Kyo, some other solution is sought. Kyo finds it, paradoxically enough, in killing. Here at least he is in direct contact with a "rationalizing" outcome. There is at least something tangible that is being accomplished.

Of course, these "solutions" do not really achieve integration. Despite the moral sanction of the church, the conflict between means and ends remains. Despite the appeal of "direct action," the problem of eventual consequences has to be faced. They serve as internal expedients, almost like the pontoon bridges that are thrown up so that soldiers can quickly move across the river to engage in the next battle.

In this essay I will explore the dynamic of alienation within political engagement. It cannot be understood without focusing on political identity, on what is sometimes termed "being political." This is not primarily a matter of action, but of self and self-experience.

Engagement and Alienation

Political engagement implies a self-identity that is rooted in political activity. This is not something that is chosen. Rather political activity has a tendency to compel this locus of self-identity upon its participants. There is a process whereby a person becomes politicized, by which I mean much more than merely becoming concerned or involved in social issues. It is a process whereby the individual comes to define himself or herself and others in terms of the political project. Politicization is not something that one does to oneself; it is something that happens to one. How and why it happens is worth considering.

There are different ways in which a person might come to have a certain self-identity. Some of the major features of our identity structures are the result of actions that we take. One might decide to join a particular religious denomination or to attend a particular college or to engage in a certain line of employment. In virtue of that choice one takes on a particular property; one is a Presbyterian or a Cornell student or a nurse. These properties may or may not play a major role in one's identity structure. And it may be that only over time and without one's being aware of it, they do come to play a role such that "being a nurse" or "being a Cornell student" becomes a central part of the individual's self-identity. But there still remains a major element of choice in that one can break that identification by leaving the organization, or by taking a different job.

Moreover, it is often the case that from the third-person point of view we do not view any of these properties as inherently identity giving. Often enough we so totally leave it up to the individual to choose his own identity that the distinction between self-identity and identity is conflated. His identity is merely the self-identity he has.

Yet sometimes it is rather different. Sometimes there is something so important about someone, be it oneself or another, that that feature defines who he is whether he accepts it or not, even whether he knows it or not. In literature there is the classic format in which the true identity of the protagonist is known to the reader or audience and the drama involves his coming to discover who he is and the implications of that fact. We find this motif in Oedipus, in the story of Moses, in the tale of King Arthur, and numerous fairy tales of princes and paupers.

In these situations it is never a matter of some incidental fact that is unknown to the individual. Rather it is a fact of such overwhelming import that it imposes itself on the individual. The mere discovery of it is instantaneously transformative or crisis generating. In literature it is the perspective of the author that affirms that these facts are of such overwhelming importance. But this author's perspective emerges from a social life that views certain properties as carrying with them enormous rights and duties and is the basis for a status of inferiority or superiority.

Involvement in deeds of enormous magnitude have this same characteristic. One cannot be the person who flew the plane that dropped the atomic bomb on Japan and merely be that person. One cannot be the man who assassinated President Lincoln and have that be merely one of many characteristics about oneself. Occasionally we find an individual who does treat such a fact about himself or herself as an incidental fact, but this is a matter of his or her self-identity. Our response to such a self-identity is that it is the result of a project of denial. He or she is a person running from themself, denying their heritage, trying to escape from themself. In short, we sometimes view people as having an objective identity that is imposed by a self-defining reality.

Because political activity involves the individual in action on a grand scale it has a tendency to confer an objective identity. And because the individual herself participates within the social world that views political activity in this way, it also has a tendency to generate the self-identity of the political agent. Thus political activity gives rise to political engagement. The activity comes to construct the self that is expressed through it. It has an inherent power to become self-actualizing. Thus it can have a hypnotizing force on the individual, both calling her into being and expressing that being within the same process. And the more important the role of the individual, the stronger is this power.

While this is a general feature of all action on a political scale, in the modern period this inherent power of political activity—its power to engage the actor, to make an agent out of her—was dramatically raised in intensity through the lens of Hegel and Marx.

Marx, Hegel, and Historical Identity

I shall try to set the stage for discussing various modes of political engagement by considering the relation of self-actualization to political activity that is inherent in Marx's politicization of Hegel. However, not even in Marx's early writings is this matter discussed directly, and one may wonder if Marx himself ever explicitly formulated this aspect of his general outlook. What I am discussing then is not Marx, and not even necessarily Marxism, but rather a certain way of viewing history and politics that emerged most strongly in Marxism. It stands, however, distinct from Marxism and does not rise or fall with beliefs that were specific to Marx.

From our ordinary perspectives, history is about human beings and the conditions of their existence, either individually or in groups. It is about the things that human beings do and the events that happen to human beings. Most early historical writing was political history, accounts of the most momentous acts and calamities that befell the powerful figures around whom history centered. Today much historical writing concerns economic and social conditions, but like political history, the ultimate subject in human life.

Hegel offers a radically different perspective. For Hegel, history is not really about human beings at all. Of course, historical study takes as its object that which happens to human beings, their groups and institutions, but the goings on of humans are not of significance in themselves. They take on significance because they embody something more fundamental: Spirit, Mind or Consciousness. History is reconceived as the study of the self-creation and self-actualization of Spirit as it comes to know itself. The great drama is the evolution of Spirit, and only secondarily and derivatively, the evolution of the finite individuals who are the vehicles through which Spirit is expressed.

This may sound less puzzling in a religious idiom. Accordingly, it would be asserted that history is not about humans but about God. Moreover, the notion of God that is involved is not God as a being that exists for all infinity as an all-knowing creator, but rather a pantheistic presence that is within everything. What occurs in history is the evolution of God; history is the story of God's coming to self-consciousness of the fact that he is God. The way a pantheistic God evolves is through the evolution of the world that is his embodiment; particularly, the evolution of human consciousness.

When Spirit comes to know itself, what it comes to know is that it is Spirit in the process of its own self-creation, which is at the same time the creation of the world. It comes to know itself when it discovers that it is the world. The discovery that Spirit makes of itself externalized as the world is for Hegel an epistemological discovery. The world is neither a given that is just there to be observed, understood, and known, nor is it a hidden reality that lies behind a world of appearances, that can never be known. Rather, the world is the externalization of Mind. Thus, in the end, Spirit comes to self-actualization through an epistemological self-understanding that destroys the subject-object distinction.

To put forward an account of this sort is in some way like writing a piece of literature within which all the characters are defined by their place within the story. The Hegelian perspective, because it presents itself as a perspective that for the first time has penetrated the most fundamental realities of all being—of humans, of God, of existence—is a perspective that cannot merely be accepted and set on the shelf. A Hegelian vision of the nature of existence is not one of many beliefs that one has. It is an overriding story that reveals the true identity of all that occurs within it.

What is the nature of self-experience for the individual who perceives history in Hegelian terms? As individuals we are meaningful as part of a greater Totality—a Totality that is itself moving from potentiality to actuality. If this is our meaning, then our most essential expression of self consists in our participation in this project of the world. Our personal potentials represent highly restricted aspects of human potential. Moreover, as individuals living in a particular stage of the evolution of Spirit, we know that our humanness is itself something undergoing transformation, and that our personal potential will be transcended by the fuller potential of those whose being expresses a more fully developed stage in the life of Spirit.

A particular individual can only achieve self-actualization in virtue of the accident of living at the end of history. This is not the end of physical time, but is the end of the story of Spirit's self-actualization. What self-actualization is possible for those of us not embodying the final stage of Spirit is that which comes through an identification of oneself as the embodiment of Spirit, and thus the discovery of oneself in the historical creation of Spirit by Spirit. On Hegel's view, it is he, Hegel, who is the first individual to fully achieve self-actualization, for it is through him that Spirit comes to know itself.

With Marx we have the "existentialization" of Hegel. Human existence is once again placed at the center. History, instead of being the story of Spirit's self-actualization through its embodiment in human culture, is the story of humanity's self-actualization. Alternatively, we may say that history is the story of the self-creation and the self-actualization of the human personality, by human beings, through the discovery that it is the human personality that makes history. The discovery of humankind as the agent of its own creation is a two-pronged discovery. In the first instance it is empirical. It is a theory of culture, and of ideology; it is the recognition of the primacy of changes in the forces of production as the cause of the evolution of human personality or personhood. This social personality is the embodiment of the dominant ideology. In the structures of beliefs, values, self-identities, hopes, perceptions, and needs of human beings, the ideology of any given period is concretely embodied. On the other hand, this discovery of the importance of economic factors is rendered a self-creation of humans by humans through a second insight that parallels Spirit's epistemological discovery that the world is the externalization of Spirit. This is the recognition that the economic relations underlying cultural development are not themselves external forces that act upon humankind, but are themselves the externalization of human reality. To think of history as governed by economic laws that are outside of humanity and act upon it, is what Marx called "the fetishism of commodities."[4] But whereas in Hegel the discovery that the world is the externalization of Spirit constitutes Spirit's self-actualization, for Marx it merely sets the stage.

One cannot achieve freedom by identifying oneself with the forces that shape one, even if those forces are an expression of the collective nature of humanity. What is necessary is to *actually gain control* over the processes whereby human beings are created. This cannot be achieved by epistemological insight. On the contrary, it is itself an historical outcome that will be brought about through self-conscious *political activity*. This political activity is self-conscious in that it recognizes itself within, and is based upon, an understanding of the historical process. Thus, in Marx as in Hegel, the self-actualization of the individual is only possible at the final stage in the development of the human personality. For Marx, it is political activity based on self-understanding that brings us towards this final stage; for Hegel full self-understanding is the final stage itself.

Of course, any individual can, at any point in history, experience himself or herself as self-actualized. But this feeling is had at the expense of understanding who one is. For Marx, selfhood is achieved only when the full range of human potentialities and needs are developed and expressed. Full self-actualization involves the expression through action of the fully developed personality. The primary locus of one's actions is one's labor within the existing economic relations of one's era. So long as these relations remain unchanged, there exist no forms for the expression through action of humankind's highest potentialities. So long as one suffers from the fetishism of commodities, one fails to understand that the limitation on the range of possible human actions is societally imposed, and one may erroneously imagine that expressing what is highest in humanity can be done merely through right conduct, personal choice, and virtue.

Those who have a sense of self-actualization during transitional historical phases are blind in a second respect. In our terms, these individuals have mistaken their persons (the person they find themselves to be) for their selves. They have identified with what is accidental and arbitrary and will be overcome in the course of historical development. They are out of touch with that which is most essentially themselves. Even if we restrict ourselves to the private sphere, what is actualized is not the human self but the historically given person. In terms of my discussion of the self as the integrated personality, we can say that in a Marxist view of the self, integration of the personality is only a necessary condition of selfhood. Selfhood, or the fully human self, is an historical product that can be understood as an integrated personality with certain specific component values, beliefs, perceptions, and notions of self-identity. These components, in general, are historical products. The existing personality types at any given point in time are a function of the forms of activity (i.e., the economic structures) of the particular age and the place of the individual within that structure. Thus, our personality, including the existing level of needs that govern our subjective sense of self-actualization, is itself a social product, and most typically a deficient one.

The person that we are, with our particular self-identity, is what is to be overcome. Thus, it is from the concrete minutia of what we are like that *we should be alienated*. For instance, our conceptions of worth, or of beauty, our values and desires that determine the things that give us pleasure, or a sense of triumph, pride or achievement—all these are corrupt. They all partake in the ideological structure of an oppressive social order. For instance, one takes pleasure and pride in those aspects of oneself that allow one to dominate others in various competitions: the competition for wealth, for status, for the better forms of work, for the most sought after members of the opposite sex. When seen properly, these aspects of one's personality are seen to be expressions of the total social order with its inherent class structures, its necessary scarcities (e.g., the means of life) and its artificial scarcities (e.g., scarcity of self-esteem and social recognition). In terms of the discussion in essay 2, the analyses of Marxism may be treated as alienness-causing beliefs that give us reasons to reperceive much that constitutes our self-identity. On a psychological level, moreover, they reveal that for many individuals there is a conflict between their moral views and self-image on the one hand and the specific realities of their personalities on the other. Thus, even the prima facie integration of the personality is shown to be erroneous. Typically, within even highly integrated personalities there are hidden contradictions—hidden, because only social analyses can reveal the nature of the elements.

Given this, one cannot throw oneself into projects that might be satisfying because one cannot identify with those aspects of one's personality that would thereby be satisfied. For instance, one cannot simply join the competitive dynamic of contemporary life; neither the qualities that allow one to succeed nor the pleasure one takes in the fruits of success is truly one's own. Thus, there is engendered an experience of the alienness of most of what we might have otherwise taken as reflecting our truest self: our desires, our tastes, our views and values. In ordinary terms, the Marxist is not at one with himself or herself. If he or she is fully aware of this inner discord, this inner contradiction, then central aspects of the person are experienced as non-self.

This experience of aspects of oneself as alien is not uncommon amongst thorough-going critics of any cultural order. However, the reaction to the political critique of personality is often a form of individual omnipotence-fantasy in which the individual believes that *he* is capable of radically transforming himself as an individual *irrespective* of the social order. In part, this split with a Marxist perspective arises from non-Marxist beliefs about the possibilities of personality change. But beyond this there is a non-Marxist perception of personality. Personality is viewed as something to be found in and only in localized interpersonal relations. But Marx's basic point is that interpersonal relations are not localized. One's personality or nature is historically fixed in the main because one's relations with others are fixed and *expressed* through economic relations. This is not primarily a matter of a causal relation between the economic forms and the nature of human beings in a given historic period. The economic form is the form of humanity in disguise.

The tendency to see the economic realm as a neutral universe within which the issues of character, of personality, of virtue, vice, identity, and spirituality are not revealed is itself an historical product that emerged only in the eighteenth century. Marx thus reaffirms in secular-historical terms an orientation towards the economic sphere that was present both in the Middle Ages and the Reformation.

Non-Marxist self-experience emerges in various forms. Those who experience themselves as existing in opposition to the present totality tend to experience themselves as outside of that totality. Thus, most social critics tend to be alienated from the society, experiencing *estrange-*

ment rather than *shame* for a totality of which one is a part. But from a Marxist perspective, the identification of self as magically outside the totality represents a flight of romanticism, a fantasy of individual transcendence that cannot be achieved. Thus, while we are all fated to not be self-actualized within the existing social world, one who sees history as Marx did knows this is her fate, and that she cannot get beyond this realization. No leap to a different social order, to a utopia, personal or social, is possible.

Thus, the politicization of Hegel brings a new form of loss. It is the loss of one who discovers that he or she is not to be. It is the discovery that not only will one always remain in potential, but that one will be in conflict with one's potential, always tending to be something incompatible with it. This is so because one is inevitably a part of one's historical epoch. The concrete meaning of this is (*a*) one is one's social activity, (*b*) one's social activity is given to one, and (*c*) one can't find in any given historical period the social activity that belongs to another period. In short, there is nothing to do that would count as self-actualizing activity. Yet one has a self-identity that recognizes one's true self in one's necessarily unexpressed and undeveloped potentialities.

Insofar as there is any role that escapes from this, it is that of the political agent (e.g. revolutionary) who knows herself. She lives in opposition to a world that is inside of her as well as outside. She is one whose self-identity consists in part in the fact that she knows that she is and must be alien to herself. More generally, the only life that to some extent escapes from this trap is that of the individual whose social activity participates in the process of the conscious creation of the human self on a social scale. Only through such activity does one gain an objective identity that is unified with those aspects of the historic person that remain as it becomes the human self. That is, only through such activity does subjective self-identity merge with objective identity. Marxism thus gives rise to a self-identity that understands itself in terms of the role it will actually play in the process of the creation of the human self, and Marxism offers itself as the guiding vehicle through which one attains the complementary objective identity.

Thus, the overwhelming psychological power of Marxism emerges because it stands as the revelatory story of the world, through which one can understand and become oneself. It retains the Hegelian conception of history as a movement towards self-actualization, but it is the self-actualization of human beings, not Spirit. In relation to this ideal and account of the human past, the meaning of individual and social reality may be discerned. That is, the relationship of events, persons, and structures to this process is experienced as their "real meaning." Thus, at one and the same time, Marxism lifts political activity to the level of vehicle for individual and historical self-actualization, and destroys all alternative conceptions of self-actualization.

The politicization of Hegel results then in not only giving to political activity unique powers as a realm of self-actualization, but it gives to *political analysis* a unique power of *revealing true identity*, and it strips away from the self many of the elements of the personality that might otherwise constitute the features of self-identity around which an active life would coalesce. Thus political activity emerges as political engagement and this engagement becomes total, subsuming all else within it.

The outcome then is an incredible tension. On the one hand, political activity becomes the locus of all that is meaningful. On the other hand, political activity is not an ideal locus for self-expression. More often than not, people are apt to feel out of touch with themselves and in danger of losing themselves in such activity. As we noted at the outset, the great problems are those of moral conflict and the unintelligibility of one's own action. Only if action is integrated with our values and beliefs can action be expressive of the self; yet because of the realities with which one deals, this contact is difficult to establish. Appeals to moral and/or tactical authorities represent attempted solutions. Where these are seen as inadequate, "direct action," whether of a violent or a humanitarian sort, has its appeal. Yet, this too is inadequate.

Three Modes of Political Engagement

It is possible to distinguish three distinct modes of political engagement. They represent more than three different styles of action; each of them represents a different way of dealing with the problem of self identity and potential alienation. The three types are (1) objectivist engagement, (2) integral engagement, and (3) rationalist engagement. I have identified each of these forms of political engagement with an historic figure, respectively, Trotsky, Gandhi, and Bentham.

Let me begin with objectivist engagement. The core of the objectivist outlook is that one's identity is determined by the actual role that one plays, not by the consequences one intends or the values one holds dear.

Leon Trotsky, maker of the Russian Revolution, is history's most dramatic and outspoken objectivist. I will use Trotsky as the exemplar of this mode of engagement, but it should be understood that this perspective is not unique to either Trotsky or Marxism.

For Trotsky the most important facts about a person bear on his or her role in the processes of historical development and class struggle. In terms of our notion of identity, the Trotskyite would say that "being bourgeois" or "being counter-revolutionary" or "being revolutionary" are part of the objective identity of those who are bourgeois, counter-revolutionary, or revolutionary. These are designations that do not depend on the individual's own view of himself (i.e., his self-identity). They are a matter of objective identity, of who someone really is irrespective of who he thinks he is or how he identifies himself. The criteria for their application specify a particular social role. Merely having certain views, intentions, and attitudes does not suffice to determine which of these identity-defining designations applies.

Thus, one is always in danger of not knowing who one is, not in the sense of lacking a self-identity, but in that one may be attributing to oneself an identity (social role) that one does not have. One may fancy oneself a revolutionary and actually be a counter-revolutionary. To be in this kind of error, where one's subjective self-identity does not accord with one's objective identity, because of political ignorance, is indeed a pathetic fate. The most damaging criticism one can make of someone or some group that regards itself as revolutionary is to maintain that it is *really* counter-revolutionary, or an unwitting lackey of the bourgeoisie, or an oppressor of the proletariat. Such "insights" are supposed to come from objective social analysis. What should be recognized is that the familiar judgments of an agent's character are suspended, because from within an objectivist engagement, character traits are not themselves central aspects of an individual's identity.

This stress on actual consequences is reflected in how the objectivist deals with the issue of justifying abhorrent means. Consider the following passage from Trotsky's essay, "Their Morals and Ours."

> A means can be justified only by its end. But the end in turn needs to be justified. From the Marxist point of view, which expresses the historical interests of the proletariat, the end is justified if it leads to increasing the power of man over nature, and to the abolition of the power of man over man.
>
> "We are to understand then that in achieving this end anything is permissible?" sarcastically demands the Philistine, demonstrating that he understands nothing. That is permissible, we answer, which *really* leads to the liberation of mankind. . . . It deduces a rule for conduct

from the laws of the development of society, thus primarily from the class struggle, this law of all laws.

"Just the same," the moralist continues to insist, "does it mean that in the class struggle against capitalists all means are permissible: lying, frame-up, betrayal, murder and so on?" Permissible and obligatory are those and only those means, we answer, which unite the revolutionary proletariat. . . . Precisely from this it follows that *not* all means are permissible. When we say that the end justifies the means, then for us the conclusion follows that the great revolutionary end spurns those base means and ways which set one part of the working class against other parts. . . .

These criteria do not, of course, give a ready answer to the question as to what is permissible and what is not permissible in each separate case. There can be no such automatic answers. . . .

Is individual terror, for example, permissible or impermissible from the point of view of "pure morals"? In this abstract form the question does not exist at all for us. . . . Our relation to the assassin remains neutral only because we know not what motives guided him. If it became known that Nikolayev acted as a conscious avenger for workers' rights . . . our sympathies would be fully on the side of the assassin. However, not the question of subjective motives, but that of *objective* expediency has for us the decisive significance. Are the means really capable of leading to the goal?[5]

When one performs an act that one views as abhorrent, one is in some degree of conflict with one's values. For Trotsky this conflict can be overcome if the means are justified in terms of overriding ends. Such a predisposition to conflict elimination may seem a necessary feature for any programmatic politics. To insist upon more integration than this is to allow historical realities to render one impotent. Given the nature of the world, one cannot be politically significant and at the same time more coherent than this. To seek a greater degree of unity is a matter of self-indulgence.

This view seems to have been held quite self-consciously by Trotsky. In his "Moralists and Sycophants Against Marxism," he lashes out at those who would propose a code of conduct for the revolution.

However, so long as this code remains unaccepted as a rule of conduct by all the oppressors and the oppressed, the warring classes will seek to gain victory *by every means*, while petty-bourgeois moralists will continue as heretofore to wander in confusion between the two camps. Subjectively, they sympathize with the oppressed—no one doubts that. Objectively, they remain captives of the morality of the ruling class and

> seek to impose it upon the oppressed instead of helping them to elaborate the morality of insurrection. . . .
>
> They openly demanded a *return* to Kant . . . if their ideas are plumbed to the bottom, it appears that they have joined an old cause, long since discredited: to subdue Marxism by means of Kantianism; to paralyze the socialist revolution by means of "absolute" norms which represent in reality the philosophical generalizations of the bourgeoisie . . . .
>
> Civilization can be saved only by the socialist revolution. To accomplish the overturn, the proletariat needs all its strength, all it resolution, all its audacity, passion and ruthlessness. Above all it must be completely free from the fictions of religion, "democracy" and transcendental morality—the spiritual chains forged by the enemy to tame and enslave it. Only that which prepares the complete and final overthrow of imperialist bestiality is moral, and nothing else. The welfare of the revolution—that is the supreme law!
>
> A clear understanding of the interrelation between the two basic classes—the bourgeoisie and the proletariat in the epoch of their mortal combat—discloses to us the objective meaning of the role of petty-bourgeois moralists. Their chief trait is impotence.[6]

In this remarkable passage, Trotsky has not only argued the necessity of ignoring moral strictures, he has provided the individual with a way of perceiving herself that will minimize the sense of moral conflict caused by her actions. One's moral inhibitions, and the sense that to act contrary to one's moral strictures is to act contrary to one's self, are the inroads that the defenders of the social order have made into one's person. The very notion of oneself that identifies self in terms of these moral values is a factor in the class struggle. The proletariat must free itself from "the spiritual chains forged by the enemy to enslave it." Thus, the inner conflict and the potentially paralyzing alienness that lies behind the "means and ends" debate are subjected to a political analysis. From the perspective of the imperative towards a positive social and historical identity, these moral strictures are themselves subjected to an alienation, an expulsion, from the self-identity. They are relegated to a bracketed position, a realm where they are mine-but-not-really-mine. They continue to exist, but now they are disconnected elements, not fully belonging to the self. Thus, the potential for experiencing one's actions as alien is avoided through a political analysis that establishes a new alienness, not now of the actions but of the moral strictures. By means of this form of analysis there is a relocation of one's sense of what is self and not-self. The therapy for paralysis is the objective understanding of its causes and functions.

What is involved here are second-order value judgments, value judgments about the values one holds. Trotsky subjects morality itself to the utilitarian standard. Through the adoption of the second-order value perspective, the Trotskian agent reestablishes his linkage with his activity. He does this by essentially estranging himself from those value judgments that tend to "divorce the actions of the body from the soul." For this to be successful, it is not necessary that the individual fully eliminate the inhibiting judgments. Rather, in judging them the individual estranges himself from them; puts them in a bracketed category in which even if they continue to have some emotional force that emotional force is seen as foreign, as not really one's own.

In functioning in this way the objectivist is not urging identification with second-order rather than first-order value judgments. She is not taking a position on where the self resides in a hierarchy of self-reflection. (See the debate between Watson and Frankfurt considered elsewhere in this volume.) Rather what she says is that you are your social or political role. If you make incorrect second-order value judgments, and thus incorrectly judge your first-order values to be supportive of the movement to a classless society (or whatever fundamental desiderata the objectivist seeks) and if you act accordingly, the fact that you identify with such objectives even in your second-order value judgments is totally irrelevant. You are determined by the consequences of your actions, not by your identifications, even on the secondary level.

Central to Trotsky's analysis is the empirical claim that by and only by means contrary to moral strictures can the liberation of humanity be achieved. Conceptions of the self and in particular criteria of identity are evaluated in terms of their role in furthering or retarding this historical process.

Trotsky's analysis of the effect of the internalization of moral principles (i.e., they lead to impotence and retard the liberation of humanity) serves as an alienating belief. That is, in virtue of coming to hold this belief about one's own values, one comes to view them as not really one's own, but as implants, as subtle means of control that have been foisted upon one as a gigantic trick designed to support the power structure.

Yet this outcome, that the individual who makes such a second-order judgment about his own values will feel alienated from them, is itself not a necessity. It is theoretically possible to reach such a conclusion about the import of one's own values and still embrace them as one's own. In saying this, I am not talking about the situation in which one simply does not care about the liberation of humanity and so is unmoved by having reached such a conclusion about one's values. Rather, it is possible to see one's values as in fact being problematic, and yet to still not feel at a distance from them. The alienation that Trotsky is able to bring off in virtue of his analysis occurs only when there is a prior internalization of the objectivist criterion for identity—that you are your social role.

The rejection of abhorrent means, even when one believes that they are the only way of attaining valuable ends, is at the core of integral engagement. It is well represented by Kierkegaard, though in his case it is not yet *integral politics,* but rather a more general integral engagement with the world. In *Purity of Heart is to Will One Thing,* he writes:

> What means do you use in order to carry out your occupation? Are the means as important to you as the end, wholly as important? Otherwise it is impossible for you to will only one thing, for in that case the irresponsible, the self-seeking, and the heterogeneous means would flow in between in confusing and corrupting fashion. . . . In time and on earth one distinguishes between the two and considers that the end is more important than the means. One thinks that the end is the main thing and demands of one who is striving that he reach the end . . . to gain an end in this fashion is an unholy act of impatience. . . .
>
> If a man sets himself a goal for his endeavor here in this life, and he fails to reach it, then, in the judgment of eternity, it is quite possible that he may be blameless. Yes, he may even be worthy of praise. . . . He might even have been prevented from reaching the goal just by being unwilling to use any other means than those which the judgment of eternity permits. In which case by his very renunciation of the impatience of passion and the inventions of cleverness, he is even worthy of praise. *He is not, therefore, eternally responsible for whether he reaches his goal within this world of time.* . . . To the temporal and earthly passion the end is unconditionally more important than the means. On that very account, it is the passionate one's torment, which if carried to its height must indeed make him sleepless and then insane, namely, that he has no control over time, and that he continually arrives too late, even if it was by merely half an hour. And what is still worse, since earthly passion is the rule, it can truthfully be said, that it is not wisdom which saves the worst ones from going insane, but indolence. On the other hand, the blessed comfort of the Eternal is like a refreshing sleep, is like "the cold of snow in the time of harvest" to the one who wills the Eternal. He whose means are invariably just as important as the end, never comes too late. Eternity is not curious and impatient as to what

> the outcome in this world of time will be. It is just because of this that the means are without exception as important as the end. To earthly and worldly passion, this observation must seem shocking and paralyzing. To it conscience must seem the most paralyzing thing of all. For conscience is indeed "a blushing innocent spirit that sets up a tumult in a man's breast and fills him with difficulties."[7]

Of course, Kierkegaard would be subjected to a ruthless class analysis and shown to be objectively promoting the interests of the status quo—and such a turning of one's back on "the world of time" would be seen to be in keeping with the general political function of the religious outlook. However, integralism is not restricted to the nonpolitical. As integral *politics*, it seeks the same degree of integration that Kierkegaard does, and situates moral strictures in a central position in the self-complex. This integral politics is most closely associated with the name of Gandhi. While we may doubt that the historical Gandhi "lived up to" the Gandhian style, the identification of him with the integral mode is well established.

In understanding integral engagements in political activity, it is important to not deny the conflicts. Thus it is possible to hold the view that only by using tactics that involve no violation of the dignity of the other is it possible to achieve the political objective. But then the conflict with the objectivist is really over who is accurate in his means-ends assessments. The objectivist himself would embrace nonviolence if he were convinced that this was the way to accomplish the end. The sharpest contrast between alternative engagements arises when there is agreement on the consequences. Needless to say, in the real world the waters are often muddied.

Thus, the crucial aspect of integral engagement is not the tactic of nonviolence; rather, it is that nonviolence is not primarily a tactical feature. As a distinctive mode of being political integral engagement is distinguished by the fact that the *factual connections between means and ends simply do not occupy crucial importance*. For a given means to be justified it is not sufficient that it produces the greatest good. Indeed it may not even be necessary that it leads to any worthy end outside itself. Instead *political activity is a necessary vehicle for the emergence and expression of selfhood*. Change may result, but then it may not. The overriding problem is that of how to be oneself in the face of social reality.

Integralism responds to the fact that the social world calls into question one's integrity. "Integrity" is meant quite literally. The wholeness that is constitutive of the self is imperiled by actions one is called upon to perform, or it may be compromised in virtue of one's past actions, or just in virtue of being alive within an unjust social order.

The paradigm of resistance to an action one is called upon to perform is conscientious objection. Luther's phrase, "I can do no other" occupies a central place in the social and legal perception of the conscientious objector. Rather than seeing this as a denial of freedom, or a bowing to external moral forces, the emphasis should be placed upon the "I"—if I did other, I would not be "I." The action in question violates the wholeness of the self; the self could not be the agent of such actions.

Similarly, acts of civil disobedience sometimes serve primarily as public declarations that define the self and limit the extent to which one is implicated by the facts of the world. As such they are direct efforts to preserve wholeness. Of course, Gandhi's activities were not mere matters of testament, but were intended to achieve specific political goals. In *Gandhi's Truth*, Erik Erikson writes:

> Truthful action, for Gandhi, was governed by the readiness to get hurt and yet not to hurt—action governed by the principle of ahimsa. . . . I think Gandhi implied in it, besides a refusal to do physical harm, a determination not to violate another person's essence. . . . Gandhi reminds us that, since we cannot possibly know the absolute truth, we are "therefore not competent to punish. . . ."
>
> And in all this, the resister must be consistently *willing to persuade* and to enlighten, even as he remains ready *to be persuaded and enlightened. He will, then, not insist on obsolete precedent or rigid principle, but will be guided by what under changing conditions will continue or come to feel true to him and his comrades, that is, will become truer through action. . . .*
>
> Gandhi, at one time, urged any individual or authority that was "fasted against" and which considered the fast to be blackmail "to refuse to yield to it even though the refusal may result in the death of the fasting person."[8]

It is clear that the "truth" that Gandhi is concerned with is not the same as that of Trotsky. For Trotsky it is a matter of actually knowing what will occur, as opposed to mere belief without certainty. For Gandhi, "truth" is a matter of "being in the truth"; it describes a state of being of the agent. This includes thoughtfulness, but does not center on factual knowledge. Rather, truth is unity, what we have called integration. Action that is true is action that is fully integrated with all the values and belief of the self. One is the true agent of it.

We must not lose sight of the centrality of personal integration to this mode of political activity. In his autobiography, *The Story of My Experiments With Truth,* Gandhi relates how his endeavor to attain full personal integration led him to vow to observe *brahmacharya* (sexual abstention) for life. He explains that the "Brahmacharya means control of the senses in thought, word and deed."[9] When it is fully achieved, this control is the peaceful, fluid control of unity rather than effort. In a passage reminiscent of Augustine, he writes, "I have yet to achieve complete mastery over thought, which is so essential. Not that the will or effort is lacking, but it is yet a problem to me wherefrom undesirable thoughts spring their insidious invasions."[10]

He sees his mode of political activity, *Satyagraha*, as arising out of this renunciation. "I can now see that all the principle events of my life, culminating in the vow of *brahmacharya*, were secretly preparing me for it."[11]

The integralist mode, then, aims at achieving full integration within political activity. There is to be no pretense in manner, no ideological deception, no false certainty and no conflict between one's values and the means one employs.

Does the integralist escape from the dilemma of political activity: self-actualization is obtainable only through a political life but political life is inherently self-alienating? Consider Trotsky's reflections on Gandhi:

> The Indian bourgeois is incapable of leading a revolutionary struggle. They are closely bound up with and dependent upon British capitalism. They tremble for their own property. They stand in fear of the masses. They seek compromises with the British imperialism no matter what the price; and they lull the Indian masses with hopes of reform from above. The leader and prophet of this bourgeoisie is Gandhi. A fake leader and a false prophet![12]

Putting the ad hominem abuse aside, this critique of Gandhian methods amounts to the claim that regardless of his subjective intentions, the social role of his approach did not promote the interests of the oppressed. Put in a larger perspective, an objectivist might regard the integralist as having suffered the horrifying fate of having acquired, in virtue of his objective role, an identity in direct opposition to that which would have been self-fulfilling. Instead, his real identity, as revealed in his objective social role, is in total conflict with his motives, intentions, and self-identity.

From the objectivist perspective this pathetic outcome is what happens when one insists on full personal integration in the face of historic conditions that do not permit it. It is not that political activity is inherently fractured, but that the degree and kind of unity it can have is dictated by the particular conditions of the historic period.

Moreover, the objectivist can point to fundamental fractures that prevent the integralist from achieving the unity he seeks. This issue does not arise if the means-ends connections are known by the integralist to support his specific behavior. But if they are believed, by the integralist himself, to not do so, then he himself has a higher order assessment of his own behavior and values, and according to this assessment he is either irrelevant to the cause that he is committed to or detrimental to its actual fulfillment. Can the integralist proceed if he reaches this kind of judgment about himself?

One option is to simply bracket these higher order judgments; to do this the integralist might, like Kierkegaard, adopt a skeptical stance towards his own ability to make such judgments. He might say that these are things that mere mortals can never know. But what if the evidence is rather persuasive? The integralist is forced to either deny the persuasive power that his own beliefs lead him to accept, or he must face up to and accept the objectivist's conclusion that (in the most difficult case) he is actually harming the values to which he is committed. And if he accepts this conclusion about his own activity, then that very activity that in one respect emerges from his deepest convictions in another respect must be viewed as alien. But this outcome defeats the entire integralist project. Thus the integralist is under enormous pressure to in fact deny or not think about the empirical claims that the objectivist puts forward.

From this perspective an ironic shift occurs: it is Trotsky, the extremist, who emerges as the political expression of the "well-adjusted" individual, emerging from a political psychotherapy or analysis able to accept his limitations and yet function in the world. (The ability to function being a formal property, equally compatible both with "functioning in accord with the social system" and with "functioning as a revolutionary in opposition to that social system.")

What Trotsky seems to have been able to accept are the limitations that his historicity placed upon him. Thus, he was able to avoid alienness because alienness, as we have seen, is not a simple function of the perceived lack of integration but is also a function of the degree and type of integration demanded by a conception of the self. From a Marxist perspective one might historicize these criteria of self and agency so that a healthy concept of the self and agency does not center on a degree of integration that is historically impossible. In particular, a healthy conception of the self would allow that the self is present in an activity even when the activity was in conflict with the individual's moral outlook, so long as the activity maximized the amount of integration permitted by the historical context and the demands of effective action. Thus, while one would always live with some degree of incompleteness and disunity, one would not experience activities that were integrated to the historically possible maximum as alien. Therefore, feelings of alienness arising from moral conflict inherent in political activity might be grasped as the expressions of regressions to bourgeois and ahistorical conceptions of self, agency, and unity. This, at any rate, is an articulation of an outlook that we find implicit within Trotsky's outlook. And it is a perspective of considerable power and sophistication.

However, even if we accept this way of understanding how to experience conflicts between one's values and one's methods, once one has reached the conclusion that such methods are necessary and that to reject them is itself to play the role of one's own enemy, the objectivist still faces the second incoherence that is inherent in political activity. Can she be reasonably sure of those means-ends connections? Or at some point is she not threatened with the terrifying realization that in fact she really does not know? Why does the objectivist have no sense of her activity as alien, as unintelligible because of the wide gap that separates what she can know from what she must know in order to act at all?

After Trotsky wrote "Their Morals and Ours," the editors of *New International* invited John Dewey to respond. The choice of Dewey was particularly appropriate, as he had just served as chairman of the Commission of Inquiry that had traveled to Mexico to hear Trotsky give testimony in his own defense against the charges of Stalin. These issues of means and ends and foresight took on worldwide significance as not only the Moscow Trials but the murder of Trotsky himself were soon to be defended as necessary means.

In his article "Means and Ends," Dewey agrees with Trotsky that "the end in the sense of consequences provides the only basis for moral ideas and action, and therefore provides the only justification that can be found for means employed."[13] He then goes on to say:

> One would expect, then, that with the idea of the liberation of mankind as the end-in-view, there would be an examination of all means that are likely to attain this end, and that every suggested means would be

> weighed and judged on the express ground of the consequences it is likely to produce.
>
> But this is *not* the course adopted in Mr. Trotsky's further discussion.[14]

And finally:

> The only conclusion I am able to reach is that in avoiding one kind of absolutism Mr. Trotsky has plunged into another kind of absolutism. There appears to be a curious transfer among orthodox Marxists of allegiance from the ideals of socialism and scientific methods of attaining them (scientific in the sense of being based on the objective relations of means and consequences) to the class struggle as the law of historical change.[15]

The "curious transfer" that Dewey notes, the "shift from one kind of absolutism to another" is what concerns us here. Of course it is possible for Trotsky to maintain that *he* does have adequate knowledge of what the future holds, and thus his actions and manner are appropriate. But surely we must reject this suggestion.

Even in everyday life, it is hard enough to have a good sense of the consequences. In discussing the experience of alienness in its everyday context, this difficulty was seen to yield a bewildering sense of openness. How much more this must be the case when we extend the horizon, when the actions in question affect thousands or millions of people.

Consider for example, the well-worn example of British appeasement of the Nazis at Munich. The effort to avoid war by allowing the Germans to take Czechoslovakia clearly failed. And it has been argued that if the Western powers had intervened militarily that the Germans were prepared to retreat. And on this basis supposedly is erected "an historical lesson." But what lesson is to be found here? What do we really know about what would have happened otherwise? Can we say with any degree of confidence that had there been an allied stand that in the long run it would have been for the better? Is it not equally likely that a stand at that point would have only postponed the German aggression, that the retreat would have only been tactical and that Germany would have continued to expand its strength. Or perhaps that under such conditions, Hitler might have ultimately been less likely to have opened a second front by attacking the Soviet Union before finishing off the Western nations? And if these are open questions, then clearly it is open as to whether or not, even in retrospect, we can do anything but guess at whether it was better or worse from a consequentialist point of view that Hitler was appeased.

So if the knowledge claims of the objectivist cannot be accepted, then there is a different question. Are the practitioners of this mode of political activity not only in error about the extent of their knowledge, but also deluding themselves? And if so, why are they engaged in a manner that is at its core committed to self-deception?

What makes the continued presence of self-deception and coarse ideology in politics so curious, is the seeming availability of an alternative. After all, why not be a well-balanced rationalist?

If objective political engagement is personified by Trotsky, rationalist political engagement is well represented by Bentham. Interestingly, Trotsky himself realized that his focus on objective consequences had a formal similarity to Bentham's principle of utility. Typical of Trotsky, he dismissed these formal similarities with a derisive comment about the bourgeoisie and the irrelevance of formal similarities.

Consider then two alternative versions of a principle of utility:

1. Do that act which has the greatest *expected* utility.
2. Do that act which will produce the greatest utility.

As similar as these principles may appear, they represent fundamentally different orientations towards political agency. As far as explicit content is concerned, principle (1) identifies the act to be done in terms of available evidence and probable consequences. The decision-making criterion is greatest *expected* utility; the act to be done is the act whose consequences when weighted by the probability of their occurrence emerges as better than any other alternative. Which act satisfies the principle in a given choice situation depends on the evidence that is available to that particular decision maker. Principle (2) focuses only on the actual consequences of the acts. It is concerned with the objective nature of the outcomes rather than with a reasonable assessment of future outcomes.

As I have noted, Trotsky's orientation is more adequately captured by (2). He is concerned with the actual outcomes. Means are justified in terms of their effects. He does not talk about choosing the means that *appear* as if they will have the most desirable effects. Bentham, on the other hand, said, "By the principle of utility is meant that principle which approves or disapproves of every action whatsoever, according to the tendency which it *appears* to have to augment or diminish the happiness of the party whose interest is in question" (emphasis mine).[16]

One might maintain that the only way one could be said to be *trying* to act in accord with (2) is by choosing the act that appears to satisfy it. And thus, one might argue, a devotion to the objectivist principle implies a devotion to the rationalist principle and thus, for the decision maker, it comes down to the same problem—trying to identify that act most likely to produce the greatest good.

But this response errs in two respects. First, the claim that the best way to satisfy the objectivist principle is to satisfy the rationalist principle is an empirical claim that when taken as a generalization applicable to all persons is surely false. For many people, simply following well-established rules or obeying the orders of some particular authority, without making any effort to establish probable utilities, would be the best strategy for actually achieving the most good.

More importantly from the point of view of the dynamics of self-identity/alienation, the two principles are part of a much more fundamental difference. It is a difference with respect to identity; in particular a difference with respect to which characteristics of a person serve to establish who he or she really is.

The rationalist engagement involves a self that is displayed in its reasonableness, balance, and above all else, in *doing one's best.* When one has done one's best one acquits oneself of one's responsibility. The objectivist outlook calls for correctness, period. The emphasis is on the objective outcome rather than upon the decision maker's rationality, responsibility, or intention. This is not to say that the rationalist approach must necessarily be less concerned with what the actual consequences are. It is possible to view the individual as having in addition to an obligation to do that act that has the greatest expected utility a second obligation to pursue with enormous diligence his effort to determine what the likely consequences will be. Yet a deep difference remains. It has to do with how the agent views his or her own identity as determined by having in fact rather than in intent acted in ways that promote the political good to which he or she is devoted.

From the point of view of one's own feelings of agency and alienness, the world is very different for a Bentham than it is for a Trotsky. The rationalist agent, who thinks of himself in terms of what he regards as identity-defining properties (e.g., motives, personality characteristics) has the validity of his self-identity largely in his control. That is, he can be something of the person he sees himself to be, merely by doing his best. He is defined by his motives, his beliefs, his propensity to forethought, his efforts, his character. Under normal circumstances these aspects of the self involve matters with which the agent is well acquainted; thus his identity is something that is known to him, and as is natural, his identity is to a large extent created and maintained by his self-identity. That is, the agent's own understanding of who he is plays a central role in shaping the self in such a way that he is in fact exactly who he thinks he is.

The objectivist, on the other hand, finds her identity always in danger of slipping out of her control. Since her self-identity is composed of the objective social roles she believes herself to play, its validity is maintained only insofar as her politics plays the historical role she imagines it to play. Psychologically this results in a far greater need to know, to actually know, what the consequences will be. Sometimes this need is met by actual knowledge and sometimes by ideologically held beliefs, that is, beliefs that are held with an unwarranted degree of certitude.

Trotsky expressed this vast confidence in his own knowledge and the possibilities of learning when he wrote:

> The "Trotskyists" learned the rhythm of history, that is, the dialectics of the class struggle. They also learned, it seems, and to a certain degree successfully, how to subordinate their subjective plans and programs to this objective rhythm.[17]

Without this certainty there is not enough sense of integration to carry on effective political action, but with it revolutionary political activity can provide whatever self-fulfillment transitional people are capable of. Thus, Trotsky writes:

> They know how to swim against the stream in the deep conviction that the new historic flood will carry them to the other shore. Not all will reach that shore, many will drown. But to participate in this movement with open eyes and with an intense will—only this can give the highest moral satisfaction to a thinking being![18]

One might point out that the Trotskyite and the Benthamite use very similar criteria in making decisions, but from the Trotskyite standpoint there is a triviality to "formal or psychological similitudes."[19] What is important is being right in fact. "Compared to revolutionary Marxists, the social-democrats and centrists appear like morons, or like quacks beside physicians: they do not think one problem through to the end."[20]

So part of the answer to the question of self-deception within the objectivist engagement is that an objectivist perspective on identity places the individual under enormous strains to believe that he knows the facts. If he accepts the rationalist perspective, if he accepts that all he has are probabilities and maybe weak ones at that, then his own self-identity becomes unglued. To say this is to say that the very fabric of his personality is in danger of being unraveled. Yet if one is driven towards self-deception in virtue of an objectivist orientation, can one instead embrace a rationalist engagement?

First, it should be remembered that the objectivist perspective on identity is not something the objectivist chooses. It is something that is carried implicit in a certain vision of history. It is a world that conforms to the tale of King Arthur: until he withdraws the sword from the stone, young Arthur is not known to himself or to others. But he is always that person who will be king, and once it is known to himself that that is who he is, that is his self-identity. The objectivist perspective on identity, which says that one's role within the story determines who one is, emerges from the power of the story itself.

Second, the rationalist outlook has problems sustaining itself in the context of political activity, however well it may be suited for the terms of everyday life. There is something self-defeating about being merely hopeful yet well aware of the way things may fail. It gives rise to a mode of nonengagement. Out of integration with one's beliefs about the limitations of what one really knows, one holds oneself back. Every action has a tentative quality. It has been chosen only because it seems more likely to lead to desired outcomes than other alternatives. This lack of engagement is itself a factor that enters into the process. Doubts and concerns may themselves prevent success.

This arises most acutely with respect to leadership. If one is only partially committed to a specific line of action, how does one get others to commit themselves? Could one, for instance, raise an army of volunteers on the grounds that *probably* the war will be won and if so, *probably* great good will come of it? The contexts of political activity demand a different manner of engagement.

Furthermore, the psychological viability of Benthamist reasonableness is limited to certain specific contexts. There is a world of difference between the relatively genteel application of Bentham's calculus to questions of legislation and welfare economics and its application to revolution. We should remember what Kierkegaard said, "It is not wisdom which saves the worst ones from going insane, but indolence."[21] Most likely no one ever was an act-utilitarian. If one is consistently and scrupulously act-utilitarian, then one strips away the familiar habitual limits to possible actions, and one breaks through the moral restraints embedded in the perceptions and conducts that govern the everyday world of interpersonal contacts. To do this is to have an explosion of imagination far greater than that of the immoralist of existential literature who announces, "Everything is lawful!" or "Everything is possible!" At least if one is outside the moral order, one is free to indulge desire, and this is limiting, stabilizing, and habitual. The act-utilitarian is inside the moral order and thus outside the realm of desire, and yet outside the realm of moral rules—that is truly dizzying. For him anything is possible and there are no other principles to limit possibility. Each possible action must be appraised individually, according to the specific consequences of performing that particular token. Existential literature notwithstanding, it is utilitarianism, adherence to a decision rule that contains a specific description of the act to be done, which results in a terrifying freedom. Anything may be required! We ward off the impact of this openness to possibility by restricting the range of actions we will consider and the range of consequences we will notice, to those of the everyday. But to do this is to abandon the political.

To apply utilitarianism to the political is to extend one's time span indefinitely, and to extend to the billions the number of persons affected. The range of possible outcomes moves towards the infinite: on the one hand there is the possible destruction of all life, and on the other the final evolution of the human spirit. Applied as best one can, in a world where a given political and economic order means millions of deaths and stunted lives, consequentialism bursts the bounds of decorum. Could it be that Trotsky, who prided himself on thinking things through to the end, was the first serious act-utilitarian?

Consider Trotsky again. His context is not that of the hypothetical introductory-ethics classroom. Yet the problems that he faced are exactly those extreme situations cited in classroom discussion to test the viability of conflicting theories. In the classroom it is possible to finally throw one's hands in the air and say, "I don't know what I would do" or to dismiss the idea that we need an ethics that can handle the most wildly imaginable situations—"What if you are in a strange country and you and your family are taken captive and you are told that unless you kill one of your children, you and all of your children will be tortured and then killed?"

For Trotsky, this is the context he operates in. And perhaps just because he was a political agent and not merely a bureaucrat with the power of a general, he was intensely aware of it. He wrote, "Stalin arrests and shoots the children of his opponents after these opponents have been themselves executed under false accusations."[22] Suddenly he faces the charge, "The detention of innocent relatives by Stalin is disgusting barbarism. But it remains a barbarism as well when it was dictated by Trotsky (1919)."[23] And it is true, Trotsky did order hostages to be taken. How then is he to distinguish himself from Stalin? He writes:

> If the revolution had displayed less superfluous generosity from the beginning, *hundreds of thousands of lives would have been saved.* Thus or otherwise I carry full responsibility for the Decree of 1919. It was a necessary measure in the struggle against oppressors. Only in the historical context of the struggle lies the justification of the decree as in general the justification of the whole civil war which too, can be called, not without foundation "disgusting barbarism."[24]

So the difference between his execution of hostages and that ordered by Stalin is that in his case they were in fact justified acts. We must try to experience the magnitudes of the consequences involved. He says, if there had been less "generosity" it would have resulted in the saving of *hundreds of thousands of lives.*

The context created by open-minded act-utilitarianism on the political landscape is not pretty. It was not paranoia that turned many socialists and trade unionists away from the Communists in disgust. Trotsky himself relates,

> . . . . an episode which in spite of its modest dimensions, does not badly illustrate the difference between *their* morals and *ours*. In 1935, through a letter to my Belgian friends, I developed the conception that the attempt of a young revolutionary party to organize "its own" trade unions is equivalent to suicide. It is necessary to find the workers where they are. But this means paying dues in order to sustain an opportunist apparatus? "Of course," I replied, "for the right to undermine the reformists it is necessary temporarily to pay them a contribution." But reformists will not permit us to undermine them? "True," I answered, "undermining demands conspirative measures. Reformists are the political police of the bourgeoisie within the working class. We must act without their permission and against their interdiction."[25]

If following a utilitarian principle leads to such actions, even if we have gotten to the point of being able to accept odious means because they lead to future good, we need to at least be sure that they do lead to the justifying ends. Once one has killed the hostages, their deaths define one in spite of one's intentions. One can no longer merely be one who thought their deaths were necessary; one is either one who killed when it was necessary or when it was not necessary. Either Trotsky was the same as Stalin or he was not.

Something happens to utilitarianism when it is political. The space within which "reasonable people may disagree" expands in the direction of including everything. No longer does utilitarianism circumscribe a friendly club within which all are good, reasonable, and well-intentioned people. All forms of monsters may enter that club. Once one seriously breaks with the unity that Kierkegaard demands and Gandhi seeks, once one is willing to let one's actions be determined by expected utility, one has let one's nature rest upon the adequacy of one's foresight. Under these circumstances, where one is willing to kill innocent hostages if this seems likely to produce the best consequences, one had best be right. In short, when fully acted out in political activity, the psychological space of the Benthamist mode drives itself into the very different space of the Trotskyist mode. The actions dictated by the rule of expected utility are such that they defeat the rationalist perspective on identity; they force one towards an objectivist position on identity.

Even outside the pressures generated by morally odious means, the objectivist perspective on identity generates pressures to believe one knows the facts. If one lives in terms of one's historical role, if one's self-identity is of a consequentialist sort because one's concept of identity is consequentialist, then it is one's highest level acts that are self-defining (i.e., the act of producing the distant consequence). When this is so, one has no actual experience of oneself as performing the acts that are self-defining. The meaning of one's present activity is not only not within one's immediate control, it is instead in the hands of others. These others exist in the historical future. One is bound to them because they will determine who you have been. Seen from the other direction, we bear the burden of determining the meaning of the actions of those long dead (e.g., the Jew who loses all Jewish self-identity renders futile the acts of those that chose to suffer rather than convert). What this means is that we cannot know the objective meaning of who we are unless we know the long-term consequences of our present activity. Without this knowledge one looks at one's present activity and knows only that it is giving one one's identity. But what that identity is, we do not know. If we have a self-identity generated out of our ideals and intentions and yet a consequentialist concept of identity, we do not know if we are really ourselves. Identity slips through our fingers. Political activity loses its capacity as a felt source of self-actualization. It becomes the realm within which our identity is established but no experienced self-actualization is ever warranted. The self we would have ourselves become may always be precisely what we are ruling out through our actions. It may not be psychologically possible to function with this awareness. Under such conditions, one must believe that one knows what one is doing; one must reject the rationalist's honesty with respect to how little he or she really knows.

This does not mean that rationalists are not to be found engaged in grand-scale political activity. What it suggests is that they have to avoid the rigorous application of the principle of expected utility. For then one enters realms of action where only a positive consequentialist self-identity can sustain one. And one will have to avoid a political view of the world and history, for this generates a political notion of identity. And finally one must act only when one knows a great deal, otherwise one's honest manner will undermine one's actions. In sum, rationalist engagement yields a self-imposed blindness and limitation. Thus, it too emerges as a mode of engagement necessarily rooted in self-deception.

Political Self-Deception

When a political agent is led to self-deception about how much he knows, he may find in extreme situations that he has to constantly maintain himself in a stance of not facing his limitations. He may have to actively screen himself from conflicting evidence. With this comes a particular form of separation of the self from activity. It is a separation that is visible in the manner with which the agent carries out his activity. It is a separation that manifests itself as the appearance of *more* engagement in the activity than one really has. This is fanaticism.

Fanaticism is not a matter of *what* is being done. An extreme act is not an act of fanaticism because of its content. If it is fanatical it is because of how it is done, in relation to the agent's beliefs and evidence. One can do an extreme act on slim grounds and not be a fanatic if one does it in a way that does not deny one's lack of knowledge. However, the extreme act often has a false manner because one feels a need for a fidelity of commitment that does not betray to oneself one's lack of confidence. One blinds oneself to one's misgivings. In this way the activity or series of activities lose their flexibility. They become stiff and mechanical; there no longer is a constant adjustment of behavior to awareness, to knowledge of new conditions. One "steels oneself up" because rigidity is required. One does not throw a bomb because one is a fanatic, nor is one a fanatic simply because one has thrown a bomb. Rather, we have to make ourselves fanatical in order to throw the bomb. Though the act itself might be justified in terms of maximum expected utility, most Benthamists cannot throw bombs.

It is not that a given activity type must be done in a specific manner. But rather that just as there are manners that reflect the degree of internal integration of the activity token, the degree to which the complex is an activity, so too different manners reflect different degrees of agency, different degrees to which the self is in the activity, to which it is self-activity. When there is a false manner, not only is much of the self not in the activity, but its falseness—by denying entry to one's beliefs and attitudes, to one's doubts and misgivings—denies entry to the self at all. In its extreme we call this madness.

It would be grossly unfair to the objectivist spirit to paint a picture in which the enormous pressure to actually know the consequences of actions leads only to coarse ideology, self-deception, and fanaticism. The most obvious response to the need to know is in fact to seek true knowledge, and Marx, for one, stands out for his understanding of the importance of social science to political activity. It is not surprising that Marx's major work falls largely within economics. The transition from what he called "utopian socialism" to "scientific socialism" is captured by the recognition of the importance of understanding the processes of social development. The abandonment of the spirit of utopianism is the abandonment of a belief in the power of individuals to create a radically different social order merely on the basis of a description of that order and the will to do so. Instead, the emphasis shifts to the necessity of understanding the nature of historical evolution, and situating political activity within the realm of possibilities revealed by an understanding of social change.

As understood by Marx, "scientific socialism" involved more than a reliance on knowledge. It involved a conception of a *method* of attaining that knowledge that is scientific. Broadly speaking we could talk of a method of experimentation, but when applied to social transformation this is not a matter of experimentation in one sphere and application in another. Rather, the actual attempt, the political process itself, is to become the method whereby one learns how to transform society. Thus in part Marxism faced the problem of the absence of knowledge by answering that the process of political change will be carried out in a manner that generates knowledge.

But beyond this, the process of transformation is seen as a way of solving the utopian's dilemma: "Who will teach the teachers?" Through the process of political activity not only does one gain necessary propositional knowledge that may be applied, but one brings into existence the kind of agents that are required to carry out the transformations. Thus the critical notion in the Marxist process is the creation of the revolutionary. This takes the explicit form of the proletariat's becoming a class that knows itself, not just in the sense of class identity but in terms of its fuller identity, which it comes to understand when it understands the nature of history and capitalism and its role in the transition to communism. Because the process involves transformations that are themselves grounded in economic development, the process is not voluntaristic. As such, it is not subject to the various forms of corruption and failure that have befallen experiments grounded solely in a moral ideal and will, most notably, the religious/utopian communities of the past, to which one might add twentieth-century Soviet Union.

All this is contained in Marx's notion of *praxis*. This notion significantly lifts the burden off the objectivist agent. She can accept the fact that it is possible that she may be in error on specifics because she sees herself as part of an extended piece of political activity carried out by an historical community of political actors who are engaged in a *method* of political activity and reflection, that in the end will generate the knowledge that they need for their success. And when this is seen as the only way in which the needed transformations can come about, then even if one is wrong, one is still part of a larger group of actors that will in the end have played the role one sees oneself as playing.

But what if there is no such praxis? Or what if we are unable to specify or to actually carry out political activity through which such learning occurs? Or what if we have no way of knowing whether it is we or others who are in fact carrying out such an activity? If this is the case, then having the idea of such a praxis is insufficient; it still remains the case that our identity is unknown and that our self-identity is subject to dissolution.

The sorry truth is that no such actual praxis has been discovered. If one is a possibility then it remains elusive. But if no such praxis has in fact been found, then how has alienness been avoided? First there is what we have discussed, false certainty and self-deception. But beyond this there is a deeper answer that does not lie in false belief. It lies in a different direction—the abandonment of the objectivist perspective on identity. For all the hardheaded analysis *of others* in terms of a consequentialist identity, for all the dismissal of intentions in favor of objective consequences, political activity has typically been made possible in the face of ignorance by a final reversal—good intentions are everything! Identity is defined ultimately in terms of intentions and thus political activity is not felt to be separated from the self because it arises from these intentions. So long as one knows what one is intending, one feels at one with oneself. This is the internal definition of voluntarism.

This retreat to intentions rather than knowledge of consequences as the source of the subjective self-identity of the objectivist political agent must be disguised from himself, for his political orientation insists that the only valid self-identity is that which is grounded in knowledge of true identity (i.e., objective consequences). And with this self-deception as to where his sense of identity is coming from, comes this as well: a turning away from a concern with truth.

Its worst manifestation within the Marxist tradition was the abandonment, by those that actually held state power through leadership in the Party, of a concern with whether what they lead is really the Party in any other sense than that they have given this name to the organization they dominate. Is it a party that will successfully lead the transformation of humanity and society? This is a question not solved but for a time resolved by silencing all voices that might question its actual identity.

In sum then, I have maintain that objectivism, especially Marxism, on the one hand deepens the sense of the alienness of aspects of self and drives one towards political activity as the one sphere in which one can truly be the agent of one's activity. Yet paradoxically, political activity is not an ideal vehicle for self-expression, and the Marxist orientation towards objective social consequences deepens the sense of alienness. On the other hand, a Marxist analysis of morality in terms of its social role helps to limit the sense of alienness that arises from moral conflict by locating one's moral strictures in a bracketed area of self (i.e., the person one finds oneself to be). But because of this freedom from moral restraint, even greater emphasis is placed on knowledge of the objective consequences. And here there are two roads to take. One tends to achieve integration of subjective self-identity with objective social identity through activity guided by knowledge of long-term consequences. The other focus is less on knowledge than on method. However, once we reject a belief in the proletariat as the transformed and transforming agent, we are left without any actual method or knowledge. Thus, the actual attainment of knowledge or the actual attainment of a self-correcting praxis becomes the only alternative to alienness, self-deception, or quietism for political beings.

It is because no actual praxis has been found, and because reality so often disconfirms the most confident expectations, that political identity and agency is unstable. Because of its comprehensive social and historical notion of identity it offers the promise of the only true self-actualization we can attain. Yet because of our finitude that same notion of identity generates contradictions too powerful to be long sustained by most people.

Notes

1. William Shakespeare, The Second Part of King Henry IV, Li. 189.
2. Andre Malraux, *Man's Fate*, trans. H. Chevalier (New York: Random House, 1961).
3. Malraux, *Man's Fate*, 145.
4. Karl Marx, *Captial*, trans. S. Moore and E. Aveling (New York: Random House, 1906), 81.
5. Leon Trotsky, "Their Morals and Ours," *New International* (June 1938):172.
6. Leon Trotsky, "Moralists and Sycophants Against Marxism," *New International* (August 1939):231-33.
7. Soren Kierkegaard, *Purity of Heart is to Will One Thing*, trans. D. Steere (New York: Harper and Row, 1956), 201-03.
8. Erik Erikson, *Gandhi's Truth* (New York: Norton, 1969), 412-17.
9. M. K. Gandhi, *An Autobiography or the Story of My Experiments With Truth* (Ahmedabad: Navajivan, 1948), 259.
10. Gandhi, *Autobiography*, 388.
11. Ibid., 384.
12. Leon Trotsky, "An Open Letter to the Workers of India," in *The Age of Permanent Revolution: A Trotsky Anthology*, ed. Isaac Deutscher (New York: Dell, 1964), 248.
13. John Dewey, "Means and Ends," *New International* (August 1938):232.
14. Dewey, "Means," 232.
15. Ibid., 232.
16. Jeremy Bentham, "Principles of Morals and Legislation" in *The Utilitarians* (Garden City: Doubleday, 1961), 17.
17. Leon Trotsky, "Ends and Means in Morality," in *The Age of Permanent Revolution*, ed. Isaac Deutscher (New York: Dell, 1964), 340.
18. Trotsky, "Ends," 340-41.
19. Ibid., 334.

20. Ibid.
21. Kierkegaard, *Purity of Heart*, 203.
22. Trotsky, "Their Morals," 169.
23. Ibid.
24. Ibid.
25. Ibid., 171.

6
How We Fooled Ourselves into Believing in Progress

Is history a story of human progress? Is it a story of human decline? Is it just a matter of ups and downs, not going anywhere? For over 2,000 years, the answers to such questions have shaped Western civilization's varying self-perception. In part, this is a matter of facts, a matter of beliefs about what will happen and about what has happened. But most centrally the disagreements have been about "what really matters, and what does not." Things occur in the world, but they do not come with labels on them that say "this is important" or "this is better than that." It is only against the backdrop of our values that we can develop a conception of what happens in time. As we shall see, the history of the notion that mankind makes progress is itself a history of the abandonment of some values in favor of others.

An inquiry into the history of the idea of progress shows how unusual it is to think about the economy as we do—as an independent realm to be evaluated in terms of the magnitude of its output rather than in terms of its contribution to a larger vision of life. Further, an inquiry in-to the history of the idea of progress shows that the issue we are concerned with, the value of simple living, has been a recurring theme in the effort to understand "what happens" in history. This should come as no surprise, for the idea of simple living is an ancient ideal and it has often represented a challenge to dominant values.

From the point of view of graceful simplicity, an inquiry of this sort is particularly illuminating. It shows that to a considerable extent the debates in the past over whether mankind makes progress in history were debates over the relative beauty of the art and literature of different historic periods. Yet when those debates ended, and there emerged something of a consensus that adhered to a belief in progress, it was not because agreement was reached in the relative merits of ancient and modern arts. Rather, what happened was a shift in the implicit definition of progress; beauty, and creative power once central concerns had been relegated to the periphery. In short, the emergence of the idea of progress reflected the dominance of new values. In particular, it represented the emergence of the modern way of thinking about economic life.

The Love of Books

I have suggested that a love of books is the hallmark of whether our schools are preparing children for living the good life. And in reading a good book, either to oneself or with others, whether with friends or children, one finds proof that the sources of both pleasure and growth are as available as fruit in an orchard.

When we think of history as the story of human progress, especially when we think of that progress as involving the progressive evolution of human sensibilities and relationships, then inevitably we postulate a radical gap between ourselves and those that lived long ago. Yet consider this ancient passage from *The Instruction of Duauf*, to which Toynbee calls our attention. I believe it's the most ancient affirmation of the wisdom of building one's life around books.

Duauf, an Egyptian scribe, is writing for his son, having installed him in the School of Books:

> I have seen him that is beaten, him that is beaten: thou art to set thine heart on books.
>
> I have beheld him that is set free from forced labor: behold, nothing surpasseth books. . . .
>
> Would that I might make thee love books more than thy mother; would that I might bring their beauty before thy face. It is greater than any calling. . . .
>
> Every artisan that wieldeth the chisel, he is wearier than him that delveth. . . .
>
> The stone-mason seeketh for work in all manner of hard stone. When he hath finished it his arms are destroyed and he is weary. . . .
>
> The field worker, his reckoning endureth for ever . . . he too is wearier than can be told, and he fareth as one fareth among lions. . . .
>
> The weaver in the workshop, he fareth more ill than any woman. His thighs are upon his belly, and he breatheth no air. . . .

> Let me tell thee, further, how it fareth with the fisherman. Is not his work upon the river, where it is mixed with the crocodiles? . . .
>
> Behold, there is no calling that is without a director except (that of) the scribe, and he is the director. . . .[1]

On one level this passage is a parent's advice to a son. As such it is advice that we have heard before. Essentially Duauf the Egyptian is telling his son to "stay in school!" While this is sound advice in our contemporary world, what is most remarkable is that Duauf gave this advice to his son over four thousand years ago. One thousand years after it was written, around the time of King David and Solomon, well before the Bible was written down, this text was being used by Egyptian schoolboys in their copy books.

How startling it is! Duauf speaks to the practical issue of human capital formation, the relationship between education and vocational life. With considerable poignancy Duauf reflects on the difficult conditions faced by laborers throughout the social order. He speaks not only of physical exhaustion but of freedom within the workplace: "there is no calling that is without a director except that of the scribe." There is even, perhaps, a fleeting recognition of the difficult condition of women ("the weaver in the workshop, he fareth more ill than any woman. His thighs are on his belly, and he breathest no air.")

What does it tell us about history that this exchange between father and son, with these sensibilities, occurred almost 4000 years ago? It is not easy to fit this ancient text into our modernistic vision. It suggests an ancient history to one of the common dilemmas of life—"What will I do when I grow up." And it bears witness to human relationships and human sensibilities which mock our distinctions between modern and traditional societies and make us wonder if we really do know what happens to man in history.

There is something else in this passage. Duauf tells his son to "set thine heart on books" and he says "Would that I might make thee love books more than thy mother; would that I might bring their beauty before thy face."

In holding up the standard of "love . . . more than thy mother," the passage attests to the bond between child and mother. But against this most fundamental standard of love, Duauf interposes books. Books, too, are a matter of the heart; they are the objects of love; a love that might appropriately surpass even the love for thy mother. Perhaps Duauf senses that books themselves are our mothers, giving birth to our ever-renewed selves. And books are, he tells us, things of beauty. But not necessarily beauty that is immediately visible. Duauf says of this beauty, "Would that I might bring [it] before thy face." The appreciation of their beauty requires instruction.

What we have in this passage is Duauf's love for his son, his love for books, and his effort to bring about a love-marriage between these two objects of his love. This is to be a marriage that will be valid in itself. Like all marriages, it is one that will take cognizance of the realities of economic life—there is a practical side to loving books. Specifically, for Duauf's son, there is his career as a scribe. How are we to fit this image in among our other images of ancient Egypt as a past world, a world of idol worship and pyramid building? From his relationship with his son, from his mixed role as affectionate father and practical guide, from his own love of books, it is clear that the world in which Duauf lived turns around remarkably fixed points of human experience. How, by the way, are we to explain Duauf's love of books? Perhaps we have yet to understand what books were and meant in ancient Egypt. Often enough we think that "back then" what was recorded was only a listing of the triumphs of the Pharaoh, or of the financial records of the Pharaoh's ministers. But for us, the "book" of ancient Egypt that *we* can love the most is itself Duauf instruction—preserved in clay tablets as a text for school children to copy. It is this writing of Duauf himself that, for us, is the book that opens up the inner world of ordinary people at the time of the Pharaohs, opens up their beauty, their loves and their anxieties.

The Problem of Homer

In our rush towards the future and our indifference towards the past we are all victims of The Idea of Progress. This is a Western idea, and any understanding of it should start with Homer. It is not that Homer wrote about progress, though it is possible to read *The Odyssey* from that perspective. It is rather that the phenomenon of Homer has always represented a problem for the Idea of Progress. This was true in the fifth century B.C.E.; it was true in the seventeenth and eighteenth centuries; it is true today.

Homer did not write. He was a poet in an oral tradition. The tales he told had been told for several hundred years. But it was his account that was written down and preserved. Possibly *The Iliad* and *The Odyssey* were the works of two different authors; we do not know for sure. But it is the Homer of *The Iliad* that is most problematic.

The Iliad is the earliest known work in Western literature. It was written down in the eighth century B.C.E. In sheer volume it is impressive, an epic poem of 600 pages. It is the story of the Trojan War. Thus, our first story was a war story. Yet it is not what one might expect. It opens nine years into the war. There is no Trojan horse in the story; there is no account of Achilles death, no mention of his vulnerable heel, and there is no account of the fall of Troy. It is a slice of experience at a critical point during the war.

It is most essentially a human story. There are no faceless, nameless, masses of soldiers. Each death, and there are many, is unique. Each is of an individual human being who is individually connected to other human beings, be they Greek or Trojan.

Perhaps *The Iliad* should be seen as the story of Hector. Hector is the great Trojan warrior, brother of Paris, whose thoughtless kidnapping of Helen started the conflict. The doomed Hector must fight Achilles who is half god. Hector curses his thoughtless brother:

> As for me, I go
> for Paris, to arouse him, if he listens.
> If only earth would swallow him here and now!
> What an affliction the Olympian
> brought up for us in him—a curse for Priam
> and Priam's children! Could I see that man
> dwindle into Death's night, I'd feel my soul
> relieved of its distress![2]

Hector has a wife and child. He knows that he is fated to die in this senseless war. He speaks with his wife, fearing that she will end up a slave in a Greek household. And she replies:

> Oh, my wild one, your bravery will be
> your own undoing. No pity for our child,
> poor little one, or me in my sad lot—
> soon to be deprived of you! Soon, soon
> Akhains as one man will set upon you
> and cut you down! Better for me, without you,
> to take cold earth for mantle. No more comfort,
> no other warmth, after you meet your doom
> but heartbreak only.[3]

When the time comes, Hector's great courage fails him. He flees from Achilles, and three times around Troy they run. But Achilles is known as the great runner; he cannot be escaped anymore than death itself. Finally, Hector turns. He will stand and fight. In short order, he is mortally wounded. As he is dying Hector speaks to Achilles:

> I beg you by your soul and by your parents,
> do not let the dogs feed on me
> in your encampment by the ships. Accept
> the bronze and gold my father will provide
> as gifts, my father and her ladyship
> my mother. Let them have my body back,
> so that our men and women may accord me
> decency of fire when I am dead.[4]

Achilles refuses, thus adding to Hector's total loss—"Dogs and birds will have you, every scrap."[5] But when old Priam, Hector's father, journeys alone to Achilles' camp, he is allowed to claim his son's body.

The Iliad is a story about human dignity. It is also about mortality and about being caught within the larger fatality of history and duty. Even in translation, it is beautiful poetry.

For centuries the study of Homer was at the center of education for ancient Greeks. Professionals who traveled from city to city recited Homer. It was believed that "Homer enshrined all wisdom and all knowledge. . . . Homer held and nourished the minds and imaginations of Greeks for generation after generation—of artists, thinkers and ordinary simple men alike. . . . Aeschylus was said to have described his own work, modestly, as 'sliced from Homer's banquet.'"[6] In the fifth century B.C.E. amidst perhaps the greatest flourishing of the human spirit, some, increasingly aware of how much they had progressed over the past, found in the greatness of this older poet a problem for their self-image, and they turned against Homer. The poet Timotheus proclaimed "I do not sing ancient melodies, my own are better by far."[7]

This was not the last time Homer served as the benchmark of human excellence. In the seventeenth century, 2,500 years after *The Iliad* many had a similarly difficult time understanding their place in history without first settling whether they had surpassed Homer. And in our own time, a full 2,800 years later, Simone Weil could say of *The Iliad*, "Nothing that Western civilization has since produced has surpassed this first poem to have appeared among them."[8]

This then is the problem of Homer. It is so good! And being so, it casts in doubt the claim that we have made progress. Nor is this just a matter of Homer's individual genius, great though it was. For he arose out of a tradition, and it was to Greek sensibilities that his poetry was directed, and it was Homer, above all others, to whom the Greeks responded. They were thus capable of recognizing Homer's genius and appreciating *The Iliad*. So the problem of Homer is really the historical problem. Given the heights that were achieved by individuals and cultures at the dawn of Western civilization, how are we to accurately orient ourselves towards the great expanse of human experience and change that followed?

Musings on the History of the Idea of Progress

When historians inquire into the history of the "idea of progress," they are arguing about the history of a specific set of beliefs about progress. They are interested in when those beliefs first arose, in who held them, in what those beliefs expressed, and in the consequences of those beliefs having been held.

What are the beliefs that constitute the idea of progress? The historian George Hildebrand has identified three elements:

- "The belief that history follows a continuous, necessary and orderly course."
- "The belief that this course is the effect of a regularly operating causal law."
- "The belief that the course of change has brought and will continue to bring improvement in the condition of mankind."[9]

There is considerable debate as to whether or not there was, in this sense, an idea of progress prior to the seventeenth and eighteenth centuries. Some writers such as Robert Nisbet find the idea of progress in virtually every era of Western history with the exception of the Renaissance. The absence of this concept in the Renaissance can perhaps be understood as following from the rediscovery of the classical world, and in the light of that rediscovery, a perception of the vast period in between as a period of decline and stagnation.[10]

Other historians argue that the ancient and medieval world lacked a full sense of the idea of progress. They emphasize several ways in which the dominant outlook of other periods varied from the key elements identified above.

It is pointed out that:

- The Greek philosophy of history typically involved the notion of decay or decline from some Golden Age.
- When the Greeks focused sharply on the progress that had occurred, they did not anticipate that it would continue indefinitely, but rather imagined that they were near the end of the process.
- The Christian view of history centered around acts of divine intervention rather than the operation of causal laws, and even when is celebrated scientific technological change, it anticipated that the world would end in the not-too-distant future.

We can accept these points, yet what is remarkable is how much of a "progressive mentality" there has been, reaching as far back in Western thought as we can go. Most important is that, for over 2,500 years, the West has been change-oriented. It has been aware of the fact that important processes of deep social change occur over time.

We tend to think of our current period, whether this be the last hundreds years, or the last two or three hundred, as a unique period of change and awareness of change. Yet something of this sort must also have been true among the ancient Greeks and possibly the Romans. Consider the following passages from Thucydides' *History of the Peloponnesian War*. They are extraordinarily rich in what they reveal about the awareness of multiple levels of rapid transformation. Thucydides is providing background about Greece:

> The country now called Hellas had no settled population in ancient times; . . . There was no commerce, and no safe communication either by land or sea; the use they made of their land was limited to the production of necessities; they had no surplus left over for capital and no regular system of agriculture.[11]

Thus, the first thing we learn about is economic change. This passage suggests an implicit theory of economic growth. The ancient peoples produced (either by necessity or design) only what they needed. There was no economic surplus that could be devoted to capital for greater productivity.

> In these early times, as communication by sea became easier, so piracy became a common profession both among the Hellenes and among the barbarians who lived on the coast in the islands. . . . At this time, such a profession, so far from being regarded as disgraceful was considered

> quite honorable. It is an attitude that can be illustrated even today by some of the inhabitant of the mainland among whom successful piracy is regarded as something to be proud of.

Thus, Thucydides tells us that one of the things that changes overtime are the moral ideas of people. What is now viewed as disgraceful, was once viewed as honorable. Some of the old customs and attitudes survive today.

> Among these people the custom of carrying arms still survives from the old days of robbery. Since houses were unprotected and communications unsafe it was the normal thing to carry arms on all occasions, and this was a general custom throughout the whole of Hellas as it is now among foreigners. The fact that the people I have mentioned still live in this way is evidence that this was once the general rule among all the Hellenes.

Though Thucydides does not say it outright, there seems an implicit view that it is not merely that there is change in our moral ideas and practices, but that such change moves in one direction, and is a change for the better.

> The Athenians were the first to give up the habit of carrying weapons and to adopt a way of living that was more relaxed and more luxurious. In fact the elder men of the rich families who had these luxurious tastes only recently gave up wearing linen undergarments and tying their hair behind their heads in a knot. . . . It was the Spartans who first began to dress simply and in accordance with our modern taste, with the rich leading a life that was as much as possible like that of the ordinary people. They, too, were the first to play games naked, to take off their clothes openly, and to rub themselves down with olive oil after their exercise. In ancient times even at the Olympic Games the athletes used to wear coverings for their loins, and indeed this practice was still in existence not very many years ago. Even today many foreigners, especially in Asia, wear these loincloths for boxing matches and wrestling bouts. Indeed, one could point to a number of other instances where the manners of the ancient Hellenic world are very similar to the manners of foreigners today.

In this last reference to ways in which the manners of foreigners are similar to those of the ancient Hellenic world we have a vision not unlike contemporary views that see the world as divided into the developed and the less-developed countries, with "our country" representing the apex of development.

Thucydides displays not merely an awareness of change, but a tremendously broad sense of the elements that undergo transformation. These include: the physical form of cities, level of technology, modes of political organization, forms of economic activity, agricultural practices, level of material well being, moral attitudes (e.g. towards piracy), attitudes towards nudity and sports, modes of dress, and even hairstyles. The fact that Thucydides moves so easily from discussing whether or not men wear underwear to how they build their warships suggests that for him all aspects of human life were part of one broad process of transformation.

He presents changes as one-directional. He gives no indication that any of them have ever been reversed, nor does Thucydides express any expectation that they will be. Rather, he talks of the Hellenes as having been "the first" to make certain changes. He apparently expects that other societies will eventually undergo similar transformations. Thus, implicitly there is a vision of a single pattern of change through which all societies move.

It is true, of course, that many believed that they had declined from a Golden Age. There were those who believed in the continuous recurrence of historical cycles, yet they too believed that there were long periods of time within which mankind gradually gained critical inventions, techniques, and institutions: the plough, use of fire, navigation, law giving, mathematics, metallurgy, and cities.

In Thucydides the picture that emerges then is one of vast change in almost all aspects of life, change that is pushed by technological innovation, and that ultimately will carry all of mankind with it. Thus, there is nothing uniquely modern about our modern self-consciousness. We are not the first to see ourselves as modern, in self-conscious contrast to a more ancient past out of which we have progressed. Rather, this way of thinking about history goes back to our earliest reflections on history. Though, just as today, there were those in the ancient world, who challenged whether all this change was indicative of real progress.

Progress and Knowledge

In ancient days, as in the current century, a more convincing case could be made that there was progress in some areas rather than others. And like today, our knowledge of the world, if not our wisdom, appeared a cumulative matter that grew as it was passed on to the next generation.

The first full and clear statement of the continued progress of knowledge into the indefinite future is to be found in the writings of the Roman stoic philosopher Seneca who wrote:

> There are many peoples today who are ignorant of the causes of eclipses of the moon, and it has only recently been demonstrated among ourselves. The day will come when time and human diligence will clear up problems which are now obscure. We divide the few years of our lives unequally between study and vice, and it will therefore be the work of many generations to explain such phenomena as comets. One day our posterity will marvel at our ignorance of causes so clear to them.
>
> How many new animals have we first come to know in the present age? In time to come men will know much that is unknown to us. Many discoveries are reserved for future ages, when our memory will have faded from men's minds. We imagine ourselves initiated in the secrets of nature; we are standing on the threshold of her temple.[12]

And,

> Much remains to do; much will remain; and no one born after thousands of centuries will be deprived of the chance of adding something.[13]

What distinguishes Seneca's vision is that unlike the seventeenth- and eighteenth-century apostles of progress, in Seneca, and in the intervening centuries, there is no broad assumption that progress with respect to knowledge means an increase in human virtue, well-being, or happiness. Either it is thought that these are independent matters or it is suspected that increased knowledge might itself be the cause of human unhappiness.

Thus in the earliest myths, be it The Garden of Eden or the Decline from the Golden Age, it is ignorance not knowledge which is associated with human virtue and happiness. Knowledge is associated with the forbidden, and its acquisition is associated with theft, dishonesty and disrespect in relation to the gods. And thus there is a heavy price to be paid for increasing knowledge.

Seneca is despairing about human virtue and happiness. Taking issue with a contemporary who celebrated their modern world, he makes a critical distinction among kinds of knowledge, distinguishing wisdom and philosophy from ingenuity, saying:

> Posidonius says: "When men were scattered over the earth, protected by caves or by the dug-out shelter of a cliff or by the trunk of a hollow tree, it was philosophy that taught them to build houses." But I, for my part, do not hold that philosophy devised these shrewdly-contrived dwellings of ours which rise story upon story, where city crowds against city, any more than that she invented fish preserves, that are enclosed for the purposes of saving men's gluttony from having to run the risk of storms and in order that, no matter how wildly the sea is raging, luxury may have its safe harbors in which to fatten fancy breeds of fish. . . . Was it not enough for man to provide himself a roof of any chance covering and to contrive for himself some natural retreat without the help of art and without trouble? Believe me that was a happy age, before the days of architects, before the days of builders! All this sort of thing was born when luxury was being born.
>
> . . . . A thatched roof once covered free men; under marble and gold dwells slavery.
>
> On another point also I differ from Posidonious, when he holds that mechanical tools were the invention of wise men . . . it was man's ingenuity, not his wisdom, that discovered all these devices.
>
> . . . . The things that are indispensable require no elaborate pains for their acquisition; it is only the luxuries that call for labour. Follow nature, and you will have no need for skilled craftsmen.[14]

Here, 2,000 years ago, we have the link being made between a doctrine of progress and a philosophy of simple living. With progress in ingenuity, that is technology, we have a variety of new products and processes. We have apartment houses, and architects and aquaculture! Invention, mechanical skill, ingenuity, labor, or to call it what it is: economic growth. All of this (for Seneca) emerges from human vice and foolishness. Before such luxury men were free and there was little need for labor. The path of wisdom and happiness lay elsewhere.

In a very severe way, Seneca advocates restricting economic activity to the satisfaction of only our most basic needs. He tells us:

> Houses, shelter, creature comforts, food, and all that has now become the source of vast trouble, were ready at hand, free to all, and obtainable for trifling pains. For the limit everywhere corresponded to the need; it is we that have made all other things valuable, we that have made them admired, we that have caused them to be sought for by extensive and manifold devices . . . that moderation which nature prescribes, which limits our desires by resources restricted to our needs, has abandoned the field . . . .[15]

Seneca's advocacy of a simple life and his despairing vision of what happens in history have a common root—his judgement about what is important. If one sees in the simple life the full resources for whatever happiness and nobility is possible for mankind, then one is not likely to see history as a story of progress.

What we do not find in Seneca's distinction between ingenuity (technology, economic growth) and wisdom, is the idea that they could indeed be combined. Neither Seneca nor Aristotle envisioned technology and the growth of productivity as opening the way for the masses of mankind to be freed from toil or freed to live a life that was economically modest but abundant in the higher aspects of life. For Seneca this would have been unnecessary for, as a stoic, he maintained that almost nothing of a material nature was really necessary for the good life. Whereas for Aristotle, the problems of the mass of humankind simply did not arise.

How They Overcame Homer

In the seventeenth century boundless confidence and pride in scientific progress expanded into the more general assertion of human progress, both that it had occurred, was occurring, and would continue to occur. These assertions were contrasted with the perspective of the Renaissance that emphasized the greatness of the classical achievements and took pride in their rediscovery and in having regained the heights achieved centuries before. As was the case with Seneca, there were those who questioned the sweeping claims. The issue was not so much whether or not there would be continued progress in the future, but rather whether or not genuine progress had in fact been made. In the seventeenth century, the issue emerged as "The Quarrel Between the Moderns and the Ancients"—a phrase used to describe an on-going intellectual exchange which lasted over a century, primarily in France and England.

This quarrel is interesting in several respects. First there is the sheer fact that for one hundred years there was an extended intellectual debate over whether mankind actually makes progress. Second, to some extent it is out of this debate that the modern idea of progress emerges, and thus the terms of the debate reveal not just the factual conclusions of the participants but their deeper definitions and values. And finally, joining this debate allows us to again enter into the big question of what happens in history. Who was right? Were (or are) the moderns superior to the ancients?

Bury, the great historian of the Idea of Progress, identifies the earliest writing on the subject as that of the Italian, Alessandro Tassoni, in his *Miscellaneous Thoughts* published in 1620. But Tassoni refers to "the quarrel" as a "current dispute," so its origins are obscure.[16] Tassoni, himself a poet and knowing his enemy, leveled an attack on Homer, identifying faults in language, plot, characterization, and imagery. He concluded that modern writers were on the whole superior to the authors of the ancient classics.

Fifteen years later, in 1635 the attack on Homer was renewed, this time in France. One of the founders of the Academie Francaise, a dramatist named Boisrobert, speaking to that body delivered a violent attack on the ancient poet. Indeed, it was Homer who was the ancient most frequently vilified.

A central voice in the attack on the ancients was Charles Perrault, remembered today as the author of *Cinderella* and *Sleeping Beauty*. Perrault made one particular contribution; in his account the issue shifts away from the simple comparison of modern and ancient works. He argues for the superiority of modern accomplishments on the basis of general processes which guarantee that that which is later will be superior. Thus knowledge advances with time. Perrault does not claim for the moderns themselves any inherent superiority of talent or genius. Rather he argues that nature is the same at all times. Those of the present have the same natural ability as those who came before, but being later, their works in both science and art are superior.

This line of thinking—that there are at work general processes whereby advance is assured—increasingly serves to build confidence in future progress. Indeed, a great deal of effort, especially in the nineteenth century, will focus on the identification and specification of such processes. Moreover, broadly opposed political philosophies will emerge based in part on whether or not these processes require for their full operation that we understand them and deliberately manipulate the world in accord with them.[17]

As Bury points out, Perrault did not extrapolate his process of progress into the indefinite future. Quite the contrary, he wrote:

> Our age had, in some sort, arrived at the summit of perfection. And since for some years the rate of the progress is much slower and appears almost insensible—as the days seem to cease lengthening when the solstice is near—it is pleasant to think that probably there are not many things for which we need envy future generations.[18]

The exposition of the fuller version of the progress of knowledge was left to Perrault's contemporary, Bernard de Fontenelle, author of *Dialogues of the Dead and Digression on the Ancients and the Moderns*. Like Perrault, Fontenelle argues from an exploration of the processes of change that in physiological terms men of his time are the same as those of ancient times. He dismisses the effects of climate as a determining factor. And he infers that whatever differences exist are due to either the passage of time or social conditions.

Fontenelle saw mathematics, physics, and medicine as cumulative, and thought it a natural process that in these areas those that come later will know more. The process envisaged was not entirely linear, but involved the elimination of a multitude of false routes. Error was part of the cumulative process whereby advance was achieved. And similarly he noted that, of necessity, those that came first would be the authors of the first discoveries. But he felt this entitled neither group to greater distinction.

Fontenelle takes a big step. He separates out from this process poetry and eloquence, arguing that they do not depend on correct reasoning and do not require a long course of experiments. In these areas he maintained that perfection might be attained in a few centuries. While the ancients might not be surpassed, they could be equaled.

With respect to the role of social circumstances, Fontenelle did not see them as playing a decisive creative or shaping role, but rather believed that they may, at points, (e.g. war) provide a breach in the ongoing process. But to the process whereby knowledge expanded there was a kind of necessity. Knowledge could be slowed down or blocked, but in time it would resume.

Fontenelle thus provided the two final ingredients to the idea of the progress of knowledge, that it would proceed indefinitely into the future and that this indefinite extension was necessarily the case. If Seneca also came to all of these conclusions, they did not take firm root in ancient times. However, with Fontenelle this concept was part of the general rationalism of the period and ultimately emerged as the wider idea of progress which encompassed social progress.

On this Fontenelle was also like Seneca. Neither believed in the connection between progress in knowledge and progress with respect to either human virtue or human well being. The difference however is that, for Seneca, if neither human virtue, nor well being, (nor, I might add, creativity and aesthetic accomplishment) progressed, then there was no progress in what is most important. In Fontenelle one finds a change in emphasis. While like Seneca, he does not believe that there is progress in wisdom or virtue, he celebrates what does progress—scientific knowledge. The difference it seems, is that Seneca believed that technological progress, in fact, makes us worse off. It draws us away from a more simple and free life towards a more artificial way of being.

In England, somewhat separately the quarrel between the ancients and the moderns was also pursued. Perhaps the most enduring contribution is Jonathon Swift's *A Full and True Account of the Battle Fought Last Friday Between the Ancient and the Modern Books in St. James's Library*. Known for short as *The Battle of the Books*, it details how inside the royal library the books of the ancients and the moderns came to life and did battle.

That Swift would conceptualize the conflict between the ancients and the moderns as a conflict between their books is more than a hint as to where he himself comes out. If ultimately the issue at stake in the debates over history is "what matters," for Swift the answer is "books." Books capture the value of a civilization, and like Duauf the ancient Egyptian scribe, Swift believes that it is books that we should love.

In a clear identification with Homer, Swift wrote the key battle scene of *The Battle of the Books* in the style of *The Iliad*. And, best of all, using a touch of Homer's own style, Homer himself becomes one of Swift's characters and enters the combat to vanquish his modern challengers:

> Then Homer slew W—sl—y with a kick of his Horse's heel; He took Perrault by mighty Force out of his Saddle, then hurl'd him at Fontenelle, with the same Blow dashing out both their Brains.[19]

The Battle ends with a defender of the Moderns (Wotton) being chased (and slain) by an ally of the Ancients (Boyle) in much the same fashion as Achilles chased Hector. Swift offers this good-bye to the dispatched Wotten: "And happy and immortal shall you be, if all my Wit and Eloquence can make you."[20] And again, Swift is right, it is Swift, through his dispatch of Wotton who has given him what immortality he has.

This final victim, Charles Wooten, in his *Reflections Upon Ancient and Modern Learning*, did, however, make an important contribution. He deepened the distinction between art and knowledge. In the former he places poetry, oratory, architecture, painting, and statuary. In the later: mathematics, natural science, physiology, and their dependencies. He maintained that in some of the arts the ancients were superior to all who came after. Here he strengthens a direction that Fontenelle was moving along. This distinction was widely accepted throughout the eighteenth century as literature and art were viewed as distinct from the general progress perceived in all other areas.

This is particularly interesting because the quarrel started roughly at the opening of the seventeenth century with the attack on Homer, and it appears to close with a sharper distinction between art and science and with a full idea of the indefinite progress of science. And in the eighteenth century it is on this basis that the extension is made to social progress as a whole. This foreshadows a notion of social progress that is divorced from aesthetic or moral progress. Indeed, this is part of the general mechanism in terms of which the Idea of Progress is able to achieve credibility: the *value base in terms of which progress is maintained gets narrower and narrower*. Now, rather than arguing that Homer has been equaled or surpassed, the entire realm of art, literature, and general sensibility is pushed to the side as a matter that no longer counts for much. The same is true of the concern with moral virtue, the central criteria employed by Seneca.

Thus, the Idea of Progress becomes plausible not merely because of the scientific revolution, but because there has been a shift in the relative weight given to the alternative criteria for assessing whether or not there has been progress.

Specifically, the emergence of the Idea of Progress required stripping from our definition of what counts as "progress" the aesthetic and moral dimensions of life. Instead, what we have left is the unstoppable progress of technology and its utilization in the production of the things of economic life. Thus, to think of history as the story of the inevitable improvement in the human condition, and to think of ourselves as fortunate consumers of an ever expanding material pie is really to think of two sides of the same coin.

Mandeville's Fable of the Bees

Aristotle, Seneca, and peoples of the quite different religious orientations which dominated both the Middle Ages and the Reformation found common ground in the impossibility of conceptualizing human progress primarily in technological and economic terms, divorced from matters of human personality, character, and behavior. Whether it was a matter of ancient virtues of creativity, of artistic and literary perfection, or of piety, honesty, and religious virtue, there was little to celebrate in economic expansion per se.

The opposite perspective emerges most powerfully in the beginning of the eighteenth century, crystalized in the works of Bernard Mandeville. In 1705, halfway between the one hundred and fifty years that separate the landing of the Puritans in the New World and the publication of *The Wealth of Nations*, Bernard Mandeville published a twenty-six page poem called "The Grumbling Hive: or Knaves Turned Honest." In 1714, the poem reappeared as part of a much larger work entitled *The Fable of the Bees: or, Private Vices, Publick Benefits*. This larger work, which ran to several hundred pages, was a detailed explanation of the various theses maintained in the poem. Subsequent editions enlarged Mandeville's commentary on his own poem.

The book created considerable scandal, and at one point was determined to be a public nuisance by the Grand Jury of Middlesex. Ultimately Mandeville's explications required an additional work: *The Fable of the Bees: Part II*.

Mandeville's poem is an attack directed at those that would live the simple life. When Mandeville wrote his poem, the great utopian experiment in religiously based simple living, the effort to build a "New England" was not yet one hundred years old; the Plymouth Colony having been founded in 1620.

All had not gone well for the project of simple living. From the pulpits of New England the clergy denounced a materialism that had betrayed the pious ideals of earlier generations. Yet the impulse towards pious simplicity was still very much alive, and the great religious awakening of the 1730's that swept through the colonies and called people back to a simple piety was still decades away.

Mandeville was not concerned with New England, but with England herself. His tale can be read as a cautionary message: look what would happen here if those seekers after the simple life of virtue were to gain the upper hand.

The basic poem appears to be a simple tale. It is the story of a flourishing hive of bees that, not having the sense to leave well enough alone, prayed to the God Jove that they be made virtuous. Jove answered their prayer, but virtue proved their ruin. My primary concern is less with Mandeville's novel empirical thesis (that private vice is beneficial to the public good), than it is with the values that are implicit in Mandeville's thought. As we shall see, it is in this respect that Mandeville can be viewed as a contemporary voice. His way of thinking about economic issues bears much in common with the way we approach questions of economic life.

Stripped to its essentials Mandeville is telling us that a thriving prosperous economy is what is important and that, if it turns out that such prosperity requires behavior and character which violates religious, moral, or spiritual ideals, then we best not trouble ourselves about such ideals.

Mandeville is the intentional voice of the great separation of economic life from any project of human transcendence. He differs in one main respect from contemporary voices. He is absolutely clear-eyed about the corruption he accepts, while in contemporary life the separation he represented has advanced to such an extent, that we do not even perceive economic life within the larger context of our ideals for human life and character.

Like many others, his tale is that of The Fall. But it is not a fall from grace, innocence, or purity. Mandeville's Eden has a very particular character. Consider the happy state in which his bees originally find themselves:

> A Spacious Hive well stockt with Bees,
> That liv'd in Luxury and Ease;
> And yet as fam'd for Laws and Arms,
> As yielding large and early Swarms;
> Was counted the great Nursery
> Of Sciences and Industry.[21]

The Hive is not just man's social life, it is life within the nation-state. It is life under a particular government "fam'd for Laws and Arms." The central accomplishment of that country is the achievement of a life of ease and luxury. It is this that will be lost; not the spiritual innocence commonly ascribed to Paradise. The bees in Mandeville's Paradise are far from innocent.

Among the inhabitants of the Hive there were "Sharpers, Parasites, Pimps, Players, Pick Pockets, Coiners, Quacks, South-sayers." This, of course, might be true of any society; there are always those that prey on it from the outside. But Mandeville tells us that while "These were call'd Knaves, . . . the grave Industrious were the same. . . . All Trades and Places knew some Cheat, No Calling was without Deceit."

He then proceeds to describe, profession by profession, the universal deceit. He describes lawyers whose art was in "raising feuds" and inflating fees, of doctors who valued "Fame and Wealth Above the Drooping Patient's Health." He tells us of a clergy that allowed men to "hide their

Sloth, Lust, Avarice and Pride," of a military in which while "Some valiant Gen'rals fought the Foe, Others took Bribes to let them go." It is the same with public servants who robbed "the very Crown they saved"; and of judges "brib'd with Gold."

Thus, Mandeville paints a picture of an entire society that is untrue to the values inherent in their social roles. It is a picture of decadence and corruption, but of a very particular kind. It is a corruption in which the pursuit of money supplants all the values that are inherent to the activity and profession in which people are engaged. It is precisely the kind of destruction of the integrity of each realm of life that Aristotle warned of. Indeed Aristotle even offered as examples of such corruption doctors and soldiers.

But Mandeville views it all with an easy eye. Having painted this vivid picture, he takes his novel turn, maintaining that all this is to the good:

> Thus every Part was full of Vice,
> Yet the whole Mass a Paradise;
> Flatter'd in Peace, and fear'd in Wars,
> They were th' Esteem of Foreigners,
> And lavish of their Wealth and Lives,
> The Balance of all other Hives.
> Such were the Blessings of that State;
> Their Crimes conspir'd to make them Great.[22]

He then proceeds to sketch how this worked. It seems that each vice produced some benefit. Thus,

> The Root of Evil, Avarice,
> That damne'd ill-natur'd baneful Vice,
> Was Slave to Prodigality,
> That nouble Sin; whilst Luxury
> Employ'd a Million of the Poor,
> And odious Pride a Million more:
> Envy it self, and Vanity,
> Were Ministers of Industry;
> Their darling Folly, Fickleness,
> In Diet, Furniture and Dress,
> That strange ridic'lous Vice, was made
> The very Wheel that turn'd the Trade.[23]

Mandeville's perception of "modern" life found its echoes two centuries later in Veblen and Galbraith. He zeroes right in on the issue of consumption; he looks at what lies behind consumer demand, and he finds vice and folly, vanity and envy, and even the fashion industry! Yet he embraces it all. And what is the central benefit he cites? It is the very luxuries and pleasures of economic growth that Seneca distained when he distinguished wisdom from ingenuity:

> Thus, Vice nurs'd Ingenuity,
> Which join'd with Time and Industry,
> Had carry'd Life's Conveniencies
> Its real Pleasures, Comforts, Ease,
> To such a Height, the very Poor
> Liv'd better than the Rich before,
> And nothing could be added more.[24]

Here we have the celebration of modern economic life. It is the sharp polar opposite of the perspective voiced by Mandeville's contemporary, the Quaker John Woolman, and sometimes it almost seems as if Mandeville and Woolman were debating before a single audience. Mandeville's values are the ones that have dominated our economic thought. Since Mandeville first stated it, it has been repeated a thousand times, jobs and income, employment and higher per capita GNP. This is the bottom line.

The tale continues. The bees are undone because of their pursuit of virtue. They failed to recognize "the Bounds of Bliss." They called out for honesty, and Jove, in anger, "rid the bawling Hive of Fraud."

Bit by bit disaster sets in. With a change in motivation and appetite market demand collapses. "The Price of Land and houses falls"; "The building Trade is quite destroyed, Artificers are not employ'd."

> The slight and fickle Age is past;
> And Clothes, as well as Fashions, last.
> Weavers, that join'd rich Silk with Plate,
> And all the Trades subordinate,
> Are gone. . . .[25]
>
> As Pride and Luxury decrease,
> So by degrees they leave the Seas,
> Not Merchants now, but Companies
> Remove whole Manufactories.
> All Arts and Craft neglected lie;
> Content, the Bane of Industry,

> Makes 'em admire their homely Store,
> And neither seek nor covet more.[26]

Ultimately, they are attacked by external foes, they fight, and are forced to retreat. Many die, and the survivors fly off to a hollow tree. Implicit in the poem is an emphasis on and an argument for enhancing the power of the nation state. The pre-Fall Hive is "fam'd for Law and Arms" and the ultimate denouement of the virtuous Hive occurs because they are attacked from without. Thus, the economy must be thought of as within a violent competitive international arena. National defense issues are central to issues of economic life.

As a diagnostician Mandeville is fascinated by the issue of human character. And the categories he is most concerned with are those of the Christian tradition: avarice, envy, vanity, pride, etc. But he simply is untroubled by finding that such characteristics and motives pervade human life. Mandeville not only doubts that much progress can be made in the elimination of base motives, he is not even attracted to such transformations. If anything, he is amused by the human spectacle.

Moreover, it is not that there are some other set of characteristics or virtues that he is concerned about (e.g. Aristotelian courage or Nietzschean vitality). He simply is not seized by the project of our becoming very different than we are. Independent of his view of the utility of vices Mandeville would not be concerned to eliminate them. He simply accepts human beings as they are, no matter how they are. In this, in fact, he echoes the contemporary "value-free" economist. The latter does not make any assessment about people's desires; he takes them as a given. In academic jargon, economic performance is to be judged in terms of the ability to move to the outermost curve on a preference map. He states that he is of the "Opinion, that whether men be good or bad, what they take delight in is their pleasure . . . we ought to dispute no more about Men's Pleasures than their Tastes."[27]

The question of what it is to really be better off is of central importance to any critique of economics. Certainly, one major criterion for the evaluation of economic circumstances and alternative economic systems is whether or not the population, or any representative individual, is better off in one or the other. Mandeville tells us that "The very Poor Liv'd better than the Rich before" and we look to his explication to reveal his understanding of what it is to have "liv'd better."

He writes:

> If we trace the most flourishing Nations in their Origin, we shall find that in the remote Beginnings of every Society, the richest and most considerable Men among them were a great while destitute of a great many Comforts of Life that are now enjoy'd by the meanest and most humble Wretches.[28]

Here his answer appears to be quite simple. One's life is better insofar as one has more of "the Comforts of Life." In the contemporary idiom, he may be said to hold an opulence notion of standard of living, those who have more things live at a higher standard than those with less.[29]

Mandeville goes on to explain how our notion of what constitutes a luxury is constantly changing:

> Many things which were once look'd upon as the Invention of Luxury, are now allow'd even to those that are so miserably poor as to become the Objects of publick Charity, nay counted so necesary, that we think no Human Creature ought to want them.[30]

He then goes on to identify some of the remarkable luxuries that are now available to all. He calls our attention to "the most ordinary Yorkshire Cloth," saying, "What depth of Thought and Ingenuity, what Toil and Labor, and what length of Time must it have cost, before Man could learn from a Seed to raise and prepare so useful a Product as Linen."[31] And he further points out:

> The Arts of Brewing, and making Bread, have by slow degrees been brought to the Perfection they now are in, but to have invented them at once, and a priori, would have required more Knowledge and a deeper Insight into the Nature of Fermentation, than the greatest Philosopher has hitherto been endowed with; yet the Fruits of both are now enjoy'ed by the meanest of our Species, and a starving Wretch knows not how to make a more humble, or a more modest Petition, than by asking for a Bit of Bread, or a Draught of Smal Beer.[32]
>
> From Caves, Huts, Hovels, Tents and Barracks, with which Mankind took up at first we are come to warm and well-wrought Houses, and the meanest habitations to be seen in Cities, are regular Buildings contriv'd by Persons skill'd in Proportions and Architecture. If the Ancient Britons and Gauls should come out of their Graves, with what Amazement wou'd they gaze on the mighty Structures everywhere rais'd for the Poor![33]

While Mandeville does not use the term "progress" to characterize the phenomenon he has focused upon, it is clear that he is offering a progressive vision of history. It moves in one direction, towards what is better. What had been thought of as luxuries are later considered necessities. It does not move in the reverse direction. It is a slow process; one which Mandeville sees as a process of human betterment, and what makes this credible is ultimately Mandeville's notion of what it is to be better off: to have more of what one desires from the marketplace.

From our point of view Mandeville's significance is that he perfectly captured in 1705 so much of the way in which we presently think about economic life. The central elements of his outlook are:

1. A lack of concern with whether higher or lower aspects of the human personality are brought to the fore in the economic realm.
2. His view of the economic realm as outside moral concerns, to be evaluated on its own terms (e.g. levels of employment, income, production, consumption).
3. His view that all classes gain as a result of economic growth.
4. His underlying identification of "living well" with living at a high level of material consumption.
5. His refusal to base policy judgments on any view of true human happiness other than those found within the actual behavior of economic agents. Desire is never in need of education, development or refinement.
6. His situating of economic policy within the world of national security and inter-state competition, with these areas providing the central criteria for policymaking.
7. His concern with the possibility of economic collapse and unemployment, and his focus on the importance of high levels of consumer demand as necessary for economic vitality.

These are all very much a part of contemporary thinking. When Mandeville wrote they represented a dramatic break with the way the Western world had heretofore thought of the economic realm. Today, we take them for granted.

In the poem, when Mandeville maintains that the poor lived better than the rich before, it might seem that he has introduced a new criterion which would in fact represent moral progress over the way Aristotle viewed the good society—namely a concern for the poor. Yet this is not the case. His comments on how the poor live better today than in previous centuries are little more than rationalization. Indeed, in his attitudes toward the poor he is worse than indifferent. He states, "I have laid down as Maxims never to be departed from, that the Poor should be kept strictly to Work, and that it was Prudence to relieve their Wants, but Folly to cure them."[34]

And further, in explaining his opposition to providing free schools and provisions for the children of the poor, he wrote:

> Abundance of hard and dirty Labour is to be done, and coarse Living is to be complied with: Where shall we find a better Nursery for these Necessities than the Children of the Poor? None certainly are nearer to it or fitter for it. Besides that the things I called Hardships, neither seem nor are such to those who have been brought up to 'em, and know no better. There is not a more contented People among us, than those who work the hardest and are the least acquainted with the Pomp and Delicacies of the World.[35]

Mandeville continues:

> It being granted then, that abundance of Work is to be done, the next thing which I think to be likewise undeniable is, that the more cheerfully it is done the better, as well for those that perform it as for the rest of the Society. To be happy is to be pleas'd, and the less Notion a Man has of a better way of Living, the more content he'll be with his own . . . .
>
> As by discouraging Idleness with art and Steadiness you may compel the Poor to labour without Force, so by bringing them up in Ignorance you may inure them to real Hardships without being ever sensible themselves that they are such.[36]

A few rhetorical gestures notwithstanding, it is clear that for Mandeville the poor are a lesser form of humanity. Indeed, he is happy enough for them to live out their lives in total ignorance of their conditions—essentially as work animals. For him they are a mere means to greater objectives. When he speaks of public benefits, or of a flourishing economy, his concern is with the aggregate features of the economy and the polity that it sustains.

The fact that Mandeville is essentially unmoved either by equity concerns or by the wretchedness of the lives of those at the bottom, helps to explain why it is that he can remain content with society as he finds it.

Woolman's linkage between the pursuit of superfluous consumption and poverty, slavery and injustice (even if Mandeville accepted the connection) would have left him unmoved. He does not share in the passion for social justice that has animated the reformers and revolutionaries of the last several centuries.

Yet it was just this passion for a better world for the ordinary man that was to explode at the end of the eighteenth century with the French Revolution. From the perspective of the Revolution, the condition of everyman matters most of all and, with a new vision of what matters, comes a new way of thinking about progress and history.

No figure better exemplifies this passion and this new vision than the French mathematician, historian, and political leader, Condorcet.

Condorcet and the Progress of Everyman

Born into a noble family, the Marquis de Condorcet was a leading figure during the French Revolution. In 1789 he was elected to the Commune of Paris and in 1791 to the Legislative Assembly, ultimately becoming its president. Yet in 1793 as the revolution devoured itself, Condorcet went into hiding. Over a nine month period he developed a two hundred page plan for his intended great work. This *Sketch for a Historical Picture of the Progress of the Human Mind* is all we have of this vision; later that year he was arrested and died in prison at the age of fifty-one.

In Condorcet we find the Idea of Progress in full bloom. He expresses it thus:

> Nature has set no term to the perfection of human faculties; . . . the perfectibility of man is truly indefinite; . . . the progress of this perfectibility, from now onwards independent of any power that might wish to halt it, has no other limit than the duration of the globe upon which nature has cast us.[37]

What is particularly interesting in Condorcet is his reconceptualization of the real subject matter of history. When history is seen as political history, it is filled with particular events: wars, assassinations, coronations, declarations, and rebellions. To Condorcet this was secondary; there are certain critical events in history, even critical political events, but this is not what history is about. These events take on their importance only insofar as they bear on something else.

For Condorcet, there is really only one story. It is the story of how mankind comes into an awareness of its ability to think for itself. It is the discovery of the power we possess in our own reason, our ability to learn and assess the world, each of us relying on our own rational abilities, free from reliance upon authority.

The issue of authority is central to Condorcet's account. The theme is reminiscent of Charles Peirce's nineteenth century essay on "The Fixation of Belief" wherein Peirce considers the different ways in which people come to have and to hold their beliefs. He contrasts the "method of authority" with "the method of science." In Condorcet's world, this ultimate releasing of mankind from authority, that is, from the intellectual control of others, is the central theme of human history. So coming to be able to think for oneself, both in virtue of freedom from the control of others, as well as in terms of the actual capability of knowledgeable reflection constitutes mankind's attainment of maturity. This, for Condorcet, is what matters.

Along these lines it is possible to take as one's subject matter "the human mind" or "the human spirit" and to see this as something that evolves over time, at first embodied most completely in one people and then in another people, great thinker, or philosophy. Hegel in fact did something of this sort. But what is most striking about Condorcet is that rather than thinking of "the human mind" as an abstraction, he took as the central subject of history the mind or mentality of the ordinary person. And going beyond this, he set this evolution of the ways of thought of the ordinary person within the context of a political struggle between the ruled and the rulers.

The central value in terms of which Condorcet distinguishes those changes that constitute progress from those which do not is the "freedom of the mind." This however has to be understood as being composed not only of a freedom from intellectual tyranny, but also a positive freedom that consists of the acquisition of the methods of rational inquiry. For Condorcet this development of the mind, a freedom from superstition, a freedom from authority, and certain mental dispositions (e.g. intellectual self-confidence, habits of rational inquiry) is of ultimate value. Condorcet, as much as anyone before or since, conceives of progress and of the history of mankind in terms of a movement towards enlightenment, understood in both its psychological and social dimensions.

Given what we said earlier about the centrality of books to the vision of progress (are those of the ancients superior to those of the moderns?) it is interesting to note that books continue, though in a different way, to be central for Condorcet. He focuses on the invention of printing. This invention serves to mark off the seventh from the eighth stage in human history. Only the invention of the alphabet, which marks the third from the fourth stage, has an equal place. In blissful ignorance of our own century, though sounding very much like those who now sing the praises of the Internet, he wrote:

> Has not printing freed the education of the people from all political and religious shackles? It would be vain for any despotism to invade all the schools; vain for it to issue cruel edicts prescribing and dictating the errors with which men's minds were to be infected, and the truths from which they were to be safeguarded. . . . The instruction that every man is free to receive from books in silence and solicitude can never be completely corrupted. It is enough for there to exist one corner of free earth from which the press can scatter its leaves. How with the multitude of different books, with the innumerable copies of each book, of reprints that can be made available at a moments notice, how could it be possible to bolt every door, to seal every crevice through which truth aspires to enter? For though this was difficult enough even when it was only a question of destroying a few copies of a manuscript to annihilate it for ever, . . . has it not become impossible today when it would be necessary to maintain an absolutely ceaseless vigilance and an unresting activity?[38]

Thus, whether as the intrinsic touchstones of progress, or as the guarantor of intellectual liberation, books were again affirmed in their import. While enlightenment is at the core of Condorcet's conception of progress, it remained for Condoret only part of the story. At the same time, he parallels enlightenment and an increase in people's happiness as the criterion of progress. Here, as before, he is exceptionally clear in directing our focus towards those invisible millions upon millions who constitute the bulk of humanity. Indeed, he tells us that what actually happens to these people is the real touchstone of progress and the subject of history.

I will quote this at length, as it represents a genuine turning point in human understanding:

> Such are the subjects that ought to enter into a historical sketch of the progress of the human mind. In presenting it, we shall endeavor above all to exhibit the influence of this progress on the opinions and the welfare of the great mass of the people, in the different nations, at the different stages of their political existence. . . .[39]

> Up till now, the history of politics, like that of philosophy or of science, has been the history of only a few individuals: that which really constitutes the human race, the vast mass of families living for the most part on the fruits of their labor, has been forgotten, and even of those who follow public professions, and work not for themselves but for society, who are engaged in teaching, ruling, protecting or healing others, it is only the leaders who have held the eye of the historian. . . .
>
> It is this most obscure and neglected chapter of the history of the human race, for which we can gather so little material from records that must occupy the foreground of our picture. And whether we are concerned with a discovery, an important theory, a new legal system, or a political revolution, we shall endeavor to determine its consequences for the majority in each society. For it is there that one finds the true subject matter of philosophy, for all intermediate consequences may be ignored except in so far as they eventually influence the greater mass of the human race.
>
> It is only when we come to this final link in the chain that our contemplation of historical events and the reflections that occur to us are of true utility. Only then can we appreciate men's true claims to fame, and can take real pleasure in the progress of their reason; only then can we truly judge the perfection of the human race.
>
> The idea that everything must be considered in relation to this single point of reference is dictated both by justice and by reason.[40, 41]

This is a great contribution. Both in its sophistication and its morality it truly represents progress over previous centuries of discourse. Here Condorcet not only puts forward a new conception of history, but a new standard in terms of which to decide whether or not history can be viewed as the story of progress: the condition of the common person.

But what does Condorcet mean by improvements in the condition of the common person? On the one hand he has this rich notion of enlightenment. On the other hand, when he speaks of human happiness and of those things that will advance it, he operates on a very basic and practical level. His predictions for progress in the future, which are in many instances prescient, include:

- voluntary birth control based on "a duty towards those who are not yet . . . not to give them existence but to give them happiness";[42]
- "New instruments, machines and looms" that "add to man's strength and can improve at once the quality and the accuracy of his productions, and *can diminish the time and labour that has to*

be expended on them [precisely what Aristotle did not understand—JMS]. The obstacles still in the way of this progress will disappear, accidents will be foreseen and prevented, the insanitary conditions that are due to the work itself or to the climate will be eliminated";[43]

- increased agricultural productivity;
- social insurance, guaranteeing people in old age a "means of livelihood produced partly by their own savings and partly by the savings of others who make the same outlay, but die before they need to reap the reward";[44]
- an indefinite expansion of the life span through improved health and "the end of infectious and hereditary diseases and illnesses brought on by climate, food, or working conditions."[45]

What we find here are many of the elements that are emphasized in the politics of simplicity—a reduction in the arduousness of work, increases in the amount of leisure, increasing economic security, and improved health. Essentially, Condorcet is fleshing out how one would think of economic progress if one took it from the point of view of the life of the common man. Not as Mandeville asserted in terms of greater and greater luxury, but in terms of finally satisfying the core economic needs of everyman.

Condorcet himself was a transitional figure, and the values that he used in defining progress still included the older criteria—the moral perfectability of mankind. But this, as well as Condorcet's rich notion of enlightenment, did not endure. What did continue, however, was the notion that in deciding whether or not mankind has made progress, one should look at the conditions of ordinary people. Here however Condorcet's concrete approach to material well being, in terms of health, food, security, leisure, and quality of work, never took hold.

Instead, what emerged was a cross between Mandeville's value-free endorsement of whatever the market produces, and Condorcet's concern for everyman. In contemporary terms, this is growth with equity. For economists it is a rise in per capita GNP coupled with a concern for the Gini coefficient (which measures the degree of inequality of income). In short it is an embrace of the ever-expanding cornucopia of consumption, but with a concern that everyone get their share.

The French social theorist Sorel maintained that the Idea of Progress was the ideology of the middle class. The values it ultimately embodies are those that Seneca rejected; they are the values associated with having more things, with expanded production, consumption, and acquisition. In short, they are the values associated with economic growth; the values of the economically rising class, the bourgeoisie. No one argued for progress on the grounds that there had been an expansion of the older values of the nobility: chivalry, military prowess, and personal fidelity. Nor was there progress to be found in terms of the Stoic values of inner freedom, self-understanding, wisdom, and peace. Nor are they successfully argued on the aesthetic grounds of art and literature. Rather the quarrel between the ancients and the moderns conceded that, in these terms, there may not have been progress. No, progress is evidenced first, as always, in the progress of knowledge and secondarily in the progress of technology and economic growth. So, one might say that given that the Idea of Progress is essentially a vision of history, the historical story that forms the dominant ideology is that of the dominant values, that of a rising and democratizing middle-class consumer.

Whatever the limitations of this conception of progress, what it represents is an assertion of the importance of what is happening to the middle class. And as almost everyone comes to think of themselves as middle class, it represents a triumph of equality. Ultimately progress comes to be defined in terms of the well-being of individuals and, at least in theory, all individuals count and count of equal significance.

The fit between the idea of progress and the middle class consumer is not accidental. For progress to be a plausible vision of history, it had to be understood in terms of a narrower range of criteria. This means abandoning as benchmarks those areas in which progress is hard to find, such as moral virtue, aesthetic sensibility and enlightenment. But if we define progress in terms of a widening array of material goods for a wider and wider group of people, then evidence abounds. And analogously, in order to sustain the middle class consumer in his getting and spending there was need for a view of history which taught that this is what life is about, this is the dimension with respect to which what happens in time is significant.

Today, we can dispense with the grand Idea of Progress, with the belief that history has been and will continue to be the story of progress. As a view of history this is both impoverished and naive. What we cannot dispense with however, is a definition of progress. Ultimately this is a matter of values, and is at the heart of any politics. For a politics of simplicity, a good starting point is the definition implicit in Condorcet: an emphasis on the ordinary person, yet a concern with the extraordinary potentials of the human mind. This includes an awareness of the aesthetic realm coupled with a concern for the practical facts of economic life. This concern is with the material world but, rather than accepting unending acquisitiveness, it focuses on meeting core needs, increasing leisure, and reducing the arduousness of work. And with this, an essential recognition of the importance of freedom is understood, in part, as each person's ability to think through for themselves the deepest questions of life and history and then to live accordingly.

Towards a More Adequate Definition of Progress

Interestingly, while the term "progress" does not play an important role in contemporary economics, the one area in economics in which there is considerable debate and innovation with respect to such matters is in what is called "development economics." Unfortunately this is generally understood as the economics of poor countries, but the issues apply to the rich countries as well. Here it is the term "development" that is the central issue.

In discussions of the Third World, the term is used with respect to a wide variety of subjects. Thus, we speak of economies as being undeveloped. We speak of political development. We speak of less-developed countries, of developing nations, and of underdeveloped societies. A comprehensive theory of development should offer an account of the relationship between these different applications.

Rather than focusing on economies, nations, or countries as that which gets developed, we might focus on societies, and say that a developed economy is one that sustains a developed society. But what is it for a society to be developed? And is this the most basic notion of development? I think not. Instead we might say that societies are developed insofar as they give rise to human beings that are developed. It is the notion of the developed human being that is our central concept.

Insofar as there are a multiplicity of alternative conceptions of a developed human being, there will be a multiplicity of notions of a developed society and quite possibly of a developed economy. The immediate question has to do with how one is to link an appraisal of societies to judgments about the kind of human beings they give rise to. One perspective emphasizes the heights of human development. Here one would look primarily for greatness or its absence. Surveying world history from this perspective is the kind of enterprise that was undertaken by those caught up in the debate between the Ancients and the Moderns. And when we do this, we do find remarkable differences. There are certain periods in which the human spirit seems to flourish, in which a kind of brilliance and power of intellect and sensibility stands out. In Western history we typically identify the classical period in ancient Greece and the Italian Renaissance as two outstanding periods of human development.

From this perspective development is not linear and progressive; it comes and goes. Thus mankind's cumulative accomplishments are of less importance and those who argued for the ancients had a plausible case. One can quite reasonably argue that the heights of human development were attained over two thousand years ago; that in ancient Greece there was more creativity and human energy and a sharper sensibility and aesthetic awareness than at any time since. Their great thinkers were bolder and wittier than ours, their command of language and rhetoric more skillful. Their artistic creations were unparalleled, their skill and imagination rarely seen in human history. By contrast we appear confused, coarse, uncertain, mechanical, depressed, and misguided.

Against such a perspective, what have we to offer to suggest that, say, twentieth- (or twenty-first-) century America represents a more developed society than Athens of the fifth century B.C.E.? Our list might look something like this:

1. We know vastly more. The Greeks lived in considerable ignorance about the nature of the human and physical world. We have all the benefits of 2,500 years of discovery.
2. Our average level of consumption is considerably higher. True, one might doubt that anyone could have lived much more luxuriously than those that lived best then, but on the average we are considerably better off.
3. Their society depended on a slave class and an agrarian class that did not significantly partake in most of those things we celebrate with respect to ancient Greece, whereas over 50 percent of our high school graduates attend college.
4. The condition of women, half of the population, is radically different now. In ancient Athens women were under the control and tutelage of men. They were married as children to mature males and rarely left the household compound. In general, they did not partake in the vast creativity nor in the democracy of Athens.
5. In terms of health and life span, we are considerably better off. True, the oldest today are much the same age as the oldest then,

but our average life span is over 70 years, while theirs was probably more like 20, with large numbers of children dying in infancy.

6. Presumably, the vast majority of the Greeks who had to work, worked much harder and longer than we have to. We have the advantage of our vast capital and technological base which provides us not only with more output, but requires less labor input.

What is interesting is that the case is not all that overwhelming. It is a strange mixture of considerations. Some seem very important; others, less so. What emerges more than anything else, however, is that our claim to be more developed stands primarily on the breadth of human development achieved rather than on the height. Broad social injustices toward slaves, women, and underclasses have been considerably overcome. Our highest peaks of education, consumption, psychic health, ease of life, and political participation may have been equaled or surpassed by many ancient Greeks, but in our society these benefits are more widespread.

The issue goes well beyond Greece. It is unlikely that there have been any societies in which some people were not more fully developed than we are as a whole. Even in societies steeped in superstition and ignorance, societies without a written history, societies attached to human sacrifice, we will find individuals learned in their traditions, masters of their oral histories, creators of art and dance and music. We may not find other societies achieving either the heights or the breadth of human excellence found in Athens. But for whatever human attribute we value, be it intelligence, wit, creativity, craft, physical attainments, compassion, or moral breadth, we will always be able to find individuals who put us to shame. There are essentially two things that we do not find. One is accurate information (or knowledge, if you will), and the other is the widespread distribution of physical well-being.

Our advantage with respect to knowledge comes little from ourselves; it is largely the accident of our being here rather than there. Most of us have absolutely no capacity for adding anything to the stock of what is known by mankind. Despite what Condorcet hoped, we are like most people have always been. We believe what we have been told. The difference is only that over the centuries mankind has made significant progress in attaining a vast stock of accurate information. Similarly, our greater incomes and wealth come not from possessing greater human capacities, but primarily because we are fortunate enough to have inherited an enormous stock of physical and intellectual capital which vastly enhances our labor productivity.

Our claim to developmental progress, then, rests on two points:

1. A vastly broader attainment of material well being and freedom;
2. Our vastly more extensive and accurate information and science.

The second of these is largely instrumental. The difference between people who believed the earth was flat and those who know it is round is simply not very important. What this suggests, then, is that our claim to greater development rests primarily on the breadth of well being. Given the horrors of human domination over others, and the terrible sufferings of starvation and early death that peoples have experienced, this is no small accomplishment. But it is only half of the story. Using both dimensions, the extent of development of various societies could be represented on a graph such as this:

Figure 6.1

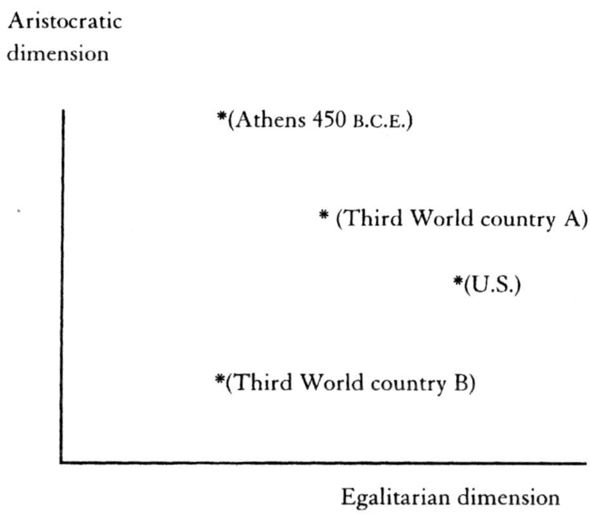

There are many ways to think of the vertical dimension. Some may consider it in terms of the spiritual level to which a society rises. Others might emphasize the moral virtues or, the aesthetics realm, or the intellectual. Taken together the two dimensions allow us to envision the developed society as an environment within which an ideal of the human person is attained both in height and in breadth—the greatest development of the greatest number.

Within this framework the case for a politics of simple living can be restated as the belief that the heights of human development are pluralistic, but that what they have in common is that they require a platform of achievement with respect to economic need. Once this platform of economic need satisfaction is achieved however, attaining fuller development requires that people turn away from the economic realm to pursue things more important, and to exercise their higher capabilities.

What we look for in a developed economy then is that it provides this general platform of freedom from the economic for all persons. And it is on this platform that we individually and collectively seek a higher form of life.

Notes

1. *The Instruction of Duauf*, quoted in Arnold Toynbee, *A Study of History*, Volume IV, (Oxford: Oxford University Press, 1951) p. 419.

2. Homer, *The Iliad*, translated by Robert Fitzgerald, (Garden City: Anchor Press, 1974) p. 150.

3. Ibid. p. 154.

4. Ibid. p. 526.

5. Ibid. p. 526.

6. Kitto, *The Greeks*, (Baltimore: Penguin Books, 1951) p. 44.

7. Ludwig Edelstein, *The Idea of Progress in Classical Antiquity* (Baltimore: Johns Hopkins Press), p. 35.

8. Simone Weil, "The Iliad: Poem of Might," *Simone Weil Reader*, ed. George A. Panichos (new York: David McKay Company, 1977), p.183.

9. Frederick Teggart, "The Idea of Progress: An Historical Analysis" in *The Idea of Progress*, ed. Frederick Teggart (Berkley: University of California Press, 1949).

10. Nisbet also rejects the idea that the "rediscovery" of the classical world occurred in the Renaissance; but what is important here is that that was the Renaissance perception.

11. Thucydides, *History of the Peloponnesian War*, translated by Rex Warner, (New York: Penguin Books, 1980), pp. 34-42. I was made aware of the significane of Thucydides for a history of the idea of progress by reading Robert Nisbet, *History of the Idea of Progress* (New York: Basic Books, 1980).

12. As quoted in J.B. Bury, *The Idea of Progress* (new York: Dover PUblications, 1960), pp 13-14. I draw heavily on Bury's account for much of this essay.

13. As quoted in Nisbet, *History of the Idea of Progress*, p.46.

14. Seneca, *Epistulae Morales*, in Teggart, *The Idea of Progress*, p. 95-96.

15. Ibid., p. 98.

16. An earlier consideration of the relative merits of the ancients and moderns can be found in Jean Bodin's *Method of Understanding History*, which was published in 1566.

Bodin cites various modern discoveries unknown to the ancients. See Nisbet, *History of the Idea of* Progress, p. 122.

17. In the seventeenth century Turgot and Adam Smith stand out among those who argued that nothing was more detrimental to economic growth than the deliberate efforts of the state to manipulate the economy.

18. Bury, *The Idea of* Progress, p.87.

19. Jonathan Swift, *The Battle of the Books*, in *A Tale of a Tub* . . . (Oxford: Clarendon Press, 1958). p 246.

20. Ibid. p. 258.

21. Bernard Mandeville, *The Fable of the Bees*, edited by F. B. Kaye, (Oxford, Oxford University Press, 1966), p. 17.

22. Ibid. p. 24.

23. Ibid. p. 25.

24. Ibid. p. 26.

25. Ibid. p. 34

26. Ibid. p. 35.

27. Ibid. p. 148.

28. Ibid. p. 169.

29. See Amartya Sen's essay in *Ethics of Consumption*, ed. David Crocker and Toby Linden (Lanham, Md.:Rowman and Littlefield, 1997).

30. Mandeville, *Fable of Bees*, 169.

31. Ibid. p. 170.

32. Ibid. p. 171.

33. Ibid. p. 171.

34. Ibid. p. 248.

35. Bernard Mandeville, "An Essay on Charity and Charity-Schools" in *Fable of the Bees*, p. 311.

36. Ibid. pp. 314-17.

37. Nicolas Condorcet, *Sketch for a Historical Picture of the History of the Progress of the Human Mind* (New York: The Noonday Press, 1955) p.4.

38. Ibid. p. 102.

39. Here, as elsewhere, he seems to be anticipating Marx. Would it be too much to say that Hegel found Condorcet standing on his feet, and stood him on his head, only to have Marx set him upright again?

40. Condorcet, *Sketch*, pp. 170-172.

41. Note that in this passage Condorcet speaks of societies at different "stages of their political existence;" in his general statement of the doctrine of the indefinite perfectibility of mankind he spoke of "the different stages of their development." Because of the centrality of enlightenment and because for Condorcet the issue of enlightenment is inextricably a political issue, he can be said to have a conception of development as political development.

42. Condorcet, *Sketch*, p. 189.

43. Ibid. p. 187.

44. Ibid. p. 181.

45. Ibid. P. 199.

7
The Monetary Illusion

If money is not the enemy, if money sometimes helps us attain a safer second-best or third-best or fourth-best life, it must be acknowledged that money does contribute to our confusion. Part of the mystery of why we go so wrong in life lies in the "illusion of money," by which I mean the illusion that the price of things tells us much about their true value.

What is fascinating about money is that we all know that it does not offer a meaningful picture of genuine wealth. For instance, is it not indisputable that much of what is most important to us—our children, our reputation, the love of another—has no price. This is a commonplace, known to all at the first instant of reflection. Yet, the moment we get up from the easy chair, we seem to set aside our reflections. Or perhaps, even while sustaining them, we cannot break away from thinking about wealth in monetary terms. We use money to measure both the income and the wealth of individuals and society. We use monetary measures to consider how income and wealth are distributed, and we use it to make comparisons with respect to standards of living—between different individuals, or between countries, or between two points in time—whether in our own life, or that of society as a whole.

We suffer from at least two kinds of blindness. First, we tend to measure the value of things in terms of their price; and second, we tend not to see the value of things that have no price. Let us consider these in turn.

The Difference Between Price and Value

Economists long ago pondered what initially seemed paradoxical, that some of the most valuable commodities, such as air and water, have little monetary value, while others, such as diamonds, are worth a great deal. In struggling with this anomaly, the distinction was made between exchange value and use value. *Exchange value* means the value that something has in virtue of its being exchangeable for some other item of value. We make these exchanges in the market, and in market economies we exchange labor and commodities for money, and money for commodities. Since money is the common element into which things are exchanged, exchange value can be measured by the amount of money that something exchanges for. The term we give to this is "price." When people inquire about the price of an item, they are asking, "How much money does one need to exchange in order to get it?" As economists came to greater clarity about these matters, explaining and predicting the prices of commodities emerged as a central task of economics.

Use value, on the other hand, was seen to mean the actual contribution to human welfare that the commodity makes. Everyone realized that when diamonds are compared to water, water is low in exchange value and high in use value, whereas diamonds were relatively low in use value but high in exchange value.

For a time, it was a challenge to economic theory to explain how this could be the case. Ultimately, the explanation was found in understanding that the price a commodity exchanges for is determined not by the importance of the commodity as a whole (e.g., water) but by its importance on the margin (e.g., one more gallon of water). Further, what was important on the margin was the cost of supplying one more unit, as well as the value to the purchaser of having one more unit.

Thus (assume that water is the only liquid), while one might exchange most of one's possessions for a gallon of water if none were available at all, one would give very little for an additional gallon if one already had plenty. Similarly, since an additional gallon can be brought to the market at very little cost, one need pay only a small price to induce the sale of an extra gallon. Whereas, if we reached a point at which bringing the extra gallon to market was very expensive (although water as a whole may remain inexpensive to provide), unless the price of water was at that high price, the last gallon would not be brought to market; and the same for the next to last and so forth. So, in order for any quantity of water to come to the market, its price must rise to the cost of supplying the last gallon. Thus, despite its almost infinite use value, water exchanges for little because it is abundant (we have limited desire for more) and because more can be obtained rather inexpensively.

What is sketched above is the solution that economists in the nineteenth century—the so-called marginalists, such as Alfred Marshall—found to the seeming paradox that things of great value (in use) could have little value (in exchange). But what is most interesting here is this: first, both before and after the paradox was explained, no one was in doubt as to the phenomenon—that there is no fixed correspondence between the market price and use value. And, second, *explaining the paradox made no difference.* We still continued to view the prices of things as adequate measures of their value, even though we knew they were not. Such is the hypnotic quality of money.

Suppose then that there are two people, and that they are in possession of exactly the same items, except that the second person has two of every item, whereas the first has only one. Thus, the second person has two houses, two cars, two blue coats, two refrigerators full of food, and so forth. The first person has only one house, one car, one blue coat, and one full refrigerator.

Insofar as we are measuring the extent of a person's assets by summing up the prices paid for the various items (or the price he could get if he sold them), the second person has twice the wealth of the first person. Having no doubt as to the difference between use value and exchange value, we know that this is nonsense. Moreover, if rather than two houses the person had a house twice as big, and rather than two cars, a car twice as long, it should be apparent to us that he still doesn't have twice the wealth of the first person. We know it is nonsense to believe that he does, yet we do so nonetheless.

The extent to which we suffer from such illusions is remarkable. It reflects something very deep about our culture, about how thoroughly our vision of things has been molded by markets and the exchanges that occur within them, and about how much of our life activity is organized around bringing things to market and bringing things back from market—most centrally, bringing ourselves (our labor, our skills) to market and bringing back home, in exchange, money or commodities.

Permanently dispelling the idea that the price you pay for something reflects its value is almost impossible. Nonetheless, it may help to reflect on the following:

- While the price of the physical necessities is often low and in some cases zero, their value is almost infinite. If they were in short supply, a billionaire would pay almost all he had for the food and water that you consume. Yet with these items of near infinite worth, having more than is necessary, or having fancy versions, is worth little more than having that which meets our needs.
- With respect to many of the commodities that we have, they would in fact be fantastically valuable (in monetary terms), if it weren't the case that they can be produced cheaply. Thus, consider your old car. Perhaps it is worth $2,000—but if, in fact, cars could not be made cheaply, or not made at all, your old car would be worth tens of thousands. If it were the only car, it would be worth millions. The same for your camera or your mirror or a pair of scissors, or a pencil or a piece of paper. Under some circumstances, these could be the most sought after, most amazing, most valuable (in monetary terms) items in the world.
- Whenever we buy something, we are doing so because we have judged that the thing is worth more to us than the price that is asked for it. That's the whole point of exchanging the money for the item. Sometimes this gap is enormous, and not merely with respect to necessities. Consider that it may only cost you $50 to buy a dog that you would not sell for thousands. What was the value of the $1 of painkiller that relieved the worst headache you ever had? How much was the best novel you ever read worth? The bicycle you had for ten years as a child—how did its value compare to the $50 paid for it?

The Value of Things That Typically Have No Price

In the 1960s and 1970s the women's movement called attention to a certain blindness with respect to the value of women's labor in the home. The basic problem was that neither the existence of women's labor nor its contribution was recognized, neither within the family nor within the larger society. In response an effort was made to "price out" women's labor at home, to point out what it would cost to hire someone to perform all these tasks. To move in this direction, to focus on monetary equivalents in order to make us appreciative of value, is both wrongheaded and quite understandable. It is wrongheaded because the price we might have to pay for the labor is not a good measure of its value; and it is understandable because being blind to all else but monetary terms, what other language can we understand?

Unfortunately, neither pointing out the monetary illusions we suffer from, nor placing monetary values on that which is not monetized, seems to make a great deal of difference. We are so thoroughly embedded in our ways of seeing that probably nothing short of being reborn in a totally different culture would really free us from the hold that money exercises upon our minds.

Still, we must try.

Consider a familiar item without a price, the human body. What is it worth? Well, if we are talking about a dead body, then perhaps very little. Medical schools, as a rule, don't have to pay for the cadavers they teach from; they are donated free of charge.

But this is not our question. Our question is not about the value of an extra body, but rather about the value of one's own body. We are not really concerned with market prices, since those reflect only: the supply and demand of that which is actually brought to market. What we really are interested in is the value of one's own body to the person himself.

Were it possible, what would someone pay to retain one's body, or perhaps to replace it? That, of course, depends on its condition and the condition of the replacement. Would an eighty-five-year-old billionaire with a life expectancy of five years pay a billion dollars to exchange bodies with someone who had fifty years to live as opposed to five? How many twenty-five year-olds with healthy bodies would rather have a billion dollars plus an eighty-five-year-old body? No doubt some, but not most people. I'd expect most people would not, for virtually any amount, exchange their bodies for significantly older, significantly less healthy bodies. I would imagine that most eighty-five-year-old billionaires would give virtually all that they own to be able to trade for a young, healthy body. Our body—our thinking, feeling, living body—is our natural wealth. It is our great property. It is from this property that our flow of experience emerges. It is this that enables us to enjoy all we enjoy, to feel all we feel. It is this that enables us to do and to be.

In this wealth, with the exception of people with illnesses, we all start out relatively equal. Each of us is given a gift that is worth billions. However, we are cursed at the same time; it is a worth that starts to dissipate the moment it arrives. It flows away from us at a steady rate, like a hole in the bank account—365 days are lost every year. There are some things we can do to make it last a bit longer, but one way or another, we end our lives completely broke.

One of the reasons that very few people see things this way is the simple fact that there is no technology for exchanging bodies. Medical science can, however, replace body parts, even vital ones, but not entire bodies. Even with respect to vital body parts, markets are largely undeveloped or underground—one cannot go out and buy a young heart.

But we are likely not far from technologies that will allow us to exchange full bodies. Let us say that we can do this, retaining perhaps enough of the brain so as to ensure continuity of memory and identity. Suppose then that body swaps between consenting adults become a real possibility. Under those conditions I expect that we would all be greatly more aware of the fundamental equality of our present situation, as well as, ironically, of the fundamental inequality; some will be buyers of sound bodies, and others will be sellers. Of course having (or occupying) a living body is not all much of a muchness—its, value can vary widely. Certainly a person facing only prolonged captivity and torture might value his living body less highly than otherwise. There are always deeply troubled, saddened, and lonely persons for whom being alive has lost all value.

Like all wealth, the wealth we have in our living body represents only the *capability* of what is good, in itself. Merely being alive is never sufficient for valued living. This wealth in our body is however necessary for any valued human functioning and experience. It is this dependence of all good experiences upon having a living body that imparts tremendous derivative value on whatever is itself necessary to sustain the life and health of that body. Thus, as noted, food, and water, and air, taken in the first increments without which life is not possible, are of extraordinary value to the individual, however little they may cost.

One implication, however, of recognizing the tremendous value of small amounts of life-sustaining necessities, and of the great wealth that we all have in our bodies, is that it seems to call into question the extent of the relative differences in income and wealth of the rich and the poor. If the marginal value of money declines rather rapidly, then the actual value of the goods possessed by the poor is substantially closer to that of those possessed by the rich than a comparison of market costs would indicate. (The use value of a liter of tap water that costs less than a penny may not be so vastly different than that of a liter of fine wine that cost 20,000 times as much; and that of a $50 bicycle may not be vastly different from that of a $30,000 car.) While this conclusion initially may be disconcerting, it takes on a different aspect when we realize that the transition we seek is not from poverty to wealth, but from poverty to simple living.

When Does Money Really Matter?

One clear circumstance where the income of the poor and the income of the rich differ enormously in value is when their income differences translate into differences in years of life. Clearly this is true in very poor countries where the life expectancy at birth of the rich and the poor is enormously different. The poor may be exposed to infant mortality rates of 1 in 5 while the rich might face rates of 1 in 100. In terms of life experience, that means that if you are poor, there is a good chance that one of your babies will die, while this is a rare tragedy if you are rich.

Consider the following table, which shows the relationship between per capita income and life expectancy for various countries in the world.

Table 7.1

Country	1994 Per Capita GDP (PPP$)	Life Expectancy at Birth
Luxembourg	34,155	75.9
United States	26,397	76.2
Japan	21,581	79.8
Canada	21,459	79.0
Denmark	21,341	75.2
France	20,510	78.7
Australia	19,285	78.1
Finland	17,417	76.3
Ireland	16,061	76.3
Israel	16,023	77.5
Spain	14,324	77.6
Mauritius	13,172	70.7
Portugal	12,326	74.6
South Korea	10,656	71.5
Chile	9,129	75.1
Mexico	7,384	72.0
Costa Rica	5,919	76.6
Brazil	5,362	66.4

Table 7.1 (cont.)

Country	1994 Per Capita GDP (PPP$)	Life Expectancy at Birth
Turkey	5,193	68.4
Poland	5,002	71.2
Jordan	4,187	68.5
Egypt	3,846	64.3
Morocco	3,681	65.3
Peru	3,645	67.4
Congo	2,410	51.3
Senegal	1,596	49.9
Kenya	1,404	53.6
India	1,348	61.3
Nepal	1,137	55.3
Haiti	896	54.4
Niger	787	47.1
Chad	700	47.0
Sierra Leone	643	33.6
Ethiopia	427	48.2

Source: Human Development Report, 1997, United Nations Development Program.[1]

The table suggests a few generalizations:

- Income matters. People in countries with higher average incomes tend to live longer.
- Income isn't all that matters. There are some countries with modest income levels, such as Costa Rica, in which people live as long as in the United States, although incomes are less than one-quarter of our level.
- Income level seems to matter less and less as income rises. Thus, comparing countries with less than $1,000 per capita income with those at about $5,000, there is a life expectancy gap of at least fifteen years. But between countries at the $5,000 level (excluding Costa Rica) and those at the $10,000 level, the gap is around nine years, and comparing those at the $10,000 with those at the $15,000 level, the gap is only around four years. Between those at the $15,000 level and those at $20,000 it is

approximately two years. Above the $20,000 level there seems hardly any relationship at all between average income and life expectancy.

These, of course, are numbers for countries as a whole. They do not say anything about the differences within the country. Thus, we must not assume that for individuals within a country, higher income translates into longer life up to the $20,000 per year level, but no further. Unfortunately, data on the relationship between income and life expectancy are not abundant. One study that was done for Canada compared the life expectancy at birth of those in the top one-fifth of the income spectrum with those in the bottom one-fifth. It found that in 1986 the life expectancy difference was 5.6 years for men and 1.8 years for women.[2] Income inequality in Canada is less than in the United States, and access to health care is greater. Thus, one would expect to see a somewhat bigger gap for the United States. One study of mortality in the United States for the period 1979-1985 concluded that, between the highest and lowest income groups, there was a difference for white men of about 10 years and for white women of 4.3 years.[3] For all the races together, these differences would be greater. This general picture is supported by a recent study that compares life expectancy of Americans, depending on what county they live in within the United States. It found a gap of about fifteen years, ranging from a low of about sixty-five years to a high of about eighty years.[4] This gap can at least be partially explained by differences in income, whether understood in its bearing on the quality of medical care available to low-income people or on the levels of homicide in the neighborhoods low-income people can afford.

On the other hand, one should not jump to the conclusion that the only reason for the gap is that the things money can buy result in higher life expectancy. Part of the explanation for the gap may lie in lifestyle choices, such as smoking, which is more prevalent at lower income levels. In part people with certain problems (e.g., self-hatred) may be both destroying their health and destroying their careers. Sometimes the link between income and health emerges not because money can sustain health, but because people who have health problems (for whatever reason) can't earn much money, sometimes being unable to work at all. Thus, in assessing the contribution that having a higher income contributes to life expectancy, these differences in life expectancy should be viewed as somewhat overstated upper limits to the importance of income. The actual significance of higher income is no doubt less, though still quite real.

In relating household income to life expectancy within countries, we can expect to find a structure similar to that found between countries: income matters, income is not all that matters, and there is a declining marginal benefit in life expectancy associated with each increment of income. An estimate for the United States appears in Figure 7.1.

Figure 7.1: Estimate of How Money Matters in the United States

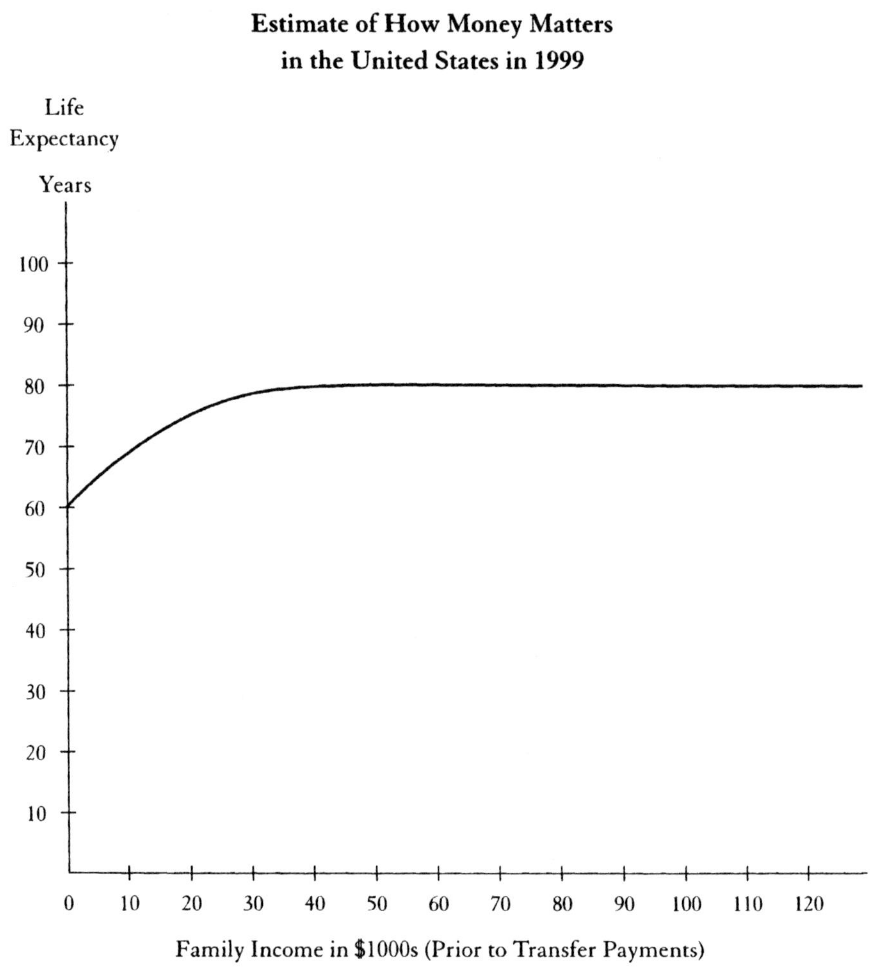

While we don't have precise figures, we can develop an informed picture of what the relationship looks like for the United States, again remembering that not all of the correlation is due to the effect that higher income has on health.

There is a dear advantage to being born into a higher-income family. Measured in terms of life expectancy, this value is of diminishing significance as income levels rise. I would conjecture that it reaches zero somewhere around family incomes of $100,000, but is quite small well before that. This, of course, is a guestimate, but it seems plausible to me.

That there is a declining marginal effect of income on life expectancy must be true. Thus, assume that at levels of family income of $10,000, each increment of $1,000 resulted in a gain in life expectancy of 1 year, and that at the $10,000 level life expectancy at birth was 65 years. If the incremental value did not decline, then at the $60,000 level of annual income life expectancy would be 50 years greater or 115 years long, and someone with $1,01,000 in annual family income would be living until they were 1,065 years old. Because we know that the effect of income on life span has reached approximately zero somewhere below life spans of 100, we know that the actual relationship can't look radically different than my guestimate.

Whatever the exact relationship, it should not be viewed as fixed for all time. It might be that new technologies will emerge such that vast incomes will enable, for a select few, life spans of 100 years or 120 years. Under those circumstances, the marginal value of money at very high income levels would become extraordinarily high. One can go further and imagine a world in which very rich people simply don't die or suffer ill health at all because new, very expensive technologies keep emerging to sustain them. The point of such speculations is that it helps to remind us of what it *would* be like if money really did continue to matter at very high levels. In the present world, the marginal value of money in yielding a longer life rapidly declines toward zero as we reach high levels of household income.

One way of responding to this recognition that beyond a certain point having more money doesn't significantly change life expectancy is to say, "Well that's a reasonable level to aspire to, and beyond that, perhaps it hardly pays to have more." From the point of view of simple living, however, this might prove a disquieting conclusion—depending on what that "zero impact" level is. It is quite different if money stops contributing to a longer life span at $20,000 in family income than if it stops being useful at $100,000 or $200,000. Moreover, we know from the county-level studies that there are pretty big differences (ten to fifteen years of life) depending on where in the United States you live.

But as stated earlier, the case for simple living does not depend upon showing that money makes no difference, any more than it depends on showing that consumption makes no difference in responding to complex human needs. Rather, the case for simple living is that high income is not necessary, either to live well or to live long. Thus, from the point of view of simple living, the conclusion is twofold: first, beyond a certain level (whatever that is), having more money yields little benefit; and second, if one lives properly, one can attain those benefits at much lower levels of income.

Here, what is important is the existence of the examples of countries like Costa Rica where, with an annul average income of about $5,000, people live as long as in the United States. As was noted above, in Canada, money seems to matter less when it comes to its contribution to life expectancy. We can have a society in which money stops making a contribution to longer life spans at very low levels of income. Such a society facilitates simple living, and is one of the objectives of a politics of simplicity.

The Value of Unpriced Personal Services

Beyond having a healthy body and a long life expectancy, in what else does human wealth reside? The Greek philosopher Epicurus identified friendship as that which was most important to human happiness. In this he was right. Clearly it is our relationships with other people that truly matter; having a loved and loving life partner, having good friends, having loved and loving children and relatives. We do not use the word "property" in these cases, nor do we speak of ownership. Yet we do some times speak of our friends and loved ones as our true wealth, or more commonly as our treasures or treasured ones.

When we own something, we have certain specific property rights with respect to it: a right to use it as we please; a right to exchange it for something else; a right to sell it; a right to whatever of value emerges from it; a right to restrict the access of others to it; a right to give it away; a right to destroy it. These property rights are what constitute economic ownership.

When it comes to other people, we have no such rights. Yet even with respect to physical property, such rights themselves confer little of economic value unless they can in fact be exercised. Where there is no expectation that such rights can be exercised, ownership is empty and, in market terms, will yield nothing. It is like being told that you own a million shares of stock in a gold mine, but no one will ever be allowed to mine the gold. The shares are worthless. Ultimately, what gives economic value to the things we own is the belief or expectation that such ownership can be transferred into a flow of things of value: in the first instance into a flow of income (through sale, rent, investment), and then, secondarily, into a flow of valued goods and services through the expenditure of that income. If not the second assumption, then the flow of monetary income is itself without economic value. Thus, it is the potential for transformation into a flow of valued goods and services that gives economic value to what we own.

How then are our human treasures, our very most valued relationships, related to goods and services? To goods, hardly at all. But what we get from each other when we have the *right* others is a unique flow of services. Consider, just three of the many things that the other, beloved and true, might provide:

- partner: someone with whom you can act in concert, not just doing things together but having a joint project;
- companion: someone with whom one can share the events of the day, someone who listens, who responds, who understands, who helps you see things more, clearly and more fully;
- affection: someone who has genuine concern, someone who thinks of you, who does things that make you feel valued, who helps you see your own worth.

The illusion of money is such that we self-blind ourselves toward these unpriced personal services, just as we do with unpaid household labor. How are we to move out of our restricted way of seeing economic life? How can we find human touchstones for thinking about political economy? How can we relate these "services" that friends and loved ones provide to the questions of wealth and income? A starting point is to rethink the notion of personal services and home production.

Personal Services and Home Production

It has long been recognized that in nonmarket economies much of what is produced is never brought to market, but is intended for home consumption and thus falls outside normal income accounting. Thus, in some Third World countries one might find, as was once the case in the United States, that 70 percent or 80 percent of the population lives on small land holdings, and that most of what they produce is used by the family itself. Thus, a very substantial portion of their income comes not in a monetized form, but rather in the goods and services directly produced.

In order to develop a more adequate picture of consumption and income and either to allow comparisons with more marketized economies or to make historical comparisons where the degree of marketization has changed, economists have sought ways of placing appropriate monetarized value (i.e., exchange value, price) on these outputs of home production. When the item in question is a good that is itself subject to market transactions (e.g., a kilo of rice, a bushel of wheat), or when it is a clear substitute for a market good, then it is easy enough to simply adjust the income and consumption figures for home production/consumption by using these market prices.

When no market price exists, an effort sometimes is made to attempt an estimate of what such items might bring if brought to market, or alternatively to estimate what price the family might have to be offered so that they would place the item in question on the market.

This all makes good sense. For most purposes our interest in income or consumption is about something more basic than the amount of money earned or spent by the household, and we can more adequately evaluate the household situation by making these adjustments for nonmarketed goods and services.

What has not been generally recognized, however, is just how wide such a principle of admission truly is. For instance, if we have agreed, as I think makes sense, that the unpaid household labor and services of women (whether as Third World farmers or in rich country homes) are both part of the income of the household and part of what it consumes, then what basis is there for not similarly treating the very same services when members of the household provide them for themselves? Thus, if it is part of the household income when the homemaker cleans five rooms, it is similarly part of household income if her husband cleans his own room, or cooks a meal for himself. In short the entire array of household tasks that encompass housework, no matter who does them, are part of the home production of the unit, and part of what must enter into a full notion of economic well-being.

But this only scratches the surface. When we think of housework we think of those activities that are somewhat arduous and often unpleasant. But this is not a defining characterization of work or of income-producing activities. Some people love their jobs; productive activity can be activity that would be done in the absence of external reward. Moreover, in wealthy economies much of our consumption expenditures are for leisure time activities. In one society a person goes out to work, earns some money, and then provides to the family a TV for their evening entertainment, indirectly paying others for a multitude of entertainment services; in another society an elder mesmerizes the children with ancient tales told around a campfire. This, too, is a contribution to family income. Once we accept the idea that goods and services produced or performed at home which substitute for market goods and services are part of family income and consumption, the range of activities that can be so viewed is wide indeed.

Often when economists attempt to adjust income numbers for home production they limit themselves to those goods and services that have a clear market substitute. But this is a matter of convenience, not because having a market substitute is a necessary condition for having economic value. Often, the absence of a clear marketplace substitute for home activities, rather than impugning the value of the home activity, is an indication of the inability of the market to actually generate a viable substitute. The most graphic examples of this occur in the area of human relationships (e.g., spending time with friends). When the market tries to provide substitutes (e.g., escort services, prostitution), they are poor imitations of the real thing, yet their prices are often very high. The high prices paid reflect the high value placed by consumers on the real thing. And of those things for which it is near impossible for the market to provide a substitute (e.g., things that have value only when provided free of monetary motivation), one is dealing with things of the greatest value.

Thus, the idea that a marketplace substitute is necessary to show that a nonmarketplace activity is of value has things backward. The economic history is typically that marketplace items take on their value by being substitutes (generally imperfect) for what is produced or done for self or others outside the market. Most of what is truly valuable are personal services, things that people do for each other or for themselves. We are drawn into market economies because of their vastly greater efficiency, even when it means that the services and, to some extent, the goods are less meaningful. Those areas that are of greatest value, or where the personal service relationships are unique, are typically areas in which market provision is so inadequate that it is not undertaken at all.

Consider then the differences between these two lists of personal services. In the first what most people seek (and need) is the engagement of a particular person who is of most importance to us:

- intimate conversation
- sex
- dinner with the family
- sitting on your father's knee
- hearing what happened with your daughter at school today
- having a holiday dinner
- watching TV together
- holding hands
- having a game of catch with your son
- playing chess with an old friend

Most of what the very wealthy hire household workers to do does not fall into these categories. Rather, it is typically the case that others are hired when the personal service has some *clear output* that is the actual objective of importance, not the doing itself by a particular person. Though people differ, rich people hire others to do things such as these:

- cleaning the house
- painting the house
- mowing the lawn
- fixing the roof
- paying the bills
- cooking dinner
- shopping for food
- taking the car in for repair
- driving the kids to soccer practice

With respect to those person-centered services (the first list) in which the value of the activity resides in the fact that it was done by or with a particular other person (a friend, a parent, a loved one), the rich are no better positioned than the poor. Neither can hire someone else to do it for them. Yet it is these person-centered services, which markets cannot provide, that are of the greatest value.

Moreover, the household is not the only nonmarket source of personal services; friends and other non household traditions also help meet our personal service needs. Thus, the market can be thought of as servicing a residue of needs that remains when we subtract those needs that are met by all nonmarket providers, be it oneself, others within the household, friends, and neighbors.

With respect to simple living, the core wisdom is that the provision of person-centered services can under certain circumstances be, not a demand on a person's time, which subtracts from their ability to live well, but rather an opportunity for them to have a meaningful existence. It is to be able to do this that we need time.

One of our deepest personal needs is the need to provide significant personal services to others. Having the psychological capacities to do that and having the social opportunities to use those capacities are among our greatest forms of wealth. Here we might remember Seneca's point that we want a friend because we need someone to sustain when he is in need. This is a major part of the contribution to our wealth that having children contributes—it gives us an opportunity to develop into our higher selves and to express those selves by giving to others.

At bottom a successful form of economic life is one that figures out how to organize society so that we are each performing and receiving such services from each other. The existence of social roles that allow this to occur is a form of national treasure; these roles are the value infrastructure that make it possible for what is truly valuable in human life to emerge. Without knowing what we do, we often sweep away such forms of human interaction in the name of a false efficiency.

This may become more obvious when we remember that fewer and fewer workers are actually engaged in the production of commodities; most are providing services, and increasingly these are personal services. For the most part economic life is merely the exchange of services, whether within the marketized segment of life or outside.[5]

Understanding the value of nonmarket services casts the familiar distinctions we make between opulence and simple living in a different light. It appears a distinction that functions only on the more superficial level of goods and marketable services. Once we reach down toward what is most valuable, the chance to give and the opportunity to receive those forms of personal services that are themselves nonmarketable, we find that the simple life can be inherently opulent if it is a life in which human bounty is constantly increased through giving to one another.

Simple Living: Wealth and Poverty

When a form of simple living is advocated, it is generally because it is believed that, by living simply on the material level one can live best in one or another of the nonmaterial dimensions.

The concept of wealth can be captured within this same framework. Being wealthy means having the diverse "assets" that allow us to live a life that partakes of diverse form of richness: material, intellectual, spiritual, aesthetic, and social.

Once approached from this angle it becomes dear that genuine wealth resides in an extraordinarily broad range of "assets":

- in our social relationships, our friendships, loves, and families;
- in our psychological capabilities, our abilities to build relationships, our ability to find meaning, to take aesthetic pleasure;
- in our cognitive capabilities, our ability to read, to understand, to learn, to reason;
- in our creative capacities, our ability to make something beautiful, to contribute something different;
- in our political rights, our ability to be a citizen of one country rather than another, our ability to build our own life, according to our own lights;
- in our historical and cultural legacy, in the riches of insight and experience that have been preserved from previous human lives and that are embodied in the great elements of human culture, be they forms of life and traditions, or great literature;
- in our natural and man-made physical environments, the beauty of Florence, or the view from the back porch.

Material wealth is not irrelevant, but its role is largely instrumental, largely in terms of how it facilitates our ability to access other forms of wealth. With clarity about genuine wealth, we may recognize how wealthy we really are (or in some cases, how poor) and, as a result, be better able to choose time rather than money, or make better use of both time and money.

The life of graceful simplicity is not a life that one can live merely by deciding to do so. To live well is an art, and to live gracefully in time is to be particularly accomplished in that art. It involves drawing on our internal capacities for creativity, appreciation, and generosity; it involves having attained some substantial level of inner peace, of security of identity and freedom from anxiety. And it involves having the good fortune of an external environment in which there is good grass and clean water and an absence of predators, but mostly essentially having space that is abundant in beauty and friendship.

Notes

1. The income figures are provided in terms of "purchasing parity," which seeks to compare income levels in different countries based on what one can buy with them rather than through reliance on international currency exchange rates.

2. R. Wilkins, O. Adams, and A. Branker, "Changes in Mortality by Income in Urban Canada from 1971 to 1986," *Health Reports* 1(2)(1989): 137-74.

3. E. Rogot, P. D. Sorlie, and N. J. Johnson, "Life Expectancy by Employment Status, Income and Education in the National Longitudinal Mortality Study," *Public Health Reports* 107(4) (Jul-Aug 1992): 457-61.

4. David Brown and Avram Goldstein, "Death Knocks Sooner for D.C.'s Black Men," *Washington Post,* 4 December 1997, 4.

5. We are actually well beyond the point in which most people are engaged in providing services rather than growing or manufacturing things. In 2001, the number of people employed in various occupations was as follows:

Total employed civilians	135,073
Managers	20,338
Professionals	21,556
Technicians	4,497
Sales	16,044
Administrative support	18,503
Household and protective	3,193
Other service (food, health, cleaning, hair)	15,166
Transporters	5,638
Precision production, craft, and repair	14,833
Machine operators, fabricators, and laborers	17,698
Farming, forestry, and fishing	3,245
Handlers, helpers, and laborers	5,326

It is only in the last four categories that we have people involved in making, growing, and building things. There were 41,102 (41 million) people with occupations of this sort in 2001, constituting 30.4 percent of those employed.

When viewed by industry, independent of exactly what the people themselves might be doing, we get a similar picture.

	1979	1992	2005 (pro)
Total	10,363	121,093	147,484
Nonfarm wage and salary	86,491	107,888	132,960
goods prod excl agriculture	26,461	23,142	23,717
mining	958	631	562
construction	4,463	4,471	5,632
manufacturing	21,040	18,040	17,523
service producing	63,030	84,746	109,243
transport, comm., utilities	5,136	5,709	6,497
wholesale trade	5,221	6,045	7,191
retail trade	14,972	19,346	23,777
finance, insurance, real estate	4,975	6,571	7,969
services	16,779	28,422	41,788
business services			
health services			
educational			
legal			
amusement			
auto repair			
government	15,947	18,653	22,021
Agriculture	3,398	3,295	3,325
Private households	1,264	1,116	802
Nonagri. self-emply/unpaid fam	7,210	8,794	10,397

Source: *SAUS*, 1995, table 654, Employment by selected industry with projection.

As a percentage of the total, those employed within agriculture or goods-producing industries is projected to fall to 18 percent within a few years (from 26 percent in 1992). As recently as 1979, those in agriculture or goods-producing industries was 29 percent of the workforce. This is a totally different world than that, say, or 1920, when those in agriculture or goods-producing industries comprised 62 percent of the workforce, or 1850 when it accounted for 81 percent of the workforce (*Historical Statistics of the United States* Series D. 152-166 Industrial Distribution of Gainful Workers. 1820-1940).

8
The Good Life and Economic Activity

When we evaluate the economic performance of any particular society, be it a wealthy country such as our own, or those of the Third World, a central criterion is whether or not there has been a general and sustained rise in the *standard of living*. If there has not been, or, if relative to the performance of other countries or its own performance in other periods the results have been mediocre, then this strongly suggests some problem with economic institutions or economic policy.

Implicitly or explicitly, such evaluations are constantly being made. They fill our news pages; they flesh out our sense of where progress is being made and where it is not; they serve as the backdrop for our ongoing policy discourse.

Of course, the validity of the evaluations and the use to which they are put rest on the adequacy of the concept of *standard of living*. If we are operating with a faulty conception of the standard of living (or of some analogous concept such as *economic well-being*), then the evaluations will be flawed and the policy prescriptions misguided.

Given the impact of how we understand the fundamental concepts, it is striking that more attention is not paid to them. Both Amartya Sen and Martha C. Nussbaum have played a significant role in insisting on the importance to public policy of alternative conceptions of the good and in challenging the dominant notions of the good that are implicit within mainstream economic discourse.

Specifically, both Sen and Nussbaum have argued against conceiving of the individual good (or well-being or standard of living) either in terms of utility or preference satisfaction, or in terms of levels of income or possession of goods. Instead, drawing on earlier thinkers, in particular Aristotle, they have articulated a general approach that emphasizes human functioning—what people actually do, feel, and experience—and their capabilities to function. In this approach, having a good life is above all else to live (and experience) in particular ways.

In her essay "The Good as Discipline, the Good as Freedom" Nussbaum opens with a quotation from Aristotle: "A person who is going to make a fruitful inquiry into the question of the best political arrangement must first set out clearly what the most choice-worthy life is. For if that is unclear, the best political arrangement must also be unclear" (Pol. 1321:14-17). She writes, "The reason [Aristotle] plausibly gives for this claim is that the goods distributed by politics, such as money, honors, and entitlements, are not good in and of themselves. They are good insofar as they are tools of human functioning."[1]

This is a perspective with which I agree, and my primary concern is with these goods: money, honors, and entitlements, not as distributed by politics but rather as generated and distributed through economic life. In this essay, I seek to use a version of the capabilities/functionings approach to shed light on one of the most fundamental questions of economics: What is the relationship between higher levels of income and increased standard of living (or economic well-being)? This question can be posed on two levels, that of each person taken individually and that of the society as a whole. For the individual the question emerges as: Does my standard of living go up as my money income rises? And for the society as a whole, the question might be posed as: To what extent does a general rise in the level of income increase economic well-being?

These crucially important questions do not even get formulated if we start off on the wrong foot, conceptually speaking. Thus, if we understand *standard of living* as identical to the income or consumption level of the individual, then economic growth that results in a general rise in the income level or in the level of consumption will have produced—by definition—a rise in the standard of living. Our question will have been answered before we even start. It is a central virtue of the capabilities/functionings approach, which understands well-being as a pattern or variety of patterns of human functionings and/or capabilities, that it blocks any automatic transition from increased consumption to increased well-being. Thus, what the dominant economic discourse approaches as a matter of logical truth is on the capabilities/functionings approach revealed to be an empirical matter of considerable complexity and subtlety.

In what follows I first review Nussbaum's explication of what she terms "the central functional capabilities" to consider the usefulness of her specific approach to the question at hand. Second, I introduce a different approach within the larger capabilities/functionings orientation, one that I believe can shed considerable light on the relationship of income growth to higher standards of living.

Nussbaum's List of Central Human Functional Capabilities

Here then is Nussbaum's list of central human functional capabilities.[2]

1. *Life*. Being able to live to the end of a human life of normal length; not dying prematurely, or before one's life is so reduced as to be not worth living.
2. *Bodily Health and Integrity*. Being able to have good health; to be adequately nourished; to have adequate shelter; having opportunities for sexual satisfaction and for choice in matters of reproduction; being able to move from place to place; being secure against violent assault, including sexual assault, marital rape, and domestic violence.
3. *Pleasure and Pain*. Being able to avoid unnecessary and nonbeneficial pain, so far as possible, and to have pleasurable experiences.
4. *Senses, Imagination, Thought*. Being able to use the senses; being able to imagine, to think, and to reason and to do these things in a way informed and cultivated by an adequate education, including, but by no means limited to, literacy and basic mathematical and scientific training. Being able to use imagination and thought in connection with experiencing and producing spiritually enriching materials and events of one's own choice (religious, literary, musical, and so forth). Being able to use one's mind in ways protected by guarantees of freedom of expression with respect to both political and artistic speech, and freedom of religious exercise.
5. *Emotions*. Being able to have attachments to things and persons outside ourselves; to love those who love and care for us, to grieve at their absence; in general, to love, to grieve, to experience longing, gratitude, and justified anger. Supporting this capability means supporting forms of human association that can be shown to be crucial in their development.
6. *Practical Reason*. Being able to form a conception of the good and to engage in critical reflection about the planning of one's own life. This includes, today, being able to seek employment outside the home (in a regime protecting the free choice of occupation) and to participate in political life.

7. *Affiliation*. Being able to live for and to others, to recognize and show concern for other human beings, to engage in various forms of social interaction; to be able to imagine the situation of another and to have compassion for that situation; to have the capability for both justice and friendship. Protecting this capability means, once again, protecting institutions that constitute such forms of affiliation, and also protecting the freedoms of assembly and political speech.
8. *Other Species*. Being able to live with concern for and in relation to animals, plants, and the world of nature.
9. *Play*. Being able to laugh, to play, to enjoy recreational activities.
10. *Separateness*. Being able to live one's own life and nobody else's. This means having certain guarantees of noninterference with certain choices that are especially personal and definitive of selfhood, such as choices regarding marriage, childbearing, sexual expression, speech, and employment.

10a. *Strong Separateness*. Being able to live one's own life in one's own surroundings and context. This means guarantees of freedom of association and of freedom from unwarranted search and seizure; it also means a certain sort of guarantee of the integrity of personal property, though this guarantee may be limited in various ways by the demands of social equality, and is always up for negotiation in connection with the interpretation of the other capabilities.

Nussbaum has presented a list of capabilities to function. Each is claimed to be necessary for the good human life. She says that "a life that *lacks any one* of these capabilities, no matter what else it has, will fall short of being a good human life."[3] And while Nussbaum is open to the possibility that the list might need to be further augmented or revised, I believe her intention is to be comprehensive, to have identified *all* of the capabilities that are necessary for the good life.

Since for every capability term there is a correlate functioning term (for instance, for the capability "being able to live a normal life span" there is the correlate functioning "living a normal life span"), Nussbaum easily could have presented her list as a set of functionings. Her reason for not doing so is that "capability, not functioning, is our political goal . . . . For political purposes it is appropriate for us to shoot for capabilities, and for those alone."[4] At the same time Nussbaum states, "It is perfectly true that functionings, not simply capabilities, are what render a life fully human: if there were no functioning of any kind in a life, we could hardly applaud it, no matter what opportunities it contained."[5]

While fear of excessive state interference might lead one to specify the specific targets of what Nussbaum refers to as "political planning" in terms of capabilities (enabling the citizenry to function in certain ways) rather than in terms of their actually functioning in a desired way, it does not seem to me that the needs of public policy can be met fully by an analysis that remains on the capabilities level.

For instance, when we seek to define and measure actual standards of living, we are legitimately concerned with the actual lives that people are living, not just what potential they might have to be living at any given standard. Thus, a family might have an income that enables them to live free from avoidable diseases, but our concern for well-being extends to at least knowing the extent to which they are doing so. What the state decides to do about it, if anything, is a separate matter.

This concern for the actual functionings on the individual level is similar to what is now a commonplace with respect to evaluating overall economic performance on the societal level. For instance, in looking at socioeconomic performance in Third World countries, we are not just concerned with whether or not the economy has the potential to reduce infant mortality to negligible levels but whether or not it has actually done so. Thus, I would argue that for policy purposes we need information not only on capabilities but also on actual functionings as well.

This point brings me to a particular problem I have in understanding how functionings and capabilities are related on Nussbaum's account. Given what she has said, that "it is perfectly true that functionings, not simply capabilities, are what render a life fully human," one might infer that in her view the good life consists of functioning in a certain manner, and the various capabilities deemed "necessary" for the good life derive their status from the logically prior necessity of the correlate functionings to the good life.

Yet, from specific passages in her account it would seem that this is *not* what she is saying. Thus, she has made clear her view that not all of the correlate functionings are necessary. She writes:

> A deeply religious person may prefer not to be well nourished but to engage in strenuous fasting. Whether for religious or other reasons, a person may prefer a celibate life to one containing sexual expression. A person may prefer to work with an intense dedication that precludes recreation and play. Are we saying that these are not fully human or flourishing lives? And are we instructing government to push people into functioning of the requisite sort, no matter what they prefer?

> Here we must answer *no*: capability, not functioning, is our political goal.[6]

Given that she has asked two questions, one about whether these functionings are necessary for a flourishing life and one about whether the state should intervene, it is not fully clear whether her "no" applies to both questions or only to the latter. As I find it implausible that these correlate functionings are each necessary for the good human life, I will interpret her as having similarly recognized that people can flourish without all the functionings.[7] But if this is her position, then for those functionings that are *not necessary* it is hard to understand why the correlative capabilities are necessary.[8]

This is not merely a theoretical point about the logic of her claim that these capabilities are necessary; it emerges again and again when we ask of specific capabilities whether they are necessary for the good human life. Examples:

1. "Having opportunities for sexual satisfaction." Some people have very little or no sex at all—certain priesthoods, certain nineteenth-century utopian communes, some people who are impotent, some people who are faithful to one who has died. Nussbaum would agree that we cannot say that none of them are living a good life. But if it is not necessarily important that these people have sexual activity, why is it necessary for their living a good human life that they have opportunities for such activity? Is the life of the monk with reduced opportunities less good than that of the priest facing daily temptation?
2. "Being able to move from place to place." If this merely means the ability to walk around, then almost everyone has it. I assume Nussbaum means something more, such as the ability to travel within one's country, a freedom that serfs did not have and that is generally lacking among the poor. But if so, then while this capability may be important to many people, it would seem excessive to say it is a necessary feature of the good life. Some people live well without ever leaving their valley; why then do they need the capability to leave?
3. "Being able to live with concern for and in relation to animals, plants, and the world of nature." I'm not sure what it means to not *be able* to live in this way. Consider this first on the level of functioning. Is it really the case that people who do not like animals, or who take little interest in them, do not live a good

life? How did Shakespeare, Aristotle, Descartes, or Balzac live in relation to animals and nature? Does it matter? Suppose we find that they lacked the capability "to live with concern for animals and plants," perhaps because they believed that animals were mechanisms without consciousness. Would this show that they did not have good human lives?

4. "Being able to laugh, to play, to enjoy recreational activities." On the level of functioning, why is it necessary that every good human life must contain play and recreation? There are good lives of dedication and devotion to ideals of religion, service to others, knowledge, political transformation, or art. Some people are very serious—and they may not be well-rounded individuals. Playing, laughing, and recreating may be absent in their lives; yet it seems that they can have a good life. Indeed, they may find pleasure, satisfaction, meaning, and even joy in what they do without playing, laughing, or recreating at all. Suppose that they not only do not play or recreate but also lack the capability of doing so—either because of the time demands of what is vital to them or because of psychological disposition. It would seem odd to maintain that because they lack this capability (which need not be actualized in any event) their lives fall short of being good human lives.
5. "Being able to live one's own life and nobody else's . . . having certain guarantees of noninterference with certain choices that are especially personal and definitive of selfhood, such as choices regarding marriage. . . ." Is it really true that no one who had an arranged marriage ever had a good life? Are entire cultures ineligible? We may want to protect the right of people to choose for other reasons—after all, everyone has an inalienable right to make mistakes—but that is very different from saying that being able to choose is a necessary feature of any good life.
6. "Being able to live one's own life in one's own surroundings and context." By this Nussbaum "means guarantees of freedom of association and of freedom from unwarranted search and seizure . . . ." Such freedoms are unfortunately rather rare in human history. Are we saying that no one who lives in a society without freedom of association lives a good life?[9] For some people this lack of freedom is utterly irrelevant; for others it may mean they are thwarted. But even for those who chafe and struggle against it, can one not find the good life in the political struggle against

> injustice? Many people have found that they flourished most intensely in political struggle—over the Vietnam war, for example, or in the civil rights movement. Such struggle can be the most meaningful part of someone's life, a kind of high point of creative energy and common cause with others against injustice.

I see no reason to deny that people may flourish without significant freedom (political or psychological) to move about, to marry whomever they wish, to participate in political activity, or to enjoy nature. We can have good lives without freedom from potential unwarranted search and seizure and without freedom from suppression of political speech or assembly. Indeed, people who have these freedoms may ask, with some despair and emptiness, "Where have all the causes gone?" This is not to say that as a general matter such capabilities and freedoms are not of great importance to the human good. It is merely to say that there are many ways and circumstances in which people can flourish. We cannot assume that those capabilities and freedoms are necessary for every good life or even that they matter in every life.

The significance of the foregoing points is this: If the list of capabilities is truly a list of necessary capabilities for the good life, then it is an extremely powerful tool. It allows us to look at societies or situations in which these capabilities are lacking and say that whatever else may be going on, these people are being denied the opportunity of the good life and, thus, that things must change. If, on the other hand, the list is, as I believe, a list not of necessary capabilities but of generally important capabilities, then it has less power. Where one or another capability is missing, the good life might still be possible, might even be compensated for by the availability of another capability. Nonetheless, if Nussbaum has provided a menu of clearly defined "building blocks" of the good life such that any concept of the good life worthy of respect is constituted by selections from the menu, she has accomplished a great deal.

Let me then turn to another question: Do these capabilities, even if one has them all, add up to the good life? Or has something important been left out?[10]

One difficulty that we encounter in trying to answer this question is that many of these functionings (or capabilities) are matters of degree. And often enough matters of degree can be very important. Thus, if someone has a great capability to love and to make friends and enjoy them—and if such capabilities are realized in his life—then one is tempted to say that he has a good life. But the case would be much less convincing if either the capacities or the functionings existed to a very limited degree. Because she is committed to explicating the good human life and not just human life per se, Nussbaum has, I believe, an intention to specify a *minimal threshold* of capability that is required. Yet, quite a few of these capabilities are articulated without any minimal threshold being evident. If there is no minimal required level, however, then nearly everyone has the capability in question, whether they are impoverished or rich, flourishing or languishing. Examples: "having opportunities for sexual satisfaction" (Nussbaum list #2); "being able to move from place to place" (#2); "being able . . . to have pleasurable experiences" (#3); "being able . . . to participate in political life" (#6); "being able . . . to engage in critical reflection about the planning of one's own life" (#6); "being able to laugh, to play, to enjoy recreational activities" (#9).

I would suggest that, at least to a minor degree, virtually everyone has such capabilities. If this is true then, without any minimal threshold being identified, the possession of all of these capabilities (and their minimal expression in the actual living of life) cannot be sufficient for the good life unless we are prepared to say that virtually everyone now leads such a life. The obvious corrective would be to identify substantial thresholds for each valuable capability. The problem with this, however, is that while having (or exercising) all of these valuable capabilities might be sufficient for the good life, it would be very implausible that it was necessary to have each capability to such a high degree.

The question of a threshold emerges from another direction as well. As I understand it, Nussbaum wants her account to accommodate a wide variety of specific visions of the good life. She believes that it is an essential part of the good life that each person work out his own conception of the good life; if this is to be meaningful, then multiple forms of the good life must be possible. The problem is that on different concrete conceptions of the good life *very different* elements are emphasized. What minimal threshold may be necessary under one conception may be viewed as quite unnecessary, even excessive, under another.

Consider, for instance, the visions of the good life represented by Aristotle (contemplative), D. H. Lawrence (sexual/experiential), Leon Trotsky (revolutionary), Cotton Mather (religious), and Caribbean Cruise Lines (pleasure/play). I am not sure that Nussbaum would accept these as alternative forms of a good human life, but they seem plausible candidates to me. Each represents a vision that has had a powerful appeal to many. Each offers opportunities for a person to flourish, at least in some important domains of the human personality.

Suppose for a moment that we view these as acceptable alternative ways of having a good human life. Note that they all have a common structural feature in that they all agree that one key element constitutes the very heart of the good life and that others are secondary, optional, or even excluded altogether. But they disagree sharply on what that one central element is. Is it self-examination, sex, political engagement, religious devotion, travel, recreation, absence of pain, fun, or what? All of these elements are represented on Nussbaum's list, but the minimal threshold that would be necessary for any one of these visions might be excessive for the others. To remain open to all of them, the list could not require high thresholds. Yet from the perspective of each of these conceptions, if Nussbaum's list only requires the most minimal level of that which it treats as central, then the entire list is thoroughly inadequate, failing to capture the essence of the good life.

If this criticism is correct, then her list fails to provide in a meaningful sense the building blocks of the good life. It is not that someone else might do better than Nussbaum; rather, it seems that the project itself is not attainable. What were to have been the building blocks of any good life emerges only as a great menu offering the elements of the multiple incompatible visions. This, of course, does not get us very far.

Nussbaum might respond by saying that each of these conceptions represents an excessive concentration on one or another element, and that they are all flawed. But I do not see how she could demonstrate this. Moreover, it seems to me that often enough the good life is somewhat lopsided. A person can have most or all of Nussbaum's items in his or her life, and yet somehow it does not come together. The lopsidedness may emerge because the good life needs some central project or conception that pulls the pieces into a kind of coherence, so that it is in fact a *life* and not just a series of episodes: getting nourished, playing the piano, taking a walk in nature, visiting a friend, reflecting on the good life, choosing a mate, having sex. This integration is one dimension of what people refer to as "meaning."

Another aspect of "meaning," I believe, has to do with feeling that it all amounts to something. People typically experience a need for some element of transcendence, a connection to something bigger than our interests and tastes—a connection to something of enduring value. This often means a life that is devoted to some ideal, be it service to others, art, knowledge, political transformation, or religion. And in this devotion, there may often be much that is good that is given up.

Finally, and independent of the above, while Nussbaum emphasizes that the capabilities approach offers those concerned with public policy "guidance . . . superior to that offered by several rivals on the development scene,"[11] her analysis fails to provide much "guidance" just where one would look for it: with respect to questions of economic life.

One way of thinking about the economic realm is to consider that most adults participate in two distinct markets. First, in the labor market we are sellers of our time and skills. In exchange we receive income and diverse nonpecuniary benefits that come with employment. Second, we enter the marketplace as consumers, purchasing, in exchange for income, a wide variety of consumption goods and services.

With respect to the economic realm, understood in terms of these two kinds of market involvement, Nussbaum's version of the capabilities/functionings approach offers relatively little for those concerned with central categories such as work, time, and consumption.

Work

For most of us, one third of our life is spent at the workplace; there is in Nussbaum's essay a striking absence of discussion of work environments. Meaningful work is absolutely central and at the core of any serious consideration of alternatives to the consumerist vision of the economic good. If it appears at all within Nussbaum's list, it is in the brief reference to choice of employment within her category of "separateness."[12]

When we think of standard of living in terms of income levels, we completely miss the fact that the value we get from what we consume with our income is only half the story. The other half involves the work itself. Far from being neutral, work—for better or worse—represents a major component of our economic well-being. The work we undertake is a major determinant of our social status, individual sense of well-being, and self-fulfillment. So central are these elements to human well-being that a case can be made that, in societies in which basic elemental needs for food, clothing, and shelter have been met, economic activity's primary impact on well-being is not through higher levels of consumption but through the work experience itself.

If we focus on "authentic work"—work that is inherently rewarding and is deeply expressive of the individual—it is possible to argue for a fundamental reconceptualization of economic life. It would be excessive to maintain that to have this kind of work is to live well and to not have this work is to live poorly no matter what else one has in life, but authentic work is surely at the heart of the good life. Above the basic needs level, economies might reasonably take the provision of authentic work as their primary objective rather than the provision of consumption goods.

Time

The choices we make when we sell our labor time have a powerful impact on the larger place of time in our lives. In purely quantitative terms, for those who seek the good life outside the realm of paid employment (and, given the nature of work in the real world, this applies to most people), the amount of time devoted to work, to getting to work, and to preparing for work determines what we have left for work in the home and for so-called leisure.

The good life has much to do with our relationship to time. Life is a passage through time, and time itself has become part of our oppression. In part this has to do with the balance between time spent doing what is inherently valuable and that which is merely instrumental and often stultifying. Less subtly, the good life has to do with leisure. Aristotle was well aware of the impossibility of living the good life if too much time is devoted to the purely instrumental. To some extent, as a result, he saw slaves and servants as a necessary part of a sound household economy.

Our lives are often sadly overburdened. This is especially true of women who work at paid employment and—more than their fair share—at home, but it is true also of men. Our lives are harried to the point that there is no gracefulness to them at all. Among the supposedly successful middle class, many live at the point of exhaustion. Even when freed from odious work, in a rage to live the good life we can drive ourselves crazy just running around. With no gracefulness to it all, without some crafting of an aesthetic of time, even an agglomeration of good activities does not constitute a good life.

Consumption

At the core of the concern with the good life, from Aristotle to the present day, has been the issue of money and the things that money can buy. There has been a sense that our appetites are insatiable and that we are trapped in a never-ending escalation of our sense of the minimally necessary level of consumption. A central role for a concept of well-being, especially one grounded in the capabilities/functionings perspective, is to help us see such issues with greater clarity. Although Nussbaum believes that beyond a certain point additional consumption not only fails to improve life but may diminish it, only in a limited way does her list come into contact with things that we purchase.

When we get to areas of major consumer expenditure—food, housing, education, transport—we get little or no guidance as to how to think about how much is enough. Nussbaum speaks of being "adequately nourished," "having adequate shelter," and "having adequate education." But adequate for what? And in whose eyes?

Presumably, Nussbaum intends "adequate" to serve a critical purpose, distinguishing what is enough from what our runaway desires may seek. And here the functionings/capabilities approach can be very useful as "adequacy" can be explicated in terms of specific valued functionings. Unfortunately, Nussbaum does not take the capabilities/functionings approach in this more concretely economic direction.

What we need is a general analysis somewhat akin to that example from Adam Smith to which Sen has called attention in recent years:

> A linen shirt, for example, is, strictly speaking, not a necessary of life. The Greeks and the Romans lived, I suppose, very comfortably, though they had no linen. But in the present times, through the greater part of Europe, a creditable day-labourer would be ashamed to appear in public without a linen shirt, the want of which would be supposed to denote that disgraceful degree of poverty which, it is presumed, no body can well fall into without extreme bad conduct. Custom, in the same manner, had rendered leather shoes a necessary of life in England. The poorest creditable person of either sex would be ashamed to appear in public without them.[13]

Smith goes on to point out that in the Scotland of his day appearing without shoes was only shameful for men, while in France both men and women could appear without shoes and not suffer social stigma.[14]

The point is that living at a high economic standard does not consist of wearing a clean linen shirt or a pair of shoes. Rather it consists (in part) of a specific functioning: *appearing in public without shame*.[15] Exactly what clothing is required changes over time and differs from society to society. But in all or almost all societies there is some association between clothing, public appearance, and shame; and, thus, there is a valid cross-cultural formulation of this element of standard of living. And in any given culture in which one's ability to be clothed depends upon one's monetary income, a central driving force behind the pursuit of money would be that it enables one to be clothed at least to the level of being able to appear in public without shame.

For our purposes, the capability "being able to appear in public without shame" has a direct connection to economic life that other capabilities, such as "being able to laugh" or "being able to form attachments," do not seem to have, even though they are pertinent to human well-being in its broader aspects.

Can we then build upon Smith's example and formulate a set of functionings that collectively explicate what it is to live at a high economic standard? And can we use that analysis to shed light upon fundamental questions such as the role of growth of income within the individual and societal quest for a better life?

Focusing on the Economic Realm

I believe the capabilities/functionings framework can forcefully illuminate some of the central issues concerning consumption, economic policy, and economic performance. To see how this approach can be brought to bear on economic issues, let us consider that aspect of life that is distinctly economic. Rather than inquire about the good life or human well-being in all its richness, we limit our focus to the notion of *standard of living*. Typically, as mentioned earlier, economists think of a person's standard of living as identical with his level of income (or consumption). Or, if they make a theoretical distinction between income (or consumption) and standard of living, they will use income (or consumption) as a proxy for standard of living.

It is just this approach that Sen has criticized, and the great value of the linen shirt example is that it allows us to view income and consumption as tools that promote or facilitate central, and possibly universally valued, functionings such as "appearing in public without shame." Moreover, the desire to appear in public without shame emerges as a key motivational factor in explaining consumption expenditures and, to some extent, labor market choices.

In his essay "The Living Standard," Sen calls for an explication of the concept of standard of living in terms of key capabilities to function rather than in terms of actual functionings.[16] Here, as with Nussbaum, I take issue with this emphasis. Merely having the capability to live well materially speaking (whether or not this is the limit of appropriate concern of the state) is not the same as actually doing so. To have a high standard of living is to actually live well economically.

Sen asks, "What about the wealthy ascetic who decides to fast and becomes undernourished despite his being rich and having the means of being excellently nourished? It seem rather odd to see him as deprived, with a low standard of living. He has chosen to fast; he was not forced to fast."[17] Sen is, of course, correct that there is a world of difference between the wealthy ascetic who decides to fast and the undernourished poor, even if both are undernourished. But this does not show that standard of living is best explicated in terms of capabilities. First, we want to keep open the possibility that a wealthy person might through choice or otherwise actually live at a very low standard. This would be foreclosed by definition if merely *being able* to live at a high standard were the same as doing so. Second, taken as functionings, fasting and starving are simply two different functionings. To fast is not to starve, even if nutritionally they come out the same. Understanding standard of living in terms of functionings does not mean that we obliterate the differences between different kinds of functionings.

Sen offers another example, saying "the *capability* to visit friends and relatives may be important for standard of living. However, a person who chooses not to make use of that capability, and curls up instead with a good book, may not be sensibly seen as being deprived and having a low standard of living."[18] Again, I do not believe Sen has made his case. It is impossible to undertake all valuable functionings at the same time. Merely forgoing one in favor of another does not show deprivation. But consider someone who, in favor of staying in his room with a good book, permanently gives up visiting relatives, or eating good meals, or any other valued functioning. At some point, I believe, we would want to say that he is living at a very low standard. Whether this is self-inflicted or a result of deprivation is yet another matter.

Whether standard of living is best explicated in terms of capabilities or functionings, or as a mix of the two, should remain an open question.

Better to judge actual analyses than to foreclose alternatives. In the current essay, I offer an account based only on functionings.

One way to approach the task of isolating economic well-being is to focus on the individual as a consumer, as an agent in the marketplace making consumption expenditures. From this perspective, we might ask if it is possible to identify one or more key functionings for each of the major categories of consumption expenditure. Such functionings would capture the forms of life experience and activity that consumer expenditures enable.

Consider table 8.1, which pairs functionings with areas of consumption expenditure. Families spend most of their money on these six areas of consumption expenditure.

Table 8.1: Areas of Expenditure and Core Functionings

Area of Expenditure	Core Functioning
Clothing	Appears in public without shame
Housing	Hosts with pride in a dwelling a reasonable distance from work and in a safe neighborhood
Transportation	Gets around relatively quickly among the central loci of everyday life (home, work, friends, schools, shops)
Food	Eats meals that are healthful, appetizing, and leisured
Health	Receives effective preventive and remediable health care
Education	Children are schooled effectively and safely

And while the core functionings identified in table 8.1 do not exhaust the functionings that may be enabled through consumer expenditures in these areas, and which motivate these expenditures, they do offer a picture of a way of life or, let us say, a level of economic life that can serve as an alternative to the level of income or consumption in appraising the standard of economic life.

One of the virtues of identifying the level of economic life (or standard of living) with a set of functionings rather than with income or expenditures is that it allows us to inquire about the role of money or expenditures in bringing about the good economic life. It does this in two ways. First, we can ask for any given individual (or family) about the connection between income and the core functionings. For each of the core functionings above, income is necessary but not sufficient. Not only must the money be spent for specific commodities but also the commodities must be utilized in a particular way. Thus, one may have the food but not the leisured meals. One may have the house and still fail to host or to host with pride. What then becomes clear is that, on the individual level, *the translation of income into a high standard of living is itself an art form*. It is very much a matter of knowing how to live and may involve a broad range of knowledges and psychological capabilities. To see things this way is a useful broadening of perspective on "the economic."

Second, however, once we begin to inquire about the set of functionings that make up a form of economic life, it becomes clear that those directly connected to expenditures are only part of the picture. There are other realms of concern than consumer expenditure that are central to our motivation as economic agents, in particular those that are central to our behavior in labor markets (where we are sellers) rather than the market for goods and services (where we are buyers).

Thus, a more complete notion of standard of living or economic functioning would have to go beyond these six areas of consumer expenditure to include the nonpecuniary labor market concerns shown in table 8.2. These four areas, and the core functionings that are identified with them, enter into the decisions we make in labor markets. To a greater extent than with consumption expenditures, these functionings may be enabled by nonmonetary aspects of our economic involvement. With respect to our desire to live in an aesthetically rich urban or natural environment, we make decisions about *which* labor markets to enter (we might look for work in Seattle, New York, or Aspen). And in pursuit of a life free from anxiety over loss of income, we may choose to trade off higher pay for greater security. (There are consumption expenditures—disability insurance policies, for instance—that also promote security functionings.) Similarly, we may prefer greater leisure to higher income. And in some circumstances the pursuit of social esteem and self-expression also may represent a trade-off against income, though clearly income level itself is a factor in attaining social esteem.

Table 8.2: Nonpecuniary Labor Market Concerns and Core Functionings

Nonpecuniary Labor Market Concern	Core Functioning
Security	Lives free from anxiety over the decline or loss of income
Beauty	Lives in an aesthetically rich human and natural environment
Leisure	Devotes ample time to enjoyment of friends and amusements
Work	Derives social esteem and personal self-expression through employment

Taken together, these ten functionings offer a vastly richer understanding of standard of living than does the focus on income or consumption expenditure. Together they extend Smith's linen shirt example to a relatively comprehensive set of functionings that, if not universally valid, have widespread cross-cultural validity.

How, then, does this analysis compare to Nussbaum's analysis, and is it vulnerable to some of the same objections I raised when discussing her approach? First, of course, it should be clear that these are not competing analyses. Nussbaum is operating within the capabilities/functionings orientation to explicate what it is to live a good life. Within the same tradition, I have focused much more sharply on the economic realm, seeking to explicate a different concept: standard of living. Living a good life and having a high standard of living are not the same thing, and how they might be related remains to be clarified.

Second, there are some parallels and some important differences between the two approaches. Nussbaum has focused on capabilities, and I have focused on functionings. Because she has only articulated capabilities, Nussbaum's analysis cannot be sufficient for having a good life. Nor does she claim that it is. She claims, rather, that each capability is necessary for the good life. This I disputed. With respect to my analysis, I would maintain that these ten functionings, collectively, are sufficient. To live in this way is to live at a high economic standard. I do not, however, maintain that to live at a high economic standard it is necessary to function in each of these ten ways. I do, however, make a claim almost as strong: to live at a high economic standard (that is, to have a high standard of living) it is necessary that one function in *almost all* of these ways; one could not forgo more than one or two and still be living well, economically speaking.

In considering Nussbaum, I argued that she faces a problem with respect to specifying thresholds of capability. The minor problem is that she did not specify thresholds, and, thus, it could be maintained that everyone (whether their life is good or not) has to some degree most of the valued capabilities. In my analysis, the differences between high, medium, and low standards of living are captured in the way the functionings are characterized. In the specific instance, I have explicated what it is to live at a *high* economic standard. But by systematically recasting the level of functioning, for instance, by replacing "hosts with pride" with "hosts without shame," one could characterize a more moderate standard of economic life. And, presumably, Nussbaum could supplement her analysis so as to provide thresholds of capability that would allow her to distinguish between what is necessary for a very good life, a moderately good life, a minimally decent life, and so forth.

The real problem Nussbaum faces is that if she specifies thresholds, which she must, she will find that what is far below what is necessary in one vision of the good life may prove excessive in another vision. This, I argued, leads to a dilemma. Either Nussbaum accommodates a wide range of visions by keeping thresholds low, thus, from the point of view of each vision, missing its essence; or she excludes many such alternatives and faces the significant burden of showing that such exclusion is not a matter of arbitrary preference.

The analysis of standard of living does not get into these difficulties because what is being explicated is a more limited economic concept.

Thus, it is quite possible, and indeed true, that in some conceptions of the good life, there might be disdain for living at a high economic standard, and, thus, these various functionings might not be a part of certain conceptions of the good life at all. However, it does not follow that the meaning of the concept *standard of living*, or *high economic standard*, would vary. A Trotskyite, for example, might have taken the stance that to live well economically is incompatible with living as a revolutionary in solidarity with the proletariat.

Similarly, there are multiple conceptions of the good life that would view it as involving life at a high (or at least a decent) economic standard plus something extra and more important that gives it its distinctive quality. Thus, it might be that D. H. Lawrence and Cotton Mather would both agree that the good life is not essentially economic, would disagree violently about the role of sexuality and piety in the good life, and yet would largely agree about the role of a moderately high economic standard.

The point, then, is that by limiting our focus to what it is to live well "economically speaking," it is possible to articulate a concept whose meaning is relatively stable across alternative visions of the good life, even though the place of economic well-being within the good life may vary.[19]

Policy Guidance and a Functionings Analysis of Standard of Living

The functionings analysis of standard of living offers a new direction when it comes to measuring standard of living, comparing levels at different times or in different cultures, and investigating causal factors responsible for growth or decline in standard of living. Unlike expenditure levels, these ten items cannot be collapsed into a single number. But we could, for instance, compare the percentage of people at a given time or in a given society that have these levels of functionings (either one by one or all of them) and then consider how those percentage levels correspond to income levels.

A functionings analysis can be expected to reveal that differences or changes in the standard of living often do not correspond to changes in real income levels. To the extent that this is so, it will offer a way of measuring what might be termed "the standard-of-living efficiency of income" for different societies or a given society at different times. This yardstick would be a measure of the extent to which changes in income convert into changes in the standard of living. Potentially, radically different standards of living are possible at the same level of per capita income and with the same pattern of income distribution. It is one of the virtues of disaggregating standard of living that inquiry into these relationships is made possible.[20]

An appropriate and vital concern for any society is how the standard of living of all of its members can be raised. As suggested above, when we understand standard of living in terms of income levels, it is a near logical truth that equitable economic growth brings about a general rise in the standard of living.[21] But once we understand standard of living in terms of the ten types of functionings detailed above, we are faced with ten complex empirical questions, each of which asks about income growth and rising levels of human functionings. Such questions include:

- When everyone's income level rises, what is the impact on the general ability of people to quickly transport themselves to the central loci of personal life?
- When everyone's income level rises, what is the impact on the extent to which people are wearing clothing that supports pride in self?
- When everyone's income level rises, what is the impact on a sufficiency of leisure?
- When everyone's income level rises, what is the impact on the extent to which people have meaningful work?

Consider these questions for a moment. They have no easy answers. Each requires independent and extensive research. It is quite possible that there will be a tight relationship between general income growth and improved functioning, but there may be no relationship or there may be a negative relationship. The answer may depend not only on the specific component of standard of living being considered but also on the specific historical period and society in question.

Here, of course, we are not asking about a single individual. For a single individual, income growth can, in many instances, result in greater levels of functioning. But what works for a given individual may not work for all of us collectively. When we all stand on tiptoe, not only does no one see the parade any better, but we all end up less comfortable.[22]

At this point, I think we can safely venture that no one knows the answers to these questions. This situation in itself is interesting. What it means is that with respect to the most fundamental of reasons for pursuing equitable economic growth, no one, neither economists nor noneconomists, is currently in a position to say with authority whether or not economic growth is the key to increasing the general level of economic well-being.

While it is clearly outside the purview of this essay to attempt to answer these questions, it is striking how weak the intuitive link between income growth and improved functionings appears to be. To a significant extent, these collective improvement problems appear to be growth resistant. For instance, functionings that are tied to pride or shame, such as appearing in public without shame, hosting with pride, or deriving social esteem through employment, all seem vulnerable to what John Kenneth Galbraith called the "squirrel wheel" phenomenon. We may run faster but not make any progress—the standards for income and expenditures that promote pride, avoid shame, and engender esteem may rise in pace with growth in the income level.

In the search for "effective schooling," so long as this is understood as schooling that enables the child to succeed in the socioeconomic competition, there may be a similar problem. If broadly shared income growth does not increase the number of winners (as may happen if success is understood in relative terms), then here too there is little or no progress.

With respect to functionings such as devotes ample time to enjoyment of friends or gets around relatively quickly among the central foci of everyday life or hosts with pride in a dwelling a reasonable distance from work or lives free from anxiety over the decline or loss of income or lives in an aesthetically rich human and natural environment; a case can be made that economic growth has lowered rather than raised these dimensions of standard of living. Surely, if we were to measure standards of living in each of these dimensions, we would not expect consistently to find that those in rich countries live better than those in poor countries.

The value of the functionings analysis should be apparent. It opens the door to new questions and to possibly surprising answers. It demonstrates the importance, as Aristotle maintained, of clarifying what we mean by a better life before we embrace public policies in our collective pursuit of it.

In reflecting on the policy dimension we are brought to the question that Nussbaum emphasized: What is the appropriate role of the state? Nussbaum views the role of government vis-a-vis the good life as merely to enable good functioning. After that, it is up to responsible adults to choose whether or not to function in these ways. She opposes using the government to shape people's desires or employing tire law to prod or (if necessary) force people to function in desirable ways.

But this dichotomy is too stark, as least if we are focused not on The Good Life writ large but on those functionings that—by and large—constitute what it is to live at a high economic standard. Here, there are many discrete smaller choices, some where it makes sense to use the law only to encourage, some where we might want to go beyond education and enablement to give a prod, and some where we do want to compel.

The reason, I believe, is similar to one I pointed out previously: across a substantial range of alternative visions of the good life, it is possible to have agreement on the meaning of economic well-being and, to a lesser degree, its general relationship to the good life. Thus, without doing violence to the autonomy of the individual in working out his or her conception of the good life, it is possible to have the state more forcefully involved in bringing about those actual functionings that constitute living at a high (or decent) standard of living.

I will conclude with examples of "functioning-promoting" as distinct from merely "functioning-enabling" policies that are within the American consensus of the appropriate role of the state in promoting a higher standard of living. This in itself does not prove that those who challenge this consensus, for instance libertarians, are wrong. But it does serve to identify what is actually involved in maintaining that the state should only enable good functionings and not go further and prod or compel them.

There would be considerable controversy about using the law to prod people to save because it is part of the virtue of frugality. Nonetheless, we do have mandatory Social Security. And while this "extraction" of income by the state can be justified in terms of preventing people from becoming a burden to others, there is substantial recognition that people may need to be forced in this way to provide for their own security. Moreover, even those who view Social Security as unduly paternalistic often enough support tax code provisions that encourage people to contribute to individual retirement accounts (IRAs) and 401 (k) plans.

Similarly, with respect to functionings in the area of health, the concern of the state is not merely with enabling people to be healthy but with their actually being healthy. True, the reason for this concern lies to a considerable degree in a concern that others might either be infected or burdened, but to some extent it lies in a concern with good functioning itself. Thus, when a decision was made to put fluoride in the water, the state was seeing to it that nonuse of fluoride would no longer be a live option.[23] Here, going beyond enabling good functioning (say by making fluoride pills available) was justifiable as an imposition not of the majority view of the good life but, rather, of the majority view of the causal relationship between fluoride and health functionings about which all share a common appraisal.

This illustrates two things. First, that the legitimacy that we accord to the state's prodding (or forcing) of a given behavior (such as saving) depends strongly on the reason for which the state is acting. And second, it illustrates that there is a line we draw between prodding in order to bring about functions that are constitutive of living at a high economic standard (such as living without anxiety over loss of income) and proddings that are designed to actualize a specific, but not shared, view of the good life.

Within this economic realm, there are also situations in which we might act to force individuals toward good functioning because when each makes his own choice the results come out in ways that collectively we judge to be inferior. Consider the decision over how many hours to work (and thus how much leisure to take). For any individual to choose more leisure and less income means a decline in his relative income standard. Left to resolution through individual choices, we have a pattern of life with too much work for good living (a lower standard of living). Thus, collectively (and democratically) we have passed legislation that prohibits consenting adults from entering into certain kinds of exchanges (for example, more than forty hours of work per week at standard pay). As a result, I would argue, we are all better off.

We might also ask, "What does it mean for the state to 'enable good functioning' if we are dealing with squirrel wheel problems?" If the efforts of each to achieve good functioning work to thwart any collective progress toward good functioning, then perhaps a stronger role for the state is warranted. I myself would not be adverse to some kind of restraint that serves to limit what we spend on cars and houses. We have luxury taxes on yachts; perhaps we should have progressive property taxes on houses so as to prevent rapid escalation in "standards of decency" that keep us running after more affluent homes.[24]

Thus, I would argue that wisdom, at least with respect to attaining higher levels of economic functioning, lies not in adopting some general view about whether government should only promote capabilities or whether it should compel functionings. One can reasonably use police power to enforce an eight-hour day and taxing powers to prod people to give to charity (for a variety of reasons) and yet fully resist any temptation to force or even encourage people to read Henry James, though it would be good for them.

Notes

I want to thank David A. Crocker for some consistent prodding and valuable comments on earlier drafts of this paper.

1. Martha C. Nussbaum, "The Good as Discipline, the Good as Freedom" in *Ethics of Consumption* (Lanham, Md.: Rowman and Littlefield Publishers, Inc., 1998), 312-13.

2. This list reproduces Nussbaum's in "The Good as Discipline," 319-20.

3. Nussbaum, "The Good as Discipline," 320; my emphasis.

4. Nussbaum, "The Good as Discipline," 321.

5. Nussbaum, "The Good as Discipline," 321.

6. Nussbaum, "The Good as Discipline," 321.

7. If it is true that not all of the correlate functionings are necessary, one might wonder if any specific ones are. To this Nussbaum does not give an answer.

8. If her position is that these correlate functionings really are necessary, but the state should not intervene, then the account is vulnerable to the examples I present below, though they would need to be recast in functionings language.

9. David A. Crocker takes the position on this and the above issues not that their lives cannot be said to be good, but that they are "less good" than they would be if they had these and other freedoms. Obviously, this is sometimes true, but as a general claim I do not find it convincing.

10. I have previously maintained that no set of capabilities could be sufficient for the good life since it is possible that they would all remain mere potential. Here I assume that some or all of Nussbaum's valuable capabilities are actualized. I am asking if this is enough.

11. Nussbaum, "The Good as Discipline," 320.

12. In "Aristotelian Social Democracy," in *Liberalism and the Good*, ed. R. Bruce Douglass, Gerald M. Mara, and Henry S. Richardson (New York: Routledge, 1990), 203-52, Nussbaum calls attention to Aristotle's view that some forms of labor are incompatible with "good human functioning" because they harm the worker, leaving him unable to adequately undertake other

functionings. However, an awareness of this potentially negative role that work can play is quite different from viewing meaningful work as a central part of the good life.

13. Adam Smith, *An Inquiry into the Nature and Causes of the Wealth of Nations* (New York: Modern Library, 1937 [1776]), 821-22, quoted in Amartya Sen, "The Living Standard," in *Ethics of Consumption* (Lanham, Md.: Rowman and Littlefield Publishers, Inc., 1998), 292.

14. Smith, *Wealth of Nations*, 822.

15. In capabilities language, having a high standard of living would involve having clothing such that one *can* appear in public without shame. I stress *actually* appearing without shame (assuming that the person appears at all). Having the clothes so that one can appear without shame is only a step removed from having the money to buy such clothes so that one can appear without shame. Unless one actually buys the clothes *and* wears them, and thus *appears* without shame, one is not *living* at a high standard, despite the potential to live so.

16. In *The Standard of Living* (Cambridge: Cambridge University Press, 1987), Sen changes his position to include functionings as well as capabilities in evaluating the living standard. (See the 1987 postscript to Sen's essay in *Ethics of Consumption* (Lanham, Md.: Rowman and Littlefield Publishers, Inc., 1998), 298).

17. Sen, "The Living Standard," in *Ethics of Consumption* (Lanham, Md.: Rowman and Littlefield Publishers, Inc., 1998), 295.

18. Sen, "The Living Standard," 295.

19. A similar point can be made about the relationship between economic well-being and well-being per se. It should not be thought that economic well-being is necessarily a part of well-being. If, for instance, the self is thought of as primarily spiritual, then much of what happens in the economic domain is largely irrelevant.

20. One of the reasons that focusing on the more narrowly economic "standard of living" offers more payoff than focusing on "the good human life" or "human well-being" is the greater consensus that exists when we focus on the narrowly economic. Thus, I would argue, when it comes to what people either want money for, or what they are seeking when they sell their labor, there is far more commonality among human beings than there is when it comes to how they understand a fuller notion of the good life.

21. I say "near" logical truth, for it remains possible that during some period (for example, a war) all of the economic growth would be channeled into increased government production and thus would not affect consumption levels.

22. Fred C. Hirsch may have been the first to use this image in his *Social Limits to Growth* (Cambridge, Mass.: Harvard University Press, 1976).

23. Those who wish to maintain a sharp line between acceptable and nonacceptable motives for state actions could respond that the good functioning that befell those who did not want to ingest fluoride was only a collateral benefit

of a public health measure favored by the majority, but not appropriately its intended purpose.

24. In *The Affluent Society* (Cambridge, Mass.: Riverside Press, 1958), Galbraith took the position that almost all private spending has reached the point at which on the margin it brings no real increase in the standard of living. Thus, he argued for preventing private spending (using taxes) to increase public spending in areas where collective improvement in the standard of living is possible (such as parks or public safety).

9
Human Activity: A Molecular Approach to Action Theory

The theory of agency that I have put forward contains the following elements:

1. A distinction is made between two questions, "What is agency?" and "What is an action?" In general, the entire field of action theory has assimilated these two questions into one. Thus, the agent causality approach invokes agent causation at one and the same time to say what it is to be an agent and to specify what an act is (to be an agent is to have agent-caused something to occur; an action is an event that is brought about through agent causation). Similarly, on mental cause theories, to be the agent of an event (my arm's going up) is for that event to have been caused by my wants and beliefs (or volition) and it is this that constitutes action.

2. Rather than treating "acts" or "actions" as the primary concept of action theory, I will instead build the theory on the concept of "activity." I will offer an account of what an activity is that does not require that a person be the agent of that activity. This account of activity, however, will be offered as an answer to the fundamental question of action theory, as posed by Wittgenstein. Broadly speaking, my analysis will be within the reductionist camp, but it will not be a matter of a mental cause that triggers a chain of events that results in a movement. Instead activity will be analyzed as a complex causally interactive process whose exact character will be specified in the analysis.

The Activity Matrix

Consider the answer to a very simple question, "What did you do today?"

- Got up
- Got dressed
- Went downstairs
- Ate breakfast
- Went outside
- Worked on the car
- Ate lunch
- Worked on the car some more
- Worked on my book
- Had dinner
- Worked some more on my book
- Called my sister

The person can be pressed for more of the details: "Exactly what did you do in working on the car?"

- Spread the tools out
- Took off the rust
- Mixed the crack filler
- Filled the cracks
- Painted the fillings

"Tell me exactly what you did in mixing the filler."

- Picked up the can
- Read the instructions
- Picked up the screwdriver
- Pried open the can

"Exactly what did you do in prying open the can?"

- Grasped the can in my left hand
- Inserted the tip of the screwdriver into the groove on the lid
- Pressed down on the screwdriver
- Put the screwdriver down
- Lifted the lid off

If we were to ask if this was exactly the way it happened we might be told, "to the best of my knowledge it happened that way." But if we focus on the pressing down with the screwdriver and ask, "Did you press down once or several times?" we may learn that there was a sequence of these pressings down. At this point the agent may not be able to tell us anything further. He may be aware of little more than of working the screwdriver around the lid, prying up as he goes. Nevertheless, there is more to it than that. There is an extraordinary richness to our simplest actions, and action theory must start with an awareness of this.

Ask someone to open a small paint can and watch what he does. Carefully observe him as he works the screwdriver around the groove. He moves his entire body. He does not simply hold the can rigidly in one hand and move the other around the can. This would put him in a position from which it would be impossible to exert any pressure on the can. Instead he rotates the can through a half circle, all the while keeping the screwdriver in roughly the same place, allowing the can to rotate past the screwdriver in much the way a record rotates past the needle. As he rotates the can in a half circle, he moves the screwdriver through a small arc of about a tenth of a circle in the opposite direction. From time to time he stops these two rotations and pries up on the lid by pressing down on the screwdriver. This he does five or six times. Each time he presses down he does so with measured force, so as to avoid bending the groove a good deal in any one spot. How does he rotate the can? Using his left hand, he pushes it along with his thumb and middle finger and guides it with the ring and index finger; occasionally the pinky helps guide the can.

And what is the other hand doing while the can is rotating? Is it merely lying in wait for its turn to press down on the screwdriver? No, the thumb is halfway up the can, the fingers are in contact near the lower edge. The screwdriver helps in the steadying process by exerting a slight pressure against the side of the groove. Is this pressure constant? I do not know. I doubt it. Probably there are many tiny motions of adjustment that escape even the keenest observer.

And the rest of the body? Is it rigidly in place? No, there is a good deal of shoulder and arm movement as the hands move. The torso moves through an arc of about a twentieth of a circle and there are slight movements of the legs and feet. He tends to "lean into" the can a bit, pressing down on the ground with his left foot, going up slightly on the ball of his right foot. His head bends over the can and moves in various ways as he rotates the can, as do his eyes and eyelids. His mouth holds to a slightly stiff position, expressing a slight tension.

This does not complete the description of "prying open the can," but I will stop here and take stock starting with the original question, "What did you do today?"

1. The response to this question was a list of several activities, each of which endured over some period of time.
2. It was possible to subdivide each of these activities into a temporally ordered series of other activities until we reached "prying open the can," which was marked by numerous cotemporal goings on.
3. At some point the agent's ability to enumerate what he was doing was exhausted.
4. Yet we could see that he was doing a number of things that he was not aware of.
5. These doings were nonetheless crucial parts of what he was aware of himself as doing.
6. Many of these cotemporal goings on were coordinated with each other.
7. Only because of this coordination was he able to accomplish his goal.
8. It is generally clear to what activity a given subactivity belongs. For example, taking the food out of the refrigerator is part of eating lunch and not part of fixing the car.
9. The activities are not mere collections or conjunctions of their parts. To agent and observer alike, they occur as, are perceivable as, and are experienced as, organic wholes.
10. These organic wholes occur on various levels. We may recognize a complex called "working on the car," a complex called "mixing the crack filler," a complex called "opening the can." The individual movements of each hand, each leg, each eye, are parts of these organic wholes.

I will now focus on the most unified level, which I shall call "the activity molecule." Above this level there are also activities, but below it there are only elements of the activity molecule. In the above example the activity molecule was "prying open the can." Consider the activity molecule a bit more thoroughly.

Point 1: The activity molecule is made up of various elements of various sorts.

a. Sequences of movements of some part of the body that play a primary role (e.g., the movements of the left hand);
b. Sequences of movements of some part of the body that play a secondary role (e.g., the movements of the legs);
c. Sequences of movements of some tool manipulated by the person;
d. Changes in some situation being effected by the above (e.g., the gradual lifting of the lid);
e. Movements of the body that allow the person to be aware of what is happening (e.g., eye movements);
f. Perceptions of and sensations arising from these various goings on.

Point 2: Activity molecules are internally integrated collections of elements. Through various modes of integration the elements are interconnected with one another. There are other events that occur at the same time as the activity and in the same general area, but these are not part of the activity. An activity is not just any sequences of events. If we consider two sequences of movements, say moving one's foot up and down and moving one's arm up and down, they may or may not belong to the same activity even though they are cotemporal. When one is shifting gears on a standard transmission car, the movements of one's arm and the movements of one's foot are both elements of a single activity. When one is keeping time to the music and waving to a friend the movements are elements in two distinct activities. In determining if two elements belong to the same activity molecule, we do not look to see if there is one volition that causes the two or a volition for each. It is a matter of the relationship between the elements. Are they integrated with each other?

Point 3: Some elements of an activity molecule may be changes in the world. Typically an activity involves some interaction between a person and some changes that he or she is causing (at least in part). In the example of prying open the can, there is the series of movements of the lid of the can as it opens. These are not to be understood as consequences of the activity, but rather as elements of the activity. In playing tennis we have the movements of the ball, including those caused by the other player. These movements are not causal consequences of two activities; we do not have each player engaged in separate instances of tennis playing. Rather, both players are engaged in a single instance of the activity: playing tennis.

Point 4: Not all of the consequences of the elements of a given activity molecule are parts of that activity molecule. Whether or not a given causal consequence of some element is itself an element of the activity depends upon how it is integrated with the other elements. If it is part of an interacting sequence such as the motions of the ball in handball then it is part of the activity. If it is tied to the elements only by virtue of the single causal connection then it is a consequence of the activity but not part of it. For example, the disturbance of the air caused by my hitting the ball is not part of the activity.

Point 5: The key to the integration is the level of awareness. Insofar as we are dealing with activities that contain sequences of events and sequences of bodily movements that produce these events, the level of awareness is not on the level of each successive bodily movement. Rather it is on the level of outcome. The sequences are integrated via this awareness of outcome. Thus, the musician's awareness is not concentrated on the blowing of air across the flute mouth. The series of events of air blowing take care of themselves. His experience is on the level of the integrated consequences of the air blowing, the music itself. An experienced driver is aware of the road; her arms move, her feet press, pedals go in and out. But these are to her as though they were goings on inside her body.

Point 6: Activity molecules are not merely integrated bundles; they have flow or internal harmony. Consider a conversation. One does not merely offer a sequence of sentences. One carries on a conversation. One point tends to follow another, or if the topic shifts there is a certain harmony that is maintained. Perhaps the conversants were really just trying to get to know one another; the emotional melody flows forward over various topics. When this rhythm is truly broken, the activity ends. Two friends stop talking politics and turn to an exchange of intimacies. To do this is to do something else. They are not unified parts of a single activity molecule of conversing. Each series of events has its own flow and internal logic. Because of this, activities appear as wholes. Phenomenologically, we do not construct them out of their elements; they are there already. This may or may not be seen by a given observer; that depends upon his or her ability to perceive the meanings that are integrated.

With this general account, it is crucial to identify the particular kind of integration that makes something an activity molecule.

The Structure of Molecular Activities

The activity molecule is a set of causally integrated events. In the most familiar cases the types of events consist of three sorts: movements, outcomes, and as awareness of these outcomes as they occur. If these events are related to each other in a particular manner, then they constitute an activity molecule. I use the term "indirect perceptual integration" to characterize that causal relationship that is constitutive of activity on the molecular level.

The activity molecule is represented in figure 9.1. The diagram shows only a fraction of the activity complex. *P* is the ongoing perceptual awareness of the outcomes O^1, O^2, . . . O^{12}. The perceptual assessment of *P* causes these outcomes to conform to some standard or form. This is represented by the circle that runs through the *O*s; it stands for the harmony that is produced in the outcomes. The route of causation is indirect. The outcomes, which might be the appearance of certain colors or shapes on a canvas, are caused via the movement of the arm and the paint brush. These movements are M^1, M^2, . . . M^{12}. While the curves running from *P* indicate the object of the awareness *P*, the straight lines running to and from the *M*'s represents the causal chain. Each movement produces some shift in outcome and this is perceived and in turn results in some adjustment of movement. *P* is thought of as continuous throughout the activity; and in a harmonious flowing activity, the number of movements and outcomes may be considered to be infinite. The duration of the activity is the length of time required by the completion of the series of movements, or alternatively, the series of outcomes.

It may be maintained that for some activities the intended outcomes never occur and hence there are no outcomes to serve as the object of awareness. First, it should be realized that there is a sense of "outcome" that is not relevant. Thus, I may be playing the guitar hoping to produce the "outcome" of impressing a listener; yet, the listener may fail to be impressed. In this case, however, impressing the listener is not the outcome necessitated by my analysis. The outcome that is the object of the ongoing awareness is the production of the music. The event that does not occur—the listener's coming to have a favorable impression— an intended causal consequence of the molecular activity, playing the guitar. The absence of this consequence is not relevant to the analysis of molecular activity. Sometimes, of course, it happens that someone tries to play the guitar and fails to produce the musical sounds. Here, there is no molecular activity of the type "playing the guitar." Of course, "trying to play the guitar" and "learning to play the guitar" are activities even if there is no molecular activity "playing the guitar." Trying to play the guitar may be a compound activity made up of a series of molecular activities such as plucking the first string, pressing the second string against a fret, and plucking the second string. When someone who is unable to play the guitar tries to play the guitar, he or she may succeed in performing these activity tokens.

Figure 9.1

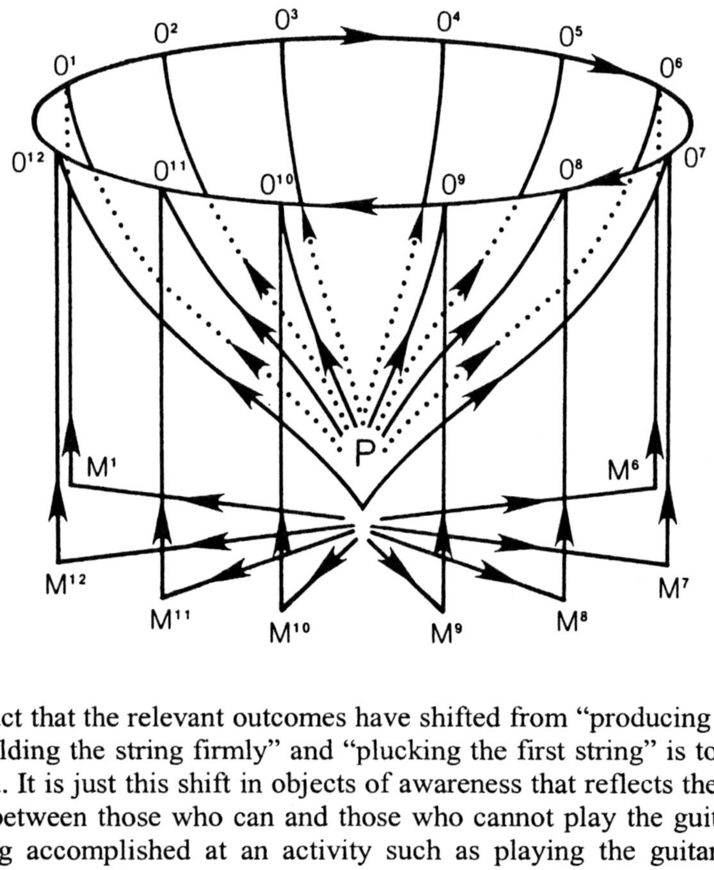

The fact that the relevant outcomes have shifted from "producing music" to "holding the string firmly" and "plucking the first string" is to be expected. It is just this shift in objects of awareness that reflects the difference between those who can and those who cannot play the guitar. Becoming accomplished at an activity such as playing the guitar is the process whereby a new molecular activity (type) enters one's repertoire. For the person who knows how, playing the guitar is not composed of a set of more basic molecular activities such as plucking the string or pressing the fret, even though it is true that he or she does pluck the string and press the fret when playing. These have now become internalized within the structure of his or her basic activity molecule.

With the above in mind, I offer the following definition of the key relationship (indirect perceptual integration):

> A set of elements is indirectly perceptually integrated if and only if it contains a series of events, a subset of the causal consequences of those events (the outcomes), and an ongoing perceptual assessment of the outcomes such that this perceptual assessment causes the series to produce an outcome that satisfies or approaches the standard implicit in the perceptual assessment.

By "perceptual assessment" I mean a form of seeing-as. The outcomes are not experienced in a phenomenologically neutral manner. They are seen critically, with some standard implicit in the perception. In the following illustrations, coffee is seen as shaking-too-much, the handwriting as not-being-clear-enough, the truck as being-too-close. In the next section I will provide a fuller discussion of these perceptual assessments and discuss their relation to wants and beliefs.

Illustration 1: I am carrying the coffee to the table; my eyes are focused on the surface of the coffee inside the cups; the coffee is seen as shaking-too-much. This perception causes my pace to slow down and my hands to grip the saucers more tightly, which causes the coffee to become more steady.

Illustration 2: I am writing a letter and perceive that my writing is illegible. This perception causes my hands to move more slowly, which causes the writing to be legible-enough.

Illustration 3: I am riding my bike through city streets. I perceive myself as too close to a moving truck; this causes my feet to move less quickly and my hands to squeeze the brakes lightly, all of which causes me to be further away from the truck.

In objection to my claim that indirect perceptual integration is sufficient for some complex to be an activity, it might be pointed out that I have not specified *how* the perceptual awareness causes the events to produce an outcome in conformity to the implicit standard. Thus, a painter with a paralyzed arm to which a brush is attached may find his arm moving the brush in conformity to his perceptual assessment of the painting being produced. A machine (or another person) may be producing the motion of the painter's arm. The machine is caused to do so by the perceptual assessments of the painter. Here we would not want to say that *the painter* was moving his arm. Thus, the account may appear vulnerable to the so-called "wayward chains" that plague accounts of action in terms of causation by a mental event.

But the above example does not constitute a problem on the analysis I have offered. I have severed the question of agency from that of activity. My claim is only that the painting of the picture is an *activity*. The wayward causal chain may defeat the claim that the person with the paralyzed arm is the agent, but not the claim that there is picture painting activity. In standard action theory approaches, this distinction is not made.

Similarly, if it is sufficient that there be indirect perceptual integration, then my account commits one to saying that something is an activity even if the person doing it finds that this process is occurring even against his or her will. I accept this implication because this bears not on the question of activity, but rather on the question of agency.

Similarly, someone may be hypnotically or electrically caused to perform an activity. She may not be an agent, but so long as the outcomes are indirectly caused by a perceptual assessment to conform to a standard implicit in her ongoing perception, it is an activity. If, however, she is hypnotically or electrically caused to make certain movements that by chance happen to conform to the perceptual assessment, but are not caused by the perceptual assessment to conform to the standard, then we do not have genuine activity. In short, if the external cause cuts in prior to the ongoing perceptual perception, then what has been caused is an activity. If it cuts in after and short-circuits the perceptual integration, then what is caused is mere behavior, not activity.

Is indirect perceptual integration also a necessary condition for action? Are there actions where indirect perceptual integration is lacking? Consider someone who is blind. Surely he performs actions, yet he does not have the perceptual awareness that people with vision have. This is correct, but it doesn't undermine the analysis. What typically happens is that some other sensory awareness becomes more acute and meaningful, whether it is auditory or tactile awareness. One can develop the skill of doing things with one's eyes closed, but one develops this skill by learning to depend more on other forms of awareness. It is just this problem of learning how to rely upon other senses that makes it so difficult to do without the senses that typically provide the indirect perceptual awareness.

Indirect perceptual integration is a particular kind of feedback process in which the perceptual awareness carries the standard against which feedback information is evaluated. The broader question is whether or not ongoing feedback is a necessary feature of action. Suppose that someone is totally anesthetized, and deprived of any sensory awareness of what she is doing. She is asked to pick up her violin and play it. And suppose that she does so. There is no ongoing perceptual awareness, indeed, no feedback at all, but there is the complex behavior of violin playing. Is this an action? Suppose that the person is participating in an experiment of some sort, and agrees to respond to a variety of commands to perform this or that activity. And suppose that she does behave accordingly despite the absence of any perceptual feedback. We might be surprised that this occurs given that the individual has no awareness of the activity as it is occurring, but certainly it is possible. How are such situations to be characterized?

I would not find it very problematic to say that such instances would be complex behavioral compounds that are not themselves actions. This is not to say that they are mere happenings, akin to processes that occur whether we want them to or not. Given that the behavior occurrences are the result of directives that the person wants to obey, in such a situation the person is making them happen. He or she is the agent of these physical processes in much the way that we can be the agent of involuntary bodily processes that once begun occur of their own accord. But agency is a different question than that of action; on my account we may or may not be the agent of our activities, and in principle we could be the agent of processes that are not actions.

It may be wondered whether or not we have indirect perceptual integration in relatively simple and brief actions such as raising one's hand or moving one's finger. First, it should be noted that such movements are most frequently parts of an activity molecule, and in those instances we would not look for indirect perceptual integration within the hand raising but between it and other elements. Still, even if only infrequently, these movements can stand alone. I may for instance raise my hand to signal someone, or to ask a question, or to give a salute.

Is there indirect perceptual integration in these cases? I think that typically there is. A hand can be raised in many different ways. The German salute we see in movies of World War II is not the same as merely lifting one's hand. The ballet dancer who raises her hand does something that is measured and graceful. At the very least when we raise our hand there is always some determination of how fast to do it and how far to extend it. In short, even something as simple as a hand raising occurs within a temporal interval during which there is perceptual feedback and adjustment.

Suppose that there are behavioral elements that are so simple and so short that there is no feedback, but simply a one-way command mechanism. These would not be molecular activities, but they would be things that we make happen and of which we would have a perceptual awareness, but no adjustment mechanism. We would be the agents of these events and in virtue of having made them happen we might perform numerous other higher level acts. And if one wished one could say that the making happen of these simple occurrences is an action. What is striking, however, is that actions of this sort, if they do occur, would operate on the margins of a theory of action, whereas classical mental cause theories have treated them as the paradigm instances of action. The activity molecule, held together through indirect perceptual integration, can serve as a relatively solid central concept for a theory of action.

Rather than stipulating that indirect perceptual integration is or is not a necessary feature of human action, it is, I think, more revealing to say that there is a spectrum of more and less active complexes of elements. What is of interest is to consider what such a spectrum of activeness might look like and what the criteria would be that determine the position of a given instance.

It is possible to distinguish between four major categories of molecular activities: bodily motions producing some change in an external object; bodily motions resulting in some effect but not in or via an external object; bodily motions in themselves; activities where no bodily movement is necessary. Associated with each of these categories are numerous manners of performance. These manners of performance are not necessarily restricted to one and only one category. The categories (with examples) and some performance modes are presented in the following list.[1]

I. Bodily motions producing some change in an external object
  A. Some examples
    1. Painting a fence
    2. Driving a car
    3. Playing a violin
    4. Drawing a picture
    5. Opening a can
  B. Some typical modes of performance
    1. Attentively
    2. Mechanically
    3. Spontaneously
    4. Relaxedly

II. Bodily motions resulting in some effect but not in or via an external object

- A. Some examples
  - 1. Speaking
  - 2. Singing
  - 3. Scratching an itch
- B. Modes of performance
  - 1. Haltingly
  - 2. Ferociously
  - 3. Softly

III. Bodily motions in themselves

- A. Some examples
  - 1. Exercising
  - 2. Dancing
  - 3. Swimming
  - 4. Diving
- B. Some typical modes of performance
  - 1. In form (gracefully, properly)
  - 2. Mindlessly
  - 3. Rigidly

IV. No bodily movement necessary

- A. Some examples
  - 1. Thinking
  - 2. Reading
  - 3. Listening to music
  - 4. Watching a sunset
- B. Some typical modes of performance
  - 1. Intently
  - 2. Carefully
  - 3. Perfunctorily

For any activity there are many manners in which it can be performed. This is not something peripheral to its being an activity. It seems that it is an essential feature of an activity that it can be performed in various manners. However, it is not the case that all instances of a type of activity performed in various manners are equally instances of activity. The manner itself reflects the extent of the activity of the performance. There might be performances so mechanical as to lack any ongoing awareness at all. Where this is truly the case we are not dealing with an activity, but merely a set of movements. And if an activity is done haltingly or spasmodically we are not dealing with a single molecular activity, but rather a series of molecular activities.

The most fully active performances are marked by indirect perceptual integration. Our best examples come from category I (bodily motions producing some change in an external object) when they are done attentively, as well as instances of category II such as speaking and singing when these are done with care. If we consider activities in category III (bodily motions in themselves) to be subject to certain norms of form, such that the outcome is, say, a graceful movement of the entire body, then we can find good instances of indirect perceptual integration when these activities are done in good form. In the last category (no necessary bodily motion) it may be difficult to find instances of indirect perceptual integration. While it is true that we may read a book critically, or watch a movie attentively, what is viewed critically is the book read or the movie seen. The book and the movie may be the objects of attention, but they are not the outcomes of the activity. The outcomes are the gradual unfolding of the plot to the reader, the perception of the sun as it sets, the hearing of the music. However, we are aware of these outcomes as they occur and this awareness affects their occurrence. If we are not understanding the book, we slow down. If the music is not being heard, there is a focusing of consciousness. Thus even here we may find examples of indirect perceptual integration, though not as clearly as in the other categories. Insofar as these outcomes are out of our control, or not subject to modification as they occur, they are not activities. This finding fits well with our preanalytic uncertainty as to whether or not examples from this category are activities.

If activity is a matter of degree, the extent to which a performance is an activity depends upon three factors: the degree to which the outcome is capable of modification; the range of causally operative criteria within the perceptual assessment; and the fineness of the discriminations of each of the causally operative criteria.

Some types of activities are susceptible to greater modification than others. If there is little way in which the outcomes can be different, then the type offers less potential for activity, or activeness. The more it can be different, the greater the opportunity the type provides for activity.

In a sense, this is like judging diving—certain dives, according to their type, are given higher multiples for difficulty. Here we are not concerned with difficulty but with degree of modifiability. Thus, filling in pictures in a coloring book is subject to less modifiability than drawing a picture on a blank page. The replacement of script by type restricted, in certain dimensions, the modifiability of writing. There is more variability between different performances of playing a violin than there is between different performances of opening a can.

When we speak of modifiability, we are concerned with a property of the activity type and not of the activity token (instance) except insofar as it was a token of a type with a certain degree of modifiability. Modifiability may be thought of as a property that reflects the variability of the possible instances that would count as instances of the type in question (e.g., there are a vast number of ways of making a sketch of a particular tree).

To some extent this distinction corresponds to that between skilled and unskilled labor. And we may understand something of the distinction between tools and machines along these lines. A farmer with a hoe uses the hoe as a tool to communicate to the outcome her vision of it. If anything, the tool enhances her ability to transmit her vision, to implement her perceptual assessments. It functions like an artist's brush. We can contrast this with machines. Consider someone working with a hand stapler. This is not a passive or partially passive performance as with an automatic can opener where the machine takes over the task. Here there is a sensory awareness that is carried through the activity to the end; there are a variety of ways the activity can turn out; there are good jobs and bad jobs. Nonetheless, the stapler permits relatively little communication of vision. There is little in the way of possible ongoing correction, adjustment, and extension of outcome, as the outcome is being produced.

While the first index to the activity of a performance dealt with the type of the activity, the second and the third deal with the actual performance. The ongoing performance includes a perceptual assessment. Within the perceptual assessment there are criteria that specify some standard or form or bench mark against which the activity's outcomes are perceived. These criteria may range over a number of dimensions of the outcome or may be restricted to just one. Thus, an individual may or may not perceive the aesthetic dimensions of the outcome. One person may be concerned only to get the job done; for him it is enough to get the message across. The range of values in his awareness is restricted. For another, matters of style may be important: economy of resources, avoiding sloppiness, pleasing appearance. These dimensions, which are present in his awareness of the outcome, were missing from the first person's awareness. But it is not enough that they be present in the perception—they must be causally operative. The artist must learn not only to perceive (to have criteria); he must learn control, craft (how to make his criteria operative). Furthermore, it is not enough that the person has the perception and the ability; the activity of the actual performance is determined by those criteria that have emerged in the outcome. Thus sometimes we are faced with an activity token that might have been performed with great attentiveness, elegance, or grace, but is in fact sloppy and gross. The complex is crude and grotesque; it barely hangs together. Here there was no necessary lack of critical perception or ability. The criteria were rendered inoperative, suspended. We may say of the agent, "he didn't care how it turned out."

Finally, there is for each operative criteria within the perceptual assessment a matter of the fineness of the discriminations. Two craftswomen may both be concerned that a surface be smooth, but one is able to perceive more finely the differences in degree. Whereas the first craftswoman quickly reaches a point at which she is no longer able to tell if she is making the surface smoother or not, the second craftswoman can still evaluate the outcomes she is producing. The first craftswoman soon reaches a point at which the edge is as straight as she can make it. The second craftswoman is able to do better because she can perceive more acutely. Two singers may both care about the rhythm and pitch of their performances. But one has far greater discrimination than the other. He hears more accurately any variation from the ideal. Here too, the finely discriminated perception must be operative.

Each molecular token must be separately appraised to determine the extent to which it is activity. If it is a clear case of indirect perceptual integration, then it is a clear case of activity. Insofar as this is not the case, we may speak of it as more or less active. As there is less modifiability of outcome, and more impoverishment of operative perception, there is a movement away from the active. As there is greater modifiability and richer operative perception we move towards the artistic. Cast in these terms this appraising may sound intellectual and arduous—in fact it is perceptual and immediate. It constitutes the aesthetic dimension of everyday life. It is something we feel in our own activity and see in the activity of others.

Perceptual Assessments

A key term in the definition of indirect perceptual integration, and thus in the analysis of activity, has been "perceptual assessment." I have characterized perceptual assessment as a form of seeing-as where what is experienced is perceived in terms of a standard. By "standard" I do not mean a value and certainly not a moral value. All I have in mind is a bench mark, something that allows us to see something as not-being-such-and-such or as conforming-more-and-more-to-such-and-such. These hyphenated expressions indicate that we are talking about a feature of the awareness itself.

This richness of perception is commonplace. Consider the following: I have just returned to my apartment. I look it over to see if everything is in order. I see it as in-order or as not-in-order. I do not first see it and then *judge* that there is a low probability that something has been disturbed in my absence.

Sometimes, of course, we do experience in this reduced way, but it is a phenomenologically different experience. Indeed, the neutralization of experience, the elimination of standards otherwise implicit in perception, is one of the characteristics of certain forms of alienation.

It might be suggested that perceptual assessments can be equated with the mental elements offered in classical accounts of action (e.g., volitions) or in their recent variants (e.g., wants, intentions, beliefs). I wish to reject any such suggestions.

First, let us dismiss the notion that perceptual assessments are beliefs. That they are closely related cannot be doubted. If I see the cup of coffee as shaking-too-much then it is typically the case that I believe that it is shaking too much. Of course, I could believe this and not have the experience of seeing it, but could I see it this way and not believe it? The answer to this question is yes. Though it is not typically the case, there are many circumstances in which we know that things are not really the way we see them to be. We have our perceptual experience but we do not accept it as veridical. Perceptual assessments, typically, are the expression of beliefs—because I believe that that amount of shaking is too-much, I see it as shaking-too-much. Typically, seeing it in this fashion emerges from beliefs that I have. But this need not always be the case. And because it need not be the case and sometimes is not, we know that perceptual assessments are not the beliefs themselves, they are simply phenomenological episodes.

Thus we can see the diagram ⊠ successively as:

a. An elevator shaft seen from above;

b. The top of the Washington Monument;

c. An "x" in a box.

Each perception is a distinct seeing-as but we need not have any beliefs that the diagram really is, or really represents, any of these possibilities. But might they be wants or desires?—the desire that it not shake any more than a certain amount, the desire that the boat sail straight for the island it is heading for, and so on? Here again, it is the case that perceptual assessments do typically express and reflect wants and desires. Typically it is only because I want it to shake less that I see it as shaking-too-much; and because I want the boat to go towards the island, I see it as going-just-right. But again, this typical interpenetration of wants into the perceptual assessments does not mean that the assessments are wants. Indeed, they may occur even when the person does not have the appropriate desire at all.

Consider the following case. Mr. Percoti is a furniture maker, a fine craftsman who because of economic circumstances has been forced to seek employment in a furniture factory. Previously, he carved his furniture with great care; now he works on the assembly line. His job is to make left front legs for bridge chairs. He works for pay and must complete seven legs each hour. His lifelong perceptual discrimination does not vanish. He knows that he is working too quickly. He sees the inadequacy of every piece he completes; they are all perceived as ill-formed. Nonetheless, it does not follow that he wants these legs to be well-formed. He may not care one way or the other. The product belongs to the boss, not to him. His only concern is that he gets seven legs finished each hour. Indeed, he may even take satisfaction in the fact that the legs are not up to his standards.

In the above example, the person has perceptual assessments of the outcome of his activity. He sees the table leg as too-fat, but he does not want it to be less fat. He might, of course, but not in this case. And since there is no desire that it be less fat, the perceptual assessment of it as too-fat is merely a perceptual assessment, it neither expresses nor is the desire that it be less fat. In this example, these are free-standing perceptual assessments; they are not causing his movements to create an outcome in conformity with their standard, rather they are "over-ridden" by a much more minimal standard.

It might be maintained that the situation is different when the assessments do enter into the activity, when they do cause the outcomes to conform to the standard implicit in the perception. It may be said that such assessments are wants or the expression of a desire that the outcomes conform to the implicit standard. This fits well with the dominant rational picture of human behavior. One might ask, "If he didn't want the outcome to conform, then why did he make it conform?"

Let us again consider the alienated craftsman. We may find that, in fact, his work is of superior quality. When we ask him why he puts so much into someone else's product, he may himself be surprised that this is so. He may remark, "That's the only way I know how to do it," or "after a lifetime of fine carving it would take an effort to not do it right, yet I don't give a damn about these table legs!" Here the indirect perceptual integration has a life of its own. The craftsman continues to perceive with his trained critical eye, and his hands respond as they have always responded despite the fact that he is *indifferent* to the quality of the outcome.

Indeed, the perceptual assessment may be operative even in direct *conflict* with the craftsman's wants. We can imagine him in a shop where his skill is causing problems for the other workers. He may be under great pressure to not work so ably. He may want to produce shoddy legs; he may want the outcomes of his activity to not conform to the standards of craft that are imbedded in his perceptions. Nonetheless, in a relaxed moment he may find himself doing work that meets his perceptual standards, despite his desire not to!

In the last example we have a normal individual operating in a marred social world, but the problem is manifest a thousand times in the life of the compulsive. She has standards that are not hers and that she may even recognize as not-hers. Nonetheless, they enter into her behavior. She tells us, and we may believe her, that she does not value her excessive neatness or cleanliness, that she does not want everything she does to be so perfect. Indeed, she may correctly regard her acute perceptions and stringent perceptual standards as parental introjects. She may wish that she did not always do everything "to perfection." In spite of herself, she is always seeing and correcting her imperfections. Now if one wishes, one may insist that she feels a need to do it that way, or that she wants to have it be perfect, or that her general desire to not be perfect is momentarily overcome by an overpowering occurrent desire to perfection, but the compulsive may not sense any such need, or feel any such desire. She just finds herself acting contrary to her desire. The existence of an overpowering need or desire are inferred by the theorist who insists that they must be there because the model admits of no alternatives.

On the account I have offered, the activity stands as activity even if it is divorced from any network of wants and beliefs. Naturally this is not the case with healthy individuals engaged in self-expressive activity. But we should not take this perhaps rare situation as the model for all activity. The link between perceptual assessments and the wants and values of the individual is one of the ways that the self achieves presence in its activities. It is not always the case.

The upshot of this discussion is to avoid any general identification of causally operative perceptual assessments with wants or beliefs. Similarly, they cannot be said to be the expressions of wants and beliefs. The main significance of this account is that it allows for an internal analysis of activities. They are what they are because of their internal structure and not because there exists a set of wants and beliefs that causes them or some of their elements (e.g., bodily movements) to occur.[2]

Notes

1. The examples are to be taken narrowly. Taken broadly they signify compound rather than molecular activities.

2. I regard the claim that activities are always caused by wants and beliefs as a sort of psychosocio myth. The tendency to so conceive human behavior is furthered by analyses of actions as events or bodily movements caused by volitions, intentions, or wants. These mental states play no necessary role in an account of activity, and I regard them as often having the status of mythic entities introduced to make behavior, which would otherwise have to be explained along other lines, seem rational. This fictional world is not the creation of philosophers; it is participated in quite generally. It is part of a general human self-perception that no doubt predates systematic philosophizing. From this self-perception there flows, in everyday life, the earnest yet erroneous attribution of wants and beliefs to oneself. Indeed, this is more than mere attribution, for such attributions play a role in the creation and wants and beliefs, though they come into being at a point subsequent to the behavior they are often thought to have prompted. This elimination of certain forms of alienness through the postulation of relevant wants and beliefs functions to make one seem less strange to oneself. It thus reduces the sense of conflict and fragmentation, and thus, drawing attention away from the causes of our alienness, it becomes morally and politically significant.

About the Author

Jerome M. Segal is a Senior Research Scholar at the University of Maryland's Institute for Philosophy and Public Policy.

As an undergraduate he received dual honors in both philosophy and economics from the City College of New York. He went on to receive a doctorate in philosophy from the University of Michigan, and taught for several years in the philosophy department of the University of Pennsylvania. Subsequently he received a degree in public affairs from the Hubert Humphrey School of the University of Minnesota.

He is the author of five previous books, (*Creating the Palestinian State, Negotiating Jerusalem, Agency and Alienation*, *Graceful Simplicity* and *Joseph's Bones*).